CUBA
MORE OR LESS

"A vivid portrait of America's alluring neighbor, *Cuba, More or Less* demonstrates the profound impact of isolation on the Cuban people and the comfort they sought in church, at great risk, after Castro's regime outlawed religion.

Part-history of the Episcopal church in Cuba, part travelogue, *Cuba, More or Less* takes readers on a journey beyond nightclubs and crumbling Colonial buildings to meet Cubans who have struggled for decades. Zachary Reid's detailed reporting provides a new perspective on this endlessly fascinating place, exposing the beauty—and frustrations—of island life while challenging the stereotypes the rest of the world holds about Cuba."

—Kristen Green,
author of *New York Times* best seller
Something Must Be Done About Price Edward County

"Everything you think about Cuba, an island of passions and heat, faith and music, of kindnesses and dangers, cars and machetes, waiting, always wanting but separate and proud and so mysteriously much more, has been movingly captured by Zachary Reid. His language is as clear as his vision, and as deep as his understanding. I've been to Cuba twice now, once on my own, and once with this book."

—David L. Robbins,
author of *The Devil's Horn* and *The Low Bird*

"Like the people and stories it describes, *Cuba, More or Less* resists simple characterizations. It is simultaneously deeply thoughtful and genuinely entertaining, and adeptly portrays a place and culture that are rich in history and meaning."

—Andrew R. H. Thompson, Ph.D.,
Postdoctoral Fellow in Environmental Ethics, The School of Theology, The University of the South.

Cuba, More or Less
by Zachary Reid

© Copyright 2016 Zachary Reid

ISBN 978-1-63393-226-5

All rights reserved. No part of this publication may be reproduced, stored in a retrieval system, or transmitted in any form or by any means – electronic, mechanical, photocopy, recording, or any other – except for brief quotations in printed reviews, without the prior written permission of the author.

Published by

210 60th Street
Virginia Beach, VA 23451
212-574-7939
www.koehlerbooks.com

CUBA

MORE OR LESS

Travel, Faith & Life in the
Waning Years of the Castro Regime

ZACHARY REID

VIRGINIA BEACH
CAPE CHARLES

For my wife Jennifer,
who possesses a patience I'll never know
&
The Rt. Rev. Griselda Delgado, the Episcopal Bishop of
Cuba, who opened her country, and her home, to me

TABLE OF CONTENTS

GALLERY	04
PROLOGUE	16
CHAPTER 1: Things I Should Have Known	19
CHAPTER 2: Havana	37
CHAPTER 3: Camagüey	74
CHAPTER 4: Santiago de Cuba	114
CHAPTER 5: Havana	157
CHAPTER 6: Epilogue	184
ACKNOWLEDGMENTS	226

Old town Havana spreads out into dense blocks of retail and residential development. This is the view from the roof of the old Bacardi building.

A man with a cigar in Pinar del Rio in western Cuba.

One of the dozens of small fishing boats anchored in the entrance to Havana harbor. The boats are ancient, but they still get daily use from the city's working watermen.

A man with a Yankees hat in a doorway in Havana. He understood capitalism: he posed for photos, then asked for dollars.

An impromptu tango broke out on the Paseo, the tree-lined boulevard that links Cuba's capitol building with the Malecon.
The promenade is one of Havana's great public spaces, hosting dancers, artists and people at leisure nearly around the clock.

A view of Havana from Morro castle, the 16th century fortification that guards the entrance to the city's harbor

The tomb of Jose Marti, in the cemetery in Santiago de Cuba. The 19th century nationalist was one of the leader's of the country's revolution against Spanish rule. Today, he's venerated as the country's greatest hero, and his bust appears across the island.

The pushpins on the map of Cuba designate outposts of the Episcopal church. The church teetered on the brink of obscurity in the decades after Fidel Castro came to power, but it survived the worst years and is making a resurgence.

A wedding party shared space with two fishermen along the Malecon in Havana. Public photo shoots are common in Cuba.

The view of Havana from Casablanca, a small working class neighborhood across the harbor. The area, and its neighbor Regla, are linked to Havana by ferry service.

The Episcopal Cathedral in Havana was built in the 1940s and survived decades of state-sponsored disdain for organized religion.

A Ferris wheel in a children's park next to San Juan Hill in Santiago. The site of Teddy Roosevelt's famed charge is now also home to a motel and a petting zoo.

The Hotel Nacional, Havana's best example of art décor grandeur. In a city of decay, the hotel is oddly resplendent.

The shadow of the Santiago's main catholic cathedral can be seen on the face of the Hotel Casa Grande. Both buildings face Cespedes Square, which is also home to Casa de Diego Velazquez, the oldest house in Cuba. It was built in 1522.

Coco taxis are a favorite with tourists in Havana, where they ply the route between old town and the Cohiba and Riveria hotels at the far end of the Malecon.

A statue of 19th century revolutionary hero Antonio Maceo stands tall in the revolutionary square in Santiago.

Havana once had a large community of Chinese immigrants. Most have assimilated or gone elsewhere, but their distinctive neighborhood remains. The green-roofed entrance leads into a pedestrian block lined with restaurants.

A taxi driver and a barber play different waiting games in Santiago.

San Lucas Episcopal Church in Santiago
is the seat of church leadership on the Eastern end of the island.

Fishing along the Malecon in Havana is a daily activity. The fishermen rarely reel in anything big enough to eat, but that never seems to slow the activity.

PROLOGUE

THE "MORE OR LESS," I borrowed from the Rev. Halbert Pons, an Episcopal priest in Santiago de Cuba with whom I once spent a few days. He'd slyly added it to the time he was supposed to pick me up: "9 o'clock, more or less," he'd told me one night so I'd know when to be ready the next morning.

He wasn't there at nine, of course. It was Cuba, and no one was ever on time for anything in Cuba. But I liked the "more or less"; it explained so much with so few words. In Cuba, everything was more or less, a sly reminder that life works out how it wants, not how you want, no matter how hard you try.

And so, too, this book. I'd spent some time with Episcopal church leaders in Havana, and I had this idea about writing a book about how they'd survived five decades of Communism. It was going to be a big and important story, and I met the people who were going to help me tell it. One man's career stretched the whole thing, and through him, I thought I could say so much. But the more time I spent in Cuba, the more people I met, the more things I saw, the more certain I became that I'd be writing another story intertwined with that story.

So here lie the two, woven together. The one about the church and how it's emerging today in fits and starts, trying to reclaim its place in a society that might not want it back. And the other about Cuba today, in the mid-teens, a country on the cusp of a freedom it hasn't seen since the 1950s, the country as I saw it from Havana to Santiago and back, by car, bus and plane. It's a place of random beauty, regular life and everything in between.

There's a lot to say about Cuba today, and this book says but a little. It's not an academic text or a political treatise, and it's certainly not a work of any spiritual weight. It's a travelogue centered around a series of interviews with church people, but it's neither a travel guide nor a religious work. It's Cuba as I saw it, more or less.

Zachary Reid
Richmond, Virginia
July 2015

CHAPTER 1

THINGS I SHOULD HAVE KNOWN

I SHOULD HAVE learned to speak Spanish before getting into this.

A better understanding of the Episcopal Church would have come in handy, too, before settling into Cuba under the pretense of studying that church there. But arrogance can be such a liberating thing: come up with an idea, convince the right people that you can do it, push on. And you're arrogant, so you never have to stop to think through the steps or figure out how you'll pull it all off. It'll work out, just because.

Which it did, much to my surprise, arrogance triumphant over the equally present and usually more powerful self-doubt for once. Go to Cuba to get material for a book?

I pulled it off.

Repeatedly.

Knowing hardly a word of Spanish.

Hola. Habla usted Ingles? Adios.

That's the language skillset I've been taking to Cuba.

I'd been there several times before I had my fit of arrogance about writing a book, and I'd made it through just fine with my English. I hadn't been trying to write this book on any of those trips, but I figured I could make it back to do the research without learning anything new, because really, writing a book, how hard can that be? I write for a newspaper. I know how to tell a story. Talk to people. Take notes. Write paragraphs. More paragraphs in a book, but still paragraphs, just the same.

And Cuba was full of stories. Fun, colorful stories, all from a place everyone knows but so few people can visit. I'd heard those stories on three previous trips. Every trip, there was something else.

I'd been there to fish, decades ago, when the Cold War was still a real thing, and I'd been there with church people to look at church things, and once, I went with a group that was half Episcopal and half Jewish and fully committed to healing old wounds of some sort, and doing a lot of sightseeing, too. That trip had been the most intensely unsatisfying week of travel I'd ever experienced, a never-ending session in group therapy for which I was ill-prepared. The sightseeing wasn't so bad, though, and it was on that trip that I first went into the Episcopal Cathedral in Havana. It was there that I met a guy named Juan Ramon and a woman named Griselda Delgado. One was the retired dean of the cathedral, a man whose career spanned the entirety of the Castro years; the other the bishop for the whole country, the first woman to be an Episcopal bishop in all of Latin America.

They were going to be my ticket back to Cuba. They didn't know it, but I did.

Ramon had been the dean of the cathedral for decades but was retired by the time I met him while I was on my tour of ecumenical appeasement. He was still retired, and still hanging out around the cathedral, a year later when I went back.

That time, I was traveling with just two others, not a dozen like the year before: the Reverend Carmen Germino, the assistant rector of St. James's Episcopal Church, in Richmond, Virginia, and DeWitt Casler, a fellow parishioner. We worked together on occasion, planning outreach and work trips for the church, and we went to Cuba that spring to talk about a summer camp for children.

Carmen went off into the office to talk to Bishop Griselda about whatever it is priests talk about when the laypeople aren't around, and DeWitt and I waited in the narrow lounge outside the office. We stared at a map of Cuba that was hanging on the wall, then we settled down on the couch and kept saying "yes" every time someone came through and offered us each a little cup of espresso. Not a bad life, going to Cuba to drink coffee while someone else does the work.

Ramon walked in and saw us and sat down in a chair at the end of the couch. I can't remember if he remembered us from the year before, but he was friendly enough either way. Cubans, we'd learned, don't mind waiting with you and they don't mind talking. They don't mind not talking, either—the guards at the gate were good at that—but Ramon was chatty. He stayed with us until the bishop came out, filling the time with stories about his career and about religious life in a country in which religion was long discouraged, if not overtly undermined, by the government.

I'm a newspaper reporter most of the time, and I like asking questions. Not Big Important Questions, with the capital letters, like those guys you see on television at news conferences who ask questions so long and complicated, no one ever really knows what they want except to prove how smart they are, being able to ask long, complicated questions. I like little questions. A prod here or there, a point of clarification, a gentle nudge to keep the story going, then get out of the way and let the guy talk. And Ramon was perfect for that. He could talk, and he didn't mind an occasional nudge. He had a story so much bigger than himself, you couldn't help but sit back and listen.

His career spanned the entirety of Castro's Cuba, from the revolution in the 1950s to the beginning of the thaw of political relations with the United States in the 2010s. If you wanted to tell the history of Cold War Cuba through a single person not named Castro, Ramon was a pretty good choice. And unlike Castro, Ramon was right there, two feet away from me, talking freely, even after I pulled out my notebook and started writing down the things he was saying.

So I peppered him with questions and took notes and made plans for what might come of it all. I knew before I got off the couch that I'd find a way to talk to him again. Even if it meant another trip. Or especially if it meant another trip, because that would give me an excuse to go back, and who didn't want to go to Cuba? Or listen to Ramon, who shared, in a perfect, if perhaps occasionally formal, English, such a good story?

He was the son of a solidly middle-class family in the 1950s, when Cuba still recognized inescapable things like class. Instead of following his father into the practice of optometry, Ramon had gone off to serve God. He went with the support of his family and the conviction that comes with knowing what you want to do and knowing you're right about it. He entered seminary in what would be the waning years of the regime of the dictator Fulgencio Batista. Cuba may not have been the most pious place at the time—the casinos and showgirls were real enough, especially in Havana, and so were the American gangsters who fueled it all—but there was still room for religion, and there were enough guilty expats around to keep the churches full. Becoming a priest was a respectable career choice.

That didn't last, of course. By the time Ramon was ordained a deacon in 1960, the country was under the full grip of Castro and his band of guerillas. The guilty expats fled, the churches emptied and then things got nasty, with Castro doing everything he could to rub religion into oblivion. Long before he went after private enterprise, Castro obliterated organized religion.

Ramon stuck to his church, but the life he would lead wasn't the life he had envisioned a few years before.

By the time I met him 54 years later, he'd reluctantly slipped into retirement—Cuba mandates it at age 72—but hadn't stopped working or talking about his church and how it found a place in a society that no longer wanted it. Cuba changed rapidly and radically, and Ramon changed, too. He figured out how to fit in.

For more than five decades, he had seen what was happening in his country and to his church. When I met him, he was learning the life of a widower, his children grown and on their own, and he was not shy in sharing those details. Maybe he'd never been shy, I don't know.

He saw what was happening to Cuba up close in Camagüey, the central province that early on tried to resist Castro and the place where Ramon worked as a parish priest for 25 years. He saw change when he traveled to Havana to visit the diocesan office. And he saw it throughout the country, as priests fled and those left behind were called on to minister in more and more places.

By the time he moved to Havana to become dean in 1992, Ramon was in charge of as many as 10 different churches. His wife Nerva Cot, also a priest and later a bishop— bishop suffragan, to be exact, a runner-up of sorts; she preceded Griselda by a few years as the first woman in Latin America to be a bishop of any type—handled a similar workload further east, in Santiago and Guantanamo.

In the 18 years he served as the dean, Ramon had seen the loosening of the state's grip on religion from as close a vantage point as a priest could attain. The cathedral and adjoining home for the dean was in the city's Vedado neighborhood, the mansion-filled former home of the rich, who fled after Castro settled in, and is still home to embassies and government offices. Less than twenty blocks from his office, up the tree-lined boulevard Avenida Paseo, is the Plaza de le Revolucion. That's where Castro's government has kept its seat of power, hidden in a hill behind the Jose Marti statue, and that's where Castro delivered many of his speeches. It was also where Pope John Paul II celebrated the mass that capped his five-day trip to Cuba in 1998, a trip often credited with beginning the slow if unsteady return to normalcy for the island's churchgoers.

Ramon was also a link to home. He was the last priest ordained by Bishop Hugo Blankingship, the only American to lead the Cuban Episcopal Church and the reason Carmen, DeWitt and I were there in the first place. We'd come to talk about a youth camp Blankingship conceived and began in the 1950s, but could never complete.

Blankingship was from Richmond, where I live, and that's where he went after fleeing Cuba in 1961. He'd retired the year before and may have planned on staying in Havana in the house he'd built adjacent to the cathedral, but when it became apparent that the revolutionaries were staying, he left.

He and his wife walked out the door one day, as empty-handed as if they were taking a casual stroll through the neighborhood. If anyone had walked in the house after they walked out, they wouldn't have suspected a thing. Their prized possessions—books and hair brushes and china and whatever else they'd collected through the years—were there. But the Blankingships were not. They'd caught a ride to the airport and taken off.

The move was so sudden, the couple arrived in Miami with nothing. The bishop had to borrow a dime from a British diplomat to make a phone call, as his daughter, Toni Donovan, would tell me years later.

They arrived in Richmond with nothing but the clothes they were wearing.

The bishop would never again see his home or Havana.

His old house is still the bishop's home, and that's where Griselda lives when she's in Havana. The first time I visited there, she proudly served lunch on the china the Blankingships left behind. They weren't just the dishes that happened to be in the house. She made a point of telling us how they had survived through the years and how they served as an important link to the past.

There were other reminders, too. A grandfather clock stood in the foyer, near the stairs and by the door that leads to the kitchen, exactly where Blankingship's daughter said it would be. She recalled it in exact detail more than a half century after last seeing it; when I looked, I matched her memories to the carvings in the wood casing and the markings on the dials. She hadn't missed a thing. The antique tables and chairs she remembered were still there, too.

In a whimsical moment, she also talked about the fishing rod one of her brothers left behind. I never saw that, but Havana is on the water: a fishing rod wasn't going to stay in a closet all those years.

She did not mention the bars on the outside of the windows, downstairs and up, or the metal gate inside the house at the top of the steps, keeping the second-floor bedrooms safe in case someone invaded the first floor, but perhaps those details had been too commonplace in the 1950s to merit memory. Bautista's Havana had not been a safe place.

The bishop had built himself a fortress there on the church grounds, walled in and protected by gates and bars and locks, so perhaps he knew what was coming.

He'd never see how it turned out. He spent the last 14 years of his life in Richmond, and died in 1975, at age 80. The church he'd help build across the island was in shambles by then, parishes empty, buildings shuttered or crumbling, little left but the fading memories of a people who had learned to keep their thoughts to themselves.

He was buried on "Bishops Row" at St. John's Episcopal Church in Richmond, just steps away from the chapel where Patrick Henry famously demanded liberty or death 200 years before, and there he could have stayed alone into eternity but for the persistence of Bishop Griselda.

She'd been to Richmond to visit the grave, and when we visited her in Havana, she opened to us the world Blankingship helped create.

More than 40 years after his death, and nearly six decades after he left, Blankingship's legacy lives on, especially in Cuba, where he is revered.

He portrait commands the wall at the top of the stairs in a part of the diocesan compound where visitors stay, giving him presence to new people nearly every day. Those who work there know him well, too, from his deeds if not his actual self. Ramon is the only priest I met who had known him, but they all know of him.

Bishop Griselda set aside days in her schedule to take us out into the countryside to the seemingly random speck on the map where Blankingship had seen potential in a piece of a land most others would have missed.

The property once dropped off just past the road, she'd said, and disappeared into the thick vegetation that covers everything that's left alone. A prior bishop filled in the ravine with gravel quarried from the mountain range in the distance, and Griselda's husband came along a decade later to clear the scrub brush that had grown back. The blue-green rocks were visible underfoot.

We stood in the open field by the road, not far from a cross Griselda had raised inside the entrance, as she pointed out where buildings would go. Her vision was as clear as Blankingship's, even as we were staring into an empty field. I think she felt the project as much as she saw it, and my friend DeWitt was right there with her, having an epiphany of his own about what he could do to help build. If I'd been more prescient, I would have had one, too. I didn't, but still, I got to walk the property with Griselda, just the two of us for a long stretch, and I felt good learning what she wanted.

We walked to an open-sided shelter at the back of the field, then we went down a hill and over a stream and back up another hill, to the hidden back half of the property, which had proved the perfect site for a working farm on which the church could grow crops that could be sold to help pay for the construction. We walked all the way to the farthest corner and climbed a small hill there. Then we stood and looked out over the whole thing. Bananas and yucca were in abundance that day, but the crops altered throughout the year, we were told, something always on its way to maturity. Griselda stood on that hill, her head protected under a purple sun hat, her arms sweeping this way and that, and told us what was to come.

The property was managed by her husband, Gerardo, and daily operations were entrusted to a cowboy who lived on a small plot nearby. He was right out of Central Casting, lean and tough and muscular in the natural way of a man who has spent his life working fields in a place where they still use oxen to pull the plows. Quiet, eyes hidden in the shadow cast by the brim of his straw hat, he was gentle enough to lean in and whisper soothing words to his horse when it became agitated. He looked like the kind of guy who'd slip whiskey into his baby's bottle and make your wife question her loyalty to you.

After a few days of looking at fields and trying to imagine the future and then visiting the bishop's old home church in the rural town of Itabo, we went back to Havana, where we again sat in the office and again listened to Ramon's stories, still in perfect English.

Back home, Carmen and DeWitt started drumming up support at St. James's for helping make Blankingship's camp a reality. The Richmond church has a long history of international outreach, so it wasn't a hard sell.

I started drumming up support for myself so I could get back to Cuba and talk to Ramon at greater length. I have a long history of being annoyingly persistent when I want something. My project was a tougher sell—my wife does not have a long history of supporting international research projects—but I pitched hard.

It never occurred to me to worry about not speaking Spanish. Ramon had been fluent in English, as had the office manager and several others we'd met, and I hadn't stopped to consider that perhaps other priests there weren't. I'd never been a language guy, and it hadn't stopped me from traveling before. Someone always knows English. It's like the Mandarin Chinese of the New World, a homogenizing comfort that's ever-present.

And it's not like I hadn't tried. I hadn't succeeded, but still. Once upon a time, I'd made a real effort to be a language guy.

When I was in high school in Norfolk, Virginia, in the 1980s, Spanish was not the language of choice for burgeoning cut-rate snobs like myself. We took French—or German, if we were serious and without humor, which I wasn't (how anyone ever gets laid in Germany, I don't know)—and perhaps some Latin. Spanish was for those kids who had to take a language but weren't smart enough to know the aristocratic appeal of French.

So with thoughts of pretty French girls and the Eiffel Tower and pretty French girls—I was a teenager; it was always about the pretty girls—I took three years of French in high school. Then I took another year in college, where the girls were even prettier, and less available.

I never really learned much beyond vocabulary. And that approach failed me almost immediately.

I first visited Cuba in 1988, at age 20, on a fishing trip with my father. Neither of us spoke Spanish, and we did just fine because we stayed at the Marina Hemingway—emphasis on the long, soft "M" and the rolled "r," as in "Muh-rina Hemingway"—a decidedly tourist-friendly enclave west of Havana. There was a canal behind our bungalow, and the property had its own dance hall and conga line and all the warm Polar beer an underaged American college boy could want.

Our fishing boat was tied up at a berth not far from our little house, and the whole time, I don't remember once stumbling over anything because of a language barrier. I don't know that the crew spoke English, but they were good and persistent at passing out beer and food, and there was really no need to talk. I may have tried to say something the first time I saw one of them throwing an empty Heineken can into the Gulf Stream, but if I did, it was ignored. All the empties went overboard that week, dozens every day. It was the first time I'd seen Heineken in cans.

It was all fine until the end of the tournament. We placed fourth of about two dozen teams, and our prize catch, a hundred-and-some-pound sailfish that was reeled in almost entirely by the crew, was going to be offered as bounty for all to enjoy. The party, we were told, would be like something from a movie: huge sailfish roasting, rum drinks, steel drums, native dancers, a zillion people, all ready to have one of those happy, fun, laughter-filled nights you see rolling by in the background in that scene when the stars meet. All we had to do was walk over.

And I had a date.

That wasn't a regular occurrence at that time, I'll admit, so I was in particularly high spirits that day.

I couldn't get a date at home, being too shy and goofy and not nearly good-looking enough or naturally charming, but I had one in Cuba. No one would believe it when I got back home, I knew, but I didn't care. I was on a Caribbean island at a marina on the ocean, and there was an actual living girl headed toward me, with me in mind. She hadn't seen me yet, but still, there was a chance I could overcome that.

She was coming my way in the company of a family connection that seemed appropriately surreal for the evening: the girl was the friend of a cousin of my stepmother's brother's wife, whose mother was Cuban and living in Havana at the time.

It was 1988, and Cuba was as Cold War Communist as could be, and a marina party with an American boy, I was told, was quite a treat.

I might have believed that, even knowing that I was the boy at the end.

The elation did not last.

We quickly established that I didn't speak Spanish and she didn't speak English—Russian was the language de rigueur at the time for aspiring Cuban intellectuals—and we kind of shrugged for a moment as we sat on the low wall of the marina, looking out over the ocean. I didn't have that thing some guys have where they can lean over and kiss the girl and everything works out, because a kiss is better than words almost all the time anyway. She didn't, either, or if she did, she wasn't going to waste it on me, two minutes into a bad idea of a blind date.

So we sat and stared at everything except each other and I probably did a nervous twitchy thing with my hands, rubbing my fingers together, and just when it was starting to look like one of those moments of missed opportunity, which my friends back home would believe, I jumped into action.

In a stroke of misguided faith in my lackluster academic career, I said something I would almost immediately regret.

"Parlez vous Francais?"

She smiled and her eyes showed what I knew to be relief, a sign that the night was going to work out after all. The tension was gone and her shoulders relaxed and she turned her whole body my way and let her beautiful brown eyes fall on me. I met her gaze and melted a little, the way I still do whenever I see beautiful brown eyes, and for that one little moment, the tiniest fraction of my life, I was the happiest guy in the world.

"Oui!" she said, pleasant and happy and maybe even with a sense of anticipation of what was to come. Not quite giddy, but close enough for me.

It could have been the beginning of a wonderful night for a 20-year-old American boy in Cuba at a conga-line dancing, gamefish-feasting party at an oceanside marina, entertaining a young woman with beautiful brown eyes, a girl who had only known the privations of Communist Cuba. I knew that scene from the movies, too, and I was, I'll quickly admit decades later, eager to play it out.

Except that asking if she spoke French was the extent of my useful French conversational skills. Three years of high school French and another year from college—including one semester when I'd earned an "A"; that had involved trying to impress a pretty girl, too—and I can't remember how many dozens of vocabulary quizzes and my opening line was, "Êtes-vous une fenêtre verte?"

"Are you a green window?"

She was not.

She was a budding Cuban intellectual schooled in Russian and well-versed in the follies of America, which was at the height of its imperialism then, Ronald Reagan still being in office and the Russians still playing the Cubans for their proximity and buying up all the bananas, and she was not amused at my ignorance.

She looked right at me and rolled her eyes in that way young women have when they realize they've been saddled with a boy not worthy of their attention. Not even close to worthy, even with free food and drink a short stroll away. So unworthy, even the roll of the eyes would seem a waste, if not for the necessity of letting the boy know how unworthy he was. I think she would have been happier if she'd been invited to babysit my nieces.

I may have said something just as dumb in English back then—I wasn't so smooth with the girls—but at least I could have tried to play it off, knowing the language and all. In French, in Cuba to a Cuban, I was a goner. That was it for me and Blind Date Girl.

The conversation quickly devolved to pointing and nodding, and then the whole experience came to an end in the conga line, when she danced one way and I another, and I never saw her again.

I was disappointed but not heartbroken. I was sharing a room with my father, so it wasn't like we had anywhere to go.

(I can't say why, but to this day, I still love the French word for window: fenêtre. It didn't serve me well then, and I've yet to see a benefit from knowing it, but I love saying it. Monet certainly didn't see his garden through something as pedestrian as a window; he took it in par le biais de la fenêtre. Through the window. I think. I had to translate that online. I'm still no good with the French.)

The thing was, that wasn't my only experience with linguistic failure on that trip. If I were ever going to learn the importance of knowing the language, it was in Cuba in 1988. But I'm more the kind of guy who picks up on the joke before he picks up on the lesson, and I didn't learn. But I did laugh. My stepmother's brother talked himself into one funny joke. Not intentionally, mind you, but funnier still because he actually spoke Spanish and still managed to botch it. His was not perfect Cuban Spanish, as he may have thought—and there's a difference, country to country—but enough Spanish to think he could get by just fine, thank you, without having to use picture menus or ask his wife, who was half-Cuban, for help, which is what my father and I had been doing.

Wherever we went, he'd order away in Spanish, and it worked out fine. Mostly, I realized later, because no matter what the menu said, you were getting a plate of pork chunks and rice and beans. One afternoon, we stopped at a little roadside pork stand way out in the country after we'd driven to a lake at the western end of the island. All four of us ordered different meals, using different words and everything, from a menu that offered many options. All four plates came out the exact same, each stacked high with roughly cut cubes of pork covered in flies.

That morning in the airport, we were sitting in the café talking away our final hours before leaving town, waiting for our Air Cubana flight back to Mexico City, when a waitress came over and asked if we'd like breakfast.

He ordered his in Spanish, and he did fine at first, huevos being huevos everywhere, but then he tried to ask for juice.

He thought he was ordering papaya juice, or jugo de papaya. The name of the fruit is the same in English as it is in Spanish. Except in Cuba, the practical word for it, the word Cubans use when they want a papaya, is fruta bomba, because papaya has come to mean something else, and it's not the kind of thing you're likely to get squeezed into a glass and served with your breakfast.

So he placed his order, then there was an awkward silence for a moment. The waitress blushed, and his wife started laughing. She laughed so hard, she nearly fell off her chair. Then the waitress laughed. My father and I laughed, too, though we weren't sure why. Laughter is contagious, and it felt good, especially not being the subject of it.

Then we figured out why they were laughing, and we laughed again. Because in Cuba, the traditional Spanish word for papaya has become a slang word for a part of the female anatomy from which it might be possible to extract a juice, but it might not be the kind of juice you'd want with your huevos.

He did not get what he ordered.

I didn't give language study another thought for two decades, until 2009, when I went to Turkey and then, months later, Peru. My wife allowed me to go both times by myself. She's a saint, to be sure, but perhaps she was also well aware that my personality—quiet and unassuming; I'm the guy in the cast of thousands, not the star out front—combined with my lack of language skills would keep me out of more trouble than they could get me into.

I didn't even try Turkish. Learning a language based on a new alphabet was well beyond my reach. I know my limits. I stayed in Istanbul the whole time and made liberal use of picture menus and frequented restaurants with food on display. I ate a lot of pizza and doner kebab that week and spent a lot of time with guys selling rugs. They all spoke perfect English.

But. for Peru, I thought about learning Spanish. I bought a phrase book and loaded instructional lessons onto my iPod and really thought I could teach myself at least the rudiments of the language on the eight-hour flight over. Which I might have done if I'd been a language guy with an inclination to learn such things. I'm not, and I didn't. I made it through a few simple phrases before realizing that speaking is only half the equation. I could por favor anything I pleased, but what was I to do when someone responded? So I went back to my music and enjoyed eight days of not understanding a word anyone said, Spanish being melodic enough to make the recitation of a grocery list a pleasant thing to hear. I think. Again, I wouldn't actually know if it were the grocery list, not knowing any of the words people were speaking.

All I picked up was learning to buy my agua sin gas if I didn't want it carbonated. I learned that through experience. Warm, carbonated water on a hot day is maybe not so refreshing.

I later tried to learn Creole—like I said, I can be persistent, even in the pursuit of failure—when I started going to Haiti on a regular basis. I figured I had a head start, what with my French skills. But I didn't know anything back then, and two decades later, I was still stuck on the green window. Fenet vet in Creole, if you're interested. Again, I think that's right. I looked it up.

I paid a hundred dollars to take a self-paced online course in Creole, but it didn't work out well. You really need someone with whom to speak, I convinced myself. I probably could have found that person—I hadn't been going to Haiti alone—but by the second or third lesson, the instruction took a dive into the romance chapter, and I realized that they and I were traveling to different Haitis. So I quit that, too, and soon thereafter lost my interest in Haiti. It's a tough place to like, much less love, in any language.

And by then, I'd switched my allegiance to Cuba.

I survived my first three trips, including the long-ago fishing expedition, without language skills, because I didn't need them: every step of the way, there had been someone who spoke perfect English.

Then I planned two weeks alone in Cuba, just me and whomever I could find to talk to. And that's when the folly hit me.

No Spanish meant no talking to most of the people I would see. And I'm a chatty guy; not talking is not good.

Not knowing the language is my own fault, I know. I've earned my living with words for most of my adult life. As a newspaper writer, I understand the beauty of clear, concise language: saying the most with the fewest words. I don't always do that, as my editors will probably tell you, but I appreciate the concept.

Clear and concise, you can learn in a vocabulary class: it's the easiest way to convey a message because you strip it to its basest form. You don't need any fancy turns of phrase: An ignorant American boy missed his chance with the pretty Cuban girl years ago. (Because really, a green window? Moron.) An arrogant American went back to Cuba as an adult.

But what has given me pleasure at home has been the capacity for language to stimulate, to entertain, its playfulness in the right hands.

There's so much more to language than simple words, and that's what I missed when that flighty, flirty woman was running Charlie Chaplin-style through the office of the Episcopal Diocese of Cuba. While I was hardly surprised by the playfulness—it was an Episcopal office, after all; they're allowed fun, and a great many make liberal use of it—I was sorry I'd cheated myself of the ability to play along. A girl like that, you need to talk to.

A language known is a powerful tool and a source for so much. It's an invitation to be chatty.

Language is nuance, innuendo, double entendre, clever turns of phrase. It makes the routine memorable, taking the same letters and words to which we all have access and doing things with them that will make someone else laugh, smile, cry, come close or run away. It's being memorable, if only for a moment.

It's being able to read Gabriel Garcia Márquez in his native Spanish and finally understanding why everyone thinks *Love in the Time of Cholera* is so good. I think. I can't actually do that, but I'm convinced something has been lost in the translation. I read it in English, and I kept wanting to strangle the guy and tell him to get over it. "She doesn't like you," I'd have said. "She never did."

Language aside, I still managed to get myself back to Cuba.

Bishop Griselda signed off on my trip and opened her office, and her country, to me in the fall of 2014. In the summer of 2015, she did it again, and also opened her home and let me spend a week in her carriage house.

But we never really worked out the details of that first trip, so I showed up in October 2014 not knowing what to expect. I had a visa and an apartment and a vague idea about interviewing people about church history. And then, once I got there, what I had the most was free time to think about that vague idea.

For four days, I sat on the couch outside the bishop's office, the same couch on which I'd sat and listened to Ramon that spring. I thought I'd spend some of my time talking to him, but he was out of town, too, so I sat on the couch alone every morning, and the people in the office took pity. They took an inventory of the staff and immediately began rationing their supply of English speakers.

They offered one a day.

One stayed for a few minutes and snuck off as soon as he could.

One stayed for an hour, so exact in his departure I thought he'd timed it. Not that that would happen in Cuba, time being a fluid concept there, but it was still suspicious.

One, the director of the diocesan office of mission and outreach projects, stayed for two hours, talking to me about everything from the church to national politics to U.S. history. He was a young version of Ramon, well versed in nearly everything and incredibly comfortable in talking about it. He finally excused himself, telling me there was a meeting going on in his office and that he should probably get back to it.

By the fourth day, some of the others who knew English but hadn't been comfortable speaking it began to talk. I learned of children and grandchildren and, in one bizarre moment, of a health supplement a woman thought my wife might like. It was a cream of some sort. I didn't buy any.

Even the flighty girl, who seemed like she'd be so much fun to be around, if only I could talk to her, was brave enough to speak, or smart enough to know that no matter how silly she sounded, she still sounded smarter than me. She agreed to take me to the bus station and help me buy a ticket.

"I can understand you," she said, finally speaking as we stood in the lobby of the bus station waiting for a clerk to finish the long process of booking my passage. "But I don't speak so good. Tomorrow. Be here. Eight o'clock."

Before tomorrow here eight o'clock and leaving Havana on a cross-country bus trip—an adventure that came with no promise of bilingual help—I took a stroll through Vedado, the once-posh suburb that's now as middle-class as it gets in Havana. Coming home from dinner that night, I passed the perpetually open windows of the apartments that line the streets. If not for the language barrier, it would have been like home, if only the people at home would turn off their air conditioners and open their sealed homes to the rest of the world for a few minutes: there was music playing, the inane chatter of television, voices here and there, the playful scream of a child (no translation needed), the equally playful chant back from the man walking in front of me, the sizzle from a stove. There were so few cars on the streets in Cuba, you could still hear what life sounded like.

And it was life for what life often is: the moment, as mundane, trivial, occasionally annoying, rarely memorable as it is, and worth every second of it.

I knew then that what I was really looking for was all of Cuba, not just the part tucked into Episcopal churches. I wanted every bit I could find, and I was hoping like hell that my lack of one sense—the good sense to learn the language—would open the way for my other senses to take it all in. Failing that, I planned to take some pictures, so at least I'd have something I could show people later.

Along the way, I'd talk about church history with church people, because my new church friends were so nice. Really, what bishop does for someone what Bishop Griselda was doing for me?

But I'd also get to see Cuba from Havana to Camagüey to Santiago and back, more than a thousand kilometers of the country, by car, bus and plane, and that was an opportunity too good to relegate to a single quest.

By the time I was done, I'd spend an afternoon with a woman who was pushing a hundred and who would tell me in beautiful detail about the day in 1930 her church opened, and how she had been going there ever since, no matter what Castro thought. She was getting ready to resume teaching Sunday school, 40 years after giving it up, because children were finally coming back.

I'd spend a morning with a couple of cut-rate hustlers in Havana who struggled for two hours to work up the courage to ask me for money, only to fail in a convoluted commission scheme involving cigars and baby formula.

I charged up San Juan Hill, the same one from the history books, only I did it in a Kia with a couple of Cuban priests, not on horseback with Teddy Roosevelt and his Rough Riders. We made it to the top without coming under fire.

Every step of the way, on that trip in October 2014, and in the three before it and two after, I saw Cuba.

Not the Cuba from television, with the handsome news anchors talking in somber tones about thawing relations and how the exiles in Miami still weren't sure they could agree. That's out there somewhere, but it's someone else's story.

Not the Cuba from the history books with Castro in fatigues and his fiery rhetoric and the mysterious disappearances of his enemies. That, too, is someone else's story. Serious, important, essential to understanding the context of Cuba and its place in the world today. But it's not my story. The closest I came to Castro was seeing one of his old limousines, which had been converted into a taxi, and reading his words on billboards.

And not the Cuba from make-believe, the one with the beautiful, busty showgirls on every corner and all the debauchery a simple boy from Virginia could handle. That one I definitely didn't see, expect maybe once when a bicycle taxi guy offered to get me a woman, but the timing was all wrong and I quickly wound up back in the company of church people.

The Cuba I saw was different.

It was mostly people being people: doing their jobs, living their lives, being as normal as anyone back home.

That could all change quickly, I guess, especially if relations really do thaw and Cuba gets sucked into that hell that swept through Russia and Eastern Europe at the end of the Cold War.

But when I went, it was still just Cuba. More or less.

A little Spanish would have helped, but I made it by fine just the same.

CHAPTER 2

HAVANA

SITTING UNDER A Lucky Strikes umbrella on the second floor veranda of a restaurant called the French Union, just up the marble stairs from a mannequin with an eerie resemblance to the late tennis player Arthur Ashe, I had the most Cuban of dinners my first night back in Havana: a Hawaiian pizza with a can of lemon-flavored soda.

The United States may have long ago cut its formal and official ties with Cuba, but Cuba never cut its ties with the rest of the world. The country is shabby at the corners, rundown top to bottom, crumbling on top of itself in places, in bad need of a good cleaning and a fresh coat of paint, but it's still a vibrant place. Unlike some of its Caribbean neighbors, especially Haiti one island to the east, Cuba is not desperate, nor has it become an island-themed resort. There's life on the streets and in the homes, easy laughter over the ubiquitous cups of espresso and the inevitable delays in nearly everything that leave people plenty of time to sit around and talk and often to laugh at, or at least accept, their fates. It's mostly functioning, with roads and schools and healthcare. Rice and beans are served daily and then some, and there are grapefruit-sized avocados and as many plantains as you can eat. But you can get a ham and pineapple pizza named after one of the United States, if that's what you prefer. About four dollars, at the French Union; less than a dollar, at a sidewalk stand a few blocks away.

In the fall of 2014, a few months before U.S. President Barack Obama's surprise announcement that he wanted to try to ease ties between the U.S. and Cuba, Havana's daily newspaper, *Granma*, still carried stories about the evils of the U.S. blockade, more than five decades after it was enacted. But outside of those pages and away from hardline government types, the rhetoric seemed a little less intense.

There are "biological factors in play," one man told me in Havana, an inevitability that change will again come to the island because nature is taking its toll on the men who brought the last round of great change. You can't live forever, even if you are *el lider*. And there's change that has already come, too, a loosening of the tight grip that for several generations separated the people into camps of "for us" and "against us," of those allowed certain perks, up to and including life itself, and those denied.

"That you're here, talking to me, tells me things are changing," another man told me, talking openly in his living room halfway across the island as I sat with notebook in hand, writing down his words. He knew who I was and why I was taking notes and what might come of his words, and he didn't care. The days of not trusting anyone were slipping into the past.

Both conversations were about religion, a topic that had been as taboo as the United States was evil almost from the beginning of the Castro revolution. Now it was coming back into acceptance, if slowly and cautiously.

"We're not friends," one priest told me about the current relationship between the church and the state. "We each have our place. I think they now understand the importance of religion to the people. Cubans never stopped being religious."

Not that Castro didn't try to make that happen. Of all the dogma he institutionalized early in his reign, distrust of and disdain for the church was among the harshest. He went after the religious leaders long before he went after the merchants. Some priests were killed, many churches closed, church schools were taken by the state and attending a Sunday service became an act of political defiance few were willing to risk.

Vladimir Lenin and Karl Marx both called religion the opiate of the masses, but it was Fidel Castro who cut off the supply.

"The church represented the power," a priest told me on the far eastern end of the island. "If you had the power, you couldn't be trusted."

And so Castro made sure the power ended. He nationalized church schools, effectively ending the system of private education for the island's middle class—which is what church schools had become during the reign of Fulgencio Bautista, as president in the 1940s and as dictator in the '50s—and helping push those people out of his way and off his island. And he made church attendance and membership in his Communist party mutually exclusive: you had to pick one or the other. You didn't have to shun the first or choose the latter, but if you chose wrong, your options were limited. The plan worked. Priests fled the island, the working class quit showing up on Sundays and the churches dwindled away.

Churches that once hosted hundreds of people on Sunday mornings soon saw their memberships decline to single figures. Many vanished altogether. Across the island, the churches themselves were either taken by the state and put into other uses, or they were abandoned, stripped of their parts and left to crumble in place.

In Santiago, which calls itself the city of heroes and claims ties to Castro. Bautista, Jose Marti and a cemetery full of other notable Cubans, the Episcopal diocese once had five churches. Two remain.

In Camagüey, a church that once had standing-room-only crowds—I saw pictures that proved it—saw its membership decline to a half-dozen people and its roof spring leaks. The state took control of the school behind the church and the boarding house for students down the street. Vandals broke or stole what little was left to it.

In the little town of Itabo, when the current bishop arrived for her first posting after seminary in the 1980s, bats were nesting in the roofless building and the front door had to be pried open. I saw those pictures, too; that the walls stood to hold the doorway was a miracle.

Across the island, it was the same.

And across the island today, things are changing.

Slowly, for sure; at least two generations of Cubans grew up without the church, and those people have been slow to adopt something they've never known. Blind obedience to one all-knowing institution proved enough for many.

But change had begun, nonetheless.

I'd seen some of that on prior trips to Cuba. There were people dressed up early on Sunday, heading off to their churches, the same as I'd see back home. Others were milling around during the week at churches that were still in use, even dominating in some neighborhoods, decades after the revolution. It wasn't the full-on evangelical church-as-your-whole-world experience you see in parts of the U.S., but it was still something.

The thought of going back to talk about that change seemed a worthy pursuit, one of those ideas that come up back home after you finish a trip and start thinking about ways to legitimize yet another to a weary spouse who stays home and tends to the business of keeping life together for the rest of the family.

"No, no," I'd say, trying out the latest spiel, "This one's for research."

Her eyes would roll a little in suspicion. She had actually done academic research and earned degrees for it.

But permission would come, eventually, because maybe I'd hit on something worth pursuing. Or maybe because I know my voice puts her to sleep at night, and I've learned how to make the most of that moment just before she slips off. That's when you ask.

But the worthiness part had some truth to it, too.

Some. After three trips, I'd seen all the picture book stuff that always comes to mind whenever someone says "Cuba": old American cars, dark-skinned women in period attire peddling big cigars and planting big red kisses on the cheeks of unsuspecting tourists, showgirls at what's left of the old luxury hotels along the waterfront, pictures of Che and the inspiring words of Fidel, displayed on billboards and walls and signs and anywhere else they could have been stenciled.

It's all there, enough to keep tourists happy the whole week they're in town. In Old Havana, it's everywhere, and elsewhere it's not so hard to find, either. But go back a few times and go alone, and you stop paying attention and start hoping for a ride in a car that's more comfortable than cool.

I'm not an historian, and I'm not much of a church member, but I do know how to take notes, and through years as a newspaper reporter, I've learned that the best way to get what you want is to ask for it. It doesn't always work out, but asking is a more reliable plan than hoping something will just appear.

So I asked.

I went to the Right Reverend Griselda Delgado, the Episcopal Bishop of Cuba, whom I'd met twice before. By telephone and email, and with the help of an acquaintance in Gainesville, Florida, we set up a plan for me to visit and talk to people about the church before and after the revolution. There was some concern that I'd stumble in and reopen old wounds the bishop had worked hard to close—church is church, even in Cuba—but I left her plenty of room to help me identify places to go and people to see, and we wrapped it all up months in advance.

I'd first see Juan Ramon, the retired Dean of the Cathedral in Havana, a man whose career had spanned the entire length of the Revolution. I'd met him before, too, and he offered the promise of hope that if nothing else worked out, at least I could put together a story about him.

Then I'd travel the country to talk to priests and parishioners.

The visa implied promise, hope that I really could study church history the way an American journalist would want: by showing up at the appointed hour, flipping open a notebook and asking questions.

But reality has a way of taking its own course, especially in the Caribbean. Cuba is a place where you go to wait your turn, and you wait whether you're a Cuban who has grown up knowing nothing else or an impatient American who thinks he's going to be presented with a reliable schedule to be followed once he walks into the office of the bishop. Because that's just not going to happen, getting that schedule.

><

I'd eventually be sent on my way to study my history, but first I had to wait my turn.

I walked into the office of the bishop on a Monday morning, getting there just before nine as instructed the day before by the person from the church who picked me up from the airport. I was directed to a couch, which I would get to know well in the days that would follow, and offered coffee, which I would come to loathe, being an American who likes his Starbucks.

My translator was there, the cheerful granddaughter of the office manager, sitting with her grandmother in the office, engrossed in a fast-moving, friendly sounding conversation.

I checked my notebooks and pens and clicked my camera on and off and back on and tried to balance the little saucer and coffee cup on the arm of the couch as I sunk further and further into the cushions. When I could sink no more, my back wedged nearly into the wall, I crossed my legs, sucked down my coffee quickly (it managed to be bitter, sweet and altogether unsatisfying) and looked around the room.

On the wall opposite the couch was the large map of Cuba I'd spent hours studying with my friend DeWitt Casler that spring. There were pushpins in the places with Episcopal churches. It was a nice map, colorful and clearly marked, and I'd buy myself two copies before the trip was over. I like maps, and I'll collect as many as I can wherever I go. I won't often consult them in public, fearing the defeat of letting people know I'm lost or uncertain, but I'll study them for hours in solitude. As long as the streets are straight and clearly marked, I can find my way around the first time... meaning that I usually wander lost, hoping I make it back to a familiar place without too much trouble.

The room also had several chairs and a coffee table with an assortment of magazines and copies of *Granma*, the tiny little daily newspaper, so thin and small it reminded me of my high school paper. There were also pictures of the bishop from the day she was ordained and doors into several offices.

I looked for the retired dean, whom I'd been told would be there and ready to talk to kick off my great project, but I didn't see him. Nor did I see the bishop. It was a small space, and neither was hiding in the back. There wasn't a back, just a little kitchen where they rinsed out the coffee cups. I checked, and they weren't there.

Neither was in town or expected back for days, the office manager told me. She was not nearly as concerned about that development as I was.

"No one's here today," she said, her voice cheerful, her upbeat delivery betraying the message she was delivering. "Would you like more coffee?"

She rubbed my shoulder, imparting tranquility the way some women can just by touching you. It was like your grandmother letting you know the world is going to be all right, no matter what, so just relax a little.

And more coffee? Of course, I would, I thought. The first cup had about two sips in it.

Then the translator, with whom I'd worked before, came out of the office and smiled the little smile you get from people who don't remember you as well as you remember them.

I could tell you about her father, the Cuban fighter pilot who had moved to Panama, and her stepfather, the construction worker who had moved to Louisville, Kentucky, where I grew up, but maybe I'm just good with random details I learn about strangers. It's what newspaper people do. I'm not so sure she could have told you my name.

"So what would you like to do today?" she asked me.

My first thought, which I didn't share because it was early in the trip and I was trying to be polite, was that I'd like to get to work. I don't mind goofing off, particularly at home, but I had suffered visa issues in Miami, where they couldn't find my name in the records and only let me board the plane after calling authorities in Havana. Then in Havana, the person with the visa disappeared between the call from Miami and the arrival of my flight, only to run into a scheduling snafu that would idle me for days where I was supposed to be working.

But fear of being that horribly demanding, pushy American kept me in check, and I just said my best, "Uh, I don't know. See something? Anything but Old Havana."

Old Havana I'd seen to death already. You can't visit Havana without someone taking you there. Fidel's old boat, the *Granma*, is there, in a whole museum devoted to his revolution. You have to see that. And the Capitol, and the art museums and days' worth of other stuff, all older than dirt and overrun by people just like you.

So the 24-year-old, a museum guide-in-training earning coveted tourist currency on her day off, took me sightseeing.

Which isn't a bad thing to do in Havana, especially in the company of someone who lives there, likes history and has the patience to stroll alongside a meandering middle-aged American who'll stop every 20 feet to take a picture of something. Plus, before getting her museum job, my guide had worked for the city's historian, an exercise in bureaucratic minutiae that prepared her well to explain to me what it was I was taking pictures of.

Somewhere on the island, my pursuit of the history of the church would come into shape.

><

But first, we were going to Chinatown.

After trading my American money for Cuba's tourist money, not to be confused with Cuba's resident money—a dual economy that creates the odd propensity to make you feel like you're getting screwed even when you're spending $25 a night to rent an entire apartment, because you know a Cuban would get the same apartment in a nice neighborhood for about three dollars—we hopped in a taxi and headed for Chinatown. The car was one of those old American tanks everyone seems to so love when they're talking about Cuba. Like many of them, this model wasn't quite right: the outside said Dodge, but the steering wheel was from a Hyundai, the back seat wasn't quite wide enough to fill the space between the doors and the whole car was coated with so much paint, it looked like a piece of ancient playground equipment, electric blue on top and descending through layers of green and yellow and red to an undercoat of rusting steel.

The car was part of the city's unofficial public transportation system for locals, not one of the tourist-friendly, spic-and-span taxis a few blocks away along the *Malecon*, the seafront highway that crosses five miles of Havana. These cars run up and down the main roads; Linea, in our case, east into Old Havana and back. Locals stand on the curb and hail them, one hand out, signaling the driver. If there's an empty seat, the driver stops; if not, he keeps going. Danella paid a peso, about four cents in my money, for the two of us to get across town, far less than the 15 tourist dollars I would spend on a taxi a few days later.

On the ride over, Danella told me that Cuba once had a sizable Chinese population, but that now it's hard to find full-blooded Chinese in Havana. Occasionally, she said, you'll see a Cuban with an Asian feature, particularly in the eyes, but that's about it. We spent more than an hour looking but didn't find one.

The Chinese may have completely assimilated, but their neighborhood has not. Chinatown remains at the edge of Old Havana, and casts its shadow, as do other Chinatowns the world over, with the requisite street-spanning gateway decorated with Chinese lettering that may or may not be of any significance to the decidedly non-Chinese population coming and going on the street below. It's not a particularly attractive touch in Havana; it's more of a low-budget version of what someone thought such an arch should maybe look like, if they'd ever seen one. There's a better example in Washington, D.C., which doesn't even have a real Chinatown: that colorful arch leads walkers past the escalator to the subway station and straight to a chain restaurant. But at least in Havana, you aren't assaulted with the sight of a hamburger joint next to the arch. The shop names there are in Chinese, and street names are in Chinese and Spanish.

The narrow streets, from an era long before the advent of motor coaches and delivery vans, are the usual Cuban combination of architectural wonder and urban decay, a telling display of the Communist-era economy's ability to undermine any aesthetic. Once-beautiful buildings in full-on decline line the streets, and people crowd the sidewalks. One corridor fans out at an angle from the main street, and the little pedestrian mall is lined on both sides with Chinese restaurants, each of which employs a small army of enthusiastic, if pushy, menu-wielding greeters who work their territory like street preachers.

A little further on, there's a building that looks like a small version of New York's Flatiron Building and then a beautiful Art Deco tower that now houses the national telephone company.

There's also a row of old movie theaters, including the Cuba, but those are mostly in that stage between hope and despair, still standing but not offering promise of much anytime soon.

Through one grimy window, we could see beautiful dresses and blown-up photographs of beautiful people in beautiful places, which they'd reach by riding in the beautifully preserved American cars visible in the background. It was a store dedicated to *quinceanera*, the celebration of a girl's 15th birthday. It's a popular rite throughout Central and Latin America, and Cuba is no exception. Later in the trip, I'd walk into a home and the most prominent photographs would be of the owner's daughter at her celebration.

But it's an expensive rite, and it's not for everyone. Danella scoffed at the whole idea, dismissing it as a waste of money. "There are better things to buy," she said.

Then she listed some of those things. At the top of her list were cell phone service, which costs more than she makes in her state job, and American shampoo.

"The Cuban shampoo is terrible for your hair," she said.

> <

Next to Chinatown, just past the gateway and heading east into Old Havana and toward the Capitol building, was the city's locomotive works. Perched on a corner lot, within sight of the classical dome of the Capitol, was a work yard with eight old steam locomotives in various stages of repair. The train station wasn't far away, but there was no rail leading into the yard.

I stopped to take a picture through a rickety chain-link fence, and one of the workers stopped to stare back at us. Then he smiled and said something to Danella.

"He said we can come in and look around," she said, sounding as surprised as I was.

Not the response I'd get back home, for sure. And not an offer I was going to pass on in Havana.

We walked to the gate, where four men were sitting in chairs and talking about something, and Danella smiled, and they let us in.

The steam engines, mostly from old sugar plantation lines, were supposedly being restored so they could return to service. Unlike U.S. repair works, which are attached to railroad lines so the locomotives can roll in, this yard was a standalone affair, with rails placed here and there and the locomotives placed by crane. Some looked steady, but others sat at precarious angles, as if they forgot to level the ground before laying out the rails. The whole yard was strewn with parts and dotted with puddles with the slick rainbow sheen of oil floating on water.

If not for the somewhat modern buses running along the

streets behind us, sharing space with the horse-drawn carts and the bicycle taxis, the scene could have been lifted from history: men in greasy overalls, some with wrenches working on steam engines, others sitting at their little tables with their demure cups of espresso, none displaying anything more modern than perhaps a wristwatch.

We made the rounds of the yard, peering into this and poking around that and generally making ourselves at home amid the environmental and physical hazards that abounded. We both took pictures without abandon—this being a sight Danella apparently didn't often see, see pulled out her phone and snapped away, too—and then we left.

> <

The religious portion of the day came several blocks away, where three imposing Catholic cathedrals sat within a few blocks of each other.

The Cathedral of San Francisco dated to 1608 and was still in use. The massive stone building had an open doorway on what seemed to be the side but was actually the back. With the difference from the blinding sun of a Caribbean morning to the darkness of the interior, you couldn't see a thing from the street. It was just a dark blob, but the sight of a small desk off to the right caught our attention. In Cuba, an open door is often an invitation to visit, and the desk, and the person behind it, offered a chance to inquire.

The girl at the desk was busy talking to a boy, and she waved us through.

Once inside, we found ourselves gawking at a stunningly detailed baroque sanctuary, rising stories into the air and stretching side to side across the entire block.

Of the many depictions shown in great detail was one of the Virgin Mary, as she once appeared to three fishermen lost offshore from a small town on the eastern end of the island. The image guided the men back to port, then Mary disappeared. Some time later, she reappeared a bit inland, near the copper mines of El Cobre, a small village near Santiago in the southeast. Twice more, she was seen, and after her third appearance, the people built her a shrine. Unfortunately, they built it atop a copper mine, and as the ground below was mined out, the building collapsed.

They built another, larger shrine nearby, and today, you can stand in the parking lot and look over a small valley and up a hill to copper mines. To this day, people still trek to the shrine in hopes of making a plea for good health. Danella's mother once took her there, decked out in the obligatory yellow gown, and prayed for her rambunctious, occasionally accident-prone daughter to live a safe life. It worked until the summer of 2014, when Danella was sickened by a piece of bad fish and was confined to her bed for nearly a month.

Down the block, on the main square facing the old customs house and across the street from the harbor, was another San Francisco, equally grand in stature. It, too, had been a working place of worship, until a brief British occupation during which the Anglicans sullied the interior by worshipping there. The Catholics refused to return, and the building had long been used as a music hall and, at least once, as the site of a wedding for a British couple. The square outside its doors is a common starting point for walking tours, so it's usually full of wide-eyed tourists and the savvy locals who know how to separate a few dollars from them.

The third was known as the main cathedral, and it sat facing Cathedral Square. It, too, had the look of its times: a massive, if less-than-inviting, stone exterior towering over the square. You could picture a fussy priest ruling there, decked out in thick, flowing wool robes in the Caribbean heat, lecturing his congregants of the evils of life in a place so beautiful.

On first glance from the square, the towers on either side looked the same, but upon further reflection they actually differed significantly.

Danella, who studied art history in college and once wrote a paper on the cathedral, said the accepted theory was that the Spanish originally built the wide, though somewhat plain, tower on the right. The British came along later and added the narrower but more ornate tower on the left. Why the Catholics had chosen to remain here even after the British occupation was a mystery, she said.

><

Around the corner from the Cathedral, at the end of a short alley that sloped gently uphill from the square, we had lunch in a room full of clocks. The building may once have been a home. When we visited, the front rooms had been converted to dining space and decorated in a peculiar antiquarian style. The furnishings looked as if they came from one of those dusty shops on a seldom-visited main street in a dying town back home: a mismatch of styles, little of real value but all with aesthetic appeal.

The clocks above us ticked and tocked and moved generally forward, but I don't think any two of the dozen or so hanging there told the same time. It reminded me of a line in a song written by a friend from Virginia, Billy Hatley:

"Time moves so slow down there/the clock don't know which way to go."

He was writing about running off to an easier life in Mexico, but the sentiment fit Havana, too. Time moves slow down there.

The menu was typical Cuban. We were served chicken and rice and black beans in quantities neither of us could fully consume, and we drank frozen lemonade, which wasn't so typical. It was delicious. Danella ordered stuffed plantains, which I'd had elsewhere in Havana and don't intend to eat again, ever. It's a taste I've yet to acquire. A two-inch-long piece of plantain is hollowed out and filled with diced ham or canned tuna. It combines the blandness of a baked plantain, tough and chewy and nearly flavorless, with a creamy filling best left to the school lunch of a child you don't much like.

They brought us too much food, which happens wherever tourists show up in Cuba. You eat and eat and eat the whole time you're there, until you're invited to dine in someone's home and you get a meal properly proportioned and you realize the gluttony of it all.

We worked hard but could not finish our lunch. Danella suggested a doggy bag, which is apparently not a common request in Cuba. The smart person just goes ahead and eats the whole thing right there and then and skips the next meal. We had to ask to take the leftovers with us. The staff struggled with wrapping the beans, and we wound up leaving with a single tinfoil packet of sticky white rice, lettuce and avocado slices. I never did eat it.

> <

Later in the day, after I'd released Danella from her tour guide obligations, I left my apartment on foot and took what would be the first of many walks that occupied my time while I waited for the bishop to return.

The Episcopal Cathedral, and the apartment I had across the street, is in Vedado, which was one of Havana's fashionable upper-crust enclaves until the revolution. It has wide, tree-lined streets, stately mansions on large lots, small parks and a peacefulness not evident in the more densely populated parts of town.

It looks old today, the banyan trees crowding the sidewalks and blocking the sun, but it has one feature that gives away its youth: its streets are laid out in a logical, easy-to-follow grid and reasonably same-sized blocks. And at each intersection, set in the ground, is a small four-sided white stone, engraved with the names of the two streets that pass by.

Old Havana fans out from the harbor inland, some blocks stretching out hundreds of feet wide, others so narrow you think you could stretch your hands across from one side to the other and touch the walls. Streets that start a block apart drift outward, only to come back together at the far side of the neighborhood. On a map, it sort of makes sense, things coming and going, being able to look past a dead end and see where it picks up again, but on the street, hidden in the canyon of walls, it's an easy place to get lost.

In Vedado, once you could have closed your eyes and counted the steps and known when to step off the curb. You can't now, of course, because decades of neglect have left gaping holes here and there, and roots have pushed their way through the concrete, and you'd likely step on a cat or a dog or trip over a random piece of garbage left beside one of the large gray bins on wheels at the intersections.

Still, you'd be reasonably safe throughout most of the neighborhood, because so few people drive, the risk of getting hit is minimal. That's also mostly true on the main roads that border the neighborhood. Cars do whizz by and aren't inclined to stop for tottering tourists, but they come with less frequency than you might expect in a city of two million people.

I kept my eyes open for my walk and headed north on *Avenida Paseo* to the *Malecon*, then east to the *Avenida de los Presidentes*—the two *avenidas*, spread wide and pedestrian friendly, dissect the neighborhood—back to *Linea*, or *Calle 9*, as it is called on some street corner markers, and looped back home.

Along the way, I saw people fishing from the wall of the *Malecon*, openly ignoring signs banning the activity. A few of the men had fishing rods but most just had spools of line. The talented among them could swing a hook with bait and sinker above their head like a cowboy with a lasso and let fly, casting their hope far into the Atlantic Ocean. I don't know what they hoped to catch, or how the fish would look after bouncing across the rocks that separate the tall wall of the *Malecon* from the sea at low tide. Lacking Cuban patience, I didn't stand around long enough to find out.

At the point where the *Avenida de los Presidentes* runs into the *Malecon*, at the grand statue of Calixto Garcia on horseback staring out to sea, a couple in white wedding attire raced through traffic with a photographer. They posed this way and that along the seawall, a happy couple recording their memories 10 or 20 feet from two fishermen working their lines. They were oblivious to the world around them, as brides and grooms can be.

One of the fishermen turned to look at the couple but the other ignored the commotion, keeping his focus on his lines.

> <

Havana is a city of grandeur and decrepitude, a place of dismay and discovery. For every building you see that you wish you could restore to its former glory, you'll find another with its front door open, or missing, and an oddly placed staircase beckoning you to uncover what lies hidden behind the darkness. Often, the buildings are one and the same, particularly along the *Malecon*.

It's also a city of grand avenues, cut in the middle and spread wide so tree-lined promenades can run their course toward the sea. There's one in Old Havana, Paseo de Marti, ending a block from where the Atlantic pours into the port, and several others further west, dissecting Vedado. They're peaceful respites, even with the low-pitched whines of underpowered motorbikes and the grind of ancient cars struggling to climb one more hill.

On a bench in the middle of *Avenida Paseo*, at *Calle 13* at the cutover that leads back to the Cathedral, a couple stopped to chat and tell me about their son, who lived in Syracuse, New York. What a shock that must be for a Cuban, I thought, finding yourself living in a place as cold as upstate New York.

They invited me to join them for dinner, or perhaps buy them dinner; I couldn't quite tell. They were talking fast and over each other and I'm not sure they knew what they wanted. I declined. I was comfortable on my bench, and some acquaintances are meant to be fleeting, blips in time, smiling faces last seen descending a hill toward the sea. Where they went, I'll never know. But I'm confident they found a warmer place than their son.

The joy of being alone in a foreign country is that it allows for a different sense of place: there's no filter between you and them, you and whatever it is that's wherever you are. There are no fellow travelers behind whom you can hide, no translator to handle the dirty work of keeping you safe from the world. It's just you and whatever comes your way.

And in Havana, that can be a relaxing thing, especially away from the touristy sections. You're mostly ignored, and even when you're engaged, it's more often than not friendly, a chance for pleasantries and casual conversation. It lacks the tension of New York or the chaos and danger of Port-au-Prince or the constant demand for sympathy of Washington, three other large cities in which I've spent time. For a big city, Havana seems small, comfortable and peaceful.

> <

The neighborhood market a block from my apartment sold almost everything: shampoo, water heaters, pressure cookers, Frosted Flakes breakfast cereal, a dozen kinds of cookies, electric tea kettles and several kinds of fruit-flavored malt liquor. But it didn't sell bottled water, which was available at a street-side kiosk out the side door and up the hill, or coffee pots, which I never found anywhere except the National Museum of Fine Arts. But more on that later.

My apartment came with a pressure cooker but not a coffee pot, which seemed an odd omission in a country that so loves its coffee. I had to settle for a jar of Colcafé Clasico instant coffee. In Cuba, known as much for its coffee as its cigars, I was relegated to stirring 100 percent pure Colombian coffee dust into a cup of boiling water. It'd be like lighting up a Swisher Sweet along the Malecon, if only I smoked.

Just boiling the water proved troublesome. The only pot in the cabinet was the kind of tub in which you might cook spaghetti. I found a small stainless steel pitcher with a hinged lid and filled it with bottled water. I struck a match and lit the stove, then balanced the pitcher on top and let it sit until the water began to roil with the tiny bubbles of a boil.

When it was time to pour, I couldn't find a potholder, so I grabbed the washcloth from the kitchen sink and grabbed the pot. I filled my cup, then set the pot down. The washcloth, apparently made of plastic fiber, stuck to the handle. I managed to pull it mostly free, but the yellow cloth was forevermore marked with a dark-rimmed hole on one side, and the handle of the pot was dotted with pieces of ripped fabric.

I set my cup of coffee on the small table, and the composition of the ceramic cup on the white lace tablecloth was so perfect, I reached for my camera so I could take a picture. When I stood up, I knocked into the edge of the plastic table, and coffee spilled all over the lace. Fortunately, it, too, was plastic, so it rinsed out easily.

><

My translator had gone back to work at the museum on Tuesday, so I was left alone for that day's wait in the church office.

Cuban Episcopals proved to be an accommodating sort, and after I finished my first coffee, the office manager, Say—pronounced *Si*—looked around and found an English speaker to entertain me until I'd decide to drift away for the rest of the day and leave her alone.

As would become apparent in the days to come, it was an act of rationing: one English speaker per day, and she'd keep me entertained until the bishop returned.

The first day, the lucky winner was the staff computer technician, a man in his early twenties who said he taught himself English by watching American movies with subtitles.

It wasn't as bad as that promised, and we mostly spent our time talking about Internet connection speeds and the computing power of my iPad, tablet computers being a small marvel there, and where in Havana I could find a reliable signal to get online.

He never once used a bad film cliché, and I decided he had good taste in movies, or at least had learned to be discerning in his vocabulary.

After lunch, he went back to work and I went in search of online access. He said it was most likely found at the tourist hotels, so I headed for the nearest: the Melia Cohiba, a huge, ugly, Spanish-built tourist hotel a block from the Malecon at the foot of *Avenida Paseo*.

The Cohiba is grand in size but little else, a V-shaped design of brownish concrete and dark windows that rises 22 stories high. From the inside looking out, there's a sweeping view of Havana heading east as the *Malecon* turns inland on its course into the historic old town and toward the entrance to the harbor. But it's sealed tight, and the windows are tinted, so there's a perpetual hint of rain, even on the sunniest day. In a city of benches and patios, a place where life can be lived outside, the Cohiba seems a tomb.

From the outside looking in, it's just another mass of the forbidden planted in the midst of long-suffering locals: a decade ago, Cubans weren't even allowed into such hotels. The whiter among them, and those with the best English skills, could occasionally pass themselves off as tourists, but not without risk. Today, they can walk in like anyone else, but their pesos won't buy much. It costs five tourist dollars for 30 minutes or 14 for a two-hour pass to use the Internet. If they could exchange their money for tourist money, it would cost 125 or 350 pesos for either.

On my first day there, struggling with the ancient speed of dated wireless equipment—getting online had a feel I remembered from the 1990s, when my home connection still went through the phone line and I always waited anxiously for the dialing to turn into the whining pitch of a connection—I watched the lobby fill near check-in time, each group proof that Americans haven't cornered the market on being unbearable on vacation.

A dozen fat, beer-drinking, cigar-smoking men clogged the line at around three o'clock, dead ringers for Americans except their conversations were in Spanish. I'll never know what they were at home, but in Havana that day, they were a cliché: rowdy men gone abroad to run amuck, talking too loud and drinking too much way too early in the day. They made each other laugh with great ease, but the staff wasn't amused.

In the lobby bar, a group of Chinese men in conservative suits and straw hats had their rum drinks and talked in hushed tones, lower yet when they noticed a lone American looking their way. They looked uncomfortable, or perhaps just unhappy, and not just because they'd allowed themselves the luxury of silly hats.

Two tables over, the Americans did come: a young couple with the obligatory wayward children fussing their way into promises of better things to come at home, if only they'd just try to behave now. The father had an armband tattoo, proving a tribal affiliation of a sort he'd probably be hard-pressed to fully explain; the mother had hair a shade too blonde for nature. They looked as if they'd stepped onto the wrong plane leaving Miami and wound up here instead of sitting beachside in Jamaica.

I left and walked the eight blocks back uphill to my apartment, where I deposited my iPad and then walked some more, another 15 blocks or so south on *Avenida Paseo* through a light sprinkle to the point where it passes the *Plaza de la Revolucion.*

On one side of the street are two government ministry buildings. The Ministry of the Interior is adorned with a black silhouette of Che Guevara, apparently based on a famous photograph, with the words *Hasta la Victoria Siempre,* or "always toward victory" mounted below the image. Next to it is the Ministry of Telecommunications, which has a mural of Camilo Cienfuegos, a Castro compatriot and fellow revolutionary who died in 1959. His depiction includes the words *Vas Bien Fidel,* or "You're going well, Fidel."

The national library is on the eastern side of the square and the national theater on the west.

The biggest attraction is the Jose Marti memorial, a 59-foot-tall statue of a seated Marti in front of a 358-foot-tall, star-shaped tower. A podium near the statue looks out over the open plaza below and has been the site of rallies, Castro speeches and papal pronouncements. The whole thing fronts the central government complex, hidden and well-guarded on the grounds that spread out behind Marti.

I tried to walk up the hill to see the statue, but an armed soldier whistled and shook his head.

"Is closed," he said, pointing to the open-air monument perched at the top of gently sloping stairs on a seemingly accessible hill. "The perimeter only."

It defied logic, closing something so early in the day and something so easily accessible without crossing a barrier, but the soldier was armed and I wasn't, so I nodded my head in a knowing way, like I'd just been making sure he'd do his job, and retreated to the sidewalk, from which I still had a clear view of Marti seated before the tower. I missed getting to the see the view of Havana from that height, but I also didn't get shot, which seemed a fair trade.

Behind Marti, buried in the grounds that stretch back for blocks, is the office of the president. I've seen the entrance before from the road—any Cuban driving past with a carload of Americans is obligated to mention it, I think—but I didn't make it that far on foot.

On the walk back, I came across a small, overgrown park hidden at the corner of *Avendia 23* and *Paseo*. It's a busy corner, with buses coming and going in all directions and the streets filled with people waiting for their rides, so it's hard to imagine anything being lost there, but the park was. At the very intersection, on the southwest corner, the land rises enough that you have to climb a dozen or more steps, turn, then climb some more before reaching the top. The whole hillside is shaded by a canopy of trees. It looks abandoned.

From the top, you descend over broken concrete into a small, decrepit square, well-hidden from the street and under enough cover to block the view from the apartments that tower near it. In America, you'd find this park in that part of town awaiting gentrification, filled with empty beer bottles and the other detritus of despair. You'd wake up someone once you got there, or at least step over the remains of their campsite.

In Cuba, it was just ignored.

At the back edge, perched against a wall, was a bust of Jorge Dimitrov, his balding bronze head covered in bird shit.

I didn't know who he was at the time, and it looked as if no one else much cared. I later learned he was the first Communist leader of Bulgaria. He died a decade before Castro's rise to power, perhaps not peacefully, so the memorial was obviously a well-considered postmortem affair, but Dimitrov seemed to have fallen out of favor by the time I visited. The only inscription on the base was his name and the years of his life, 1882-1949.

I took a couple of pictures and looked around for anything else interesting but couldn't find it. I climbed back up top, then trotted down the steps and slipped into the crowd on the street and waited for the light to turn so I could cross.

Four blocks down, just past the British Embassy, which backs up to the North Korean Embassy—an odd juxtaposition, diplomats from two countries fighting so hard to find their relevance in a changing world, sitting so close to each other—is a museum dedicated to the painter Servando Cabrera Moreno, once a staunch supporter of the revolution.

The Colonial-style mansion featured several rooms of his work: abstract and sensual in an almost brutal way. There were also pieces from Moreno's personal collection of Central and South American art. A small room across the back had a surprising, impressive array of beautiful stained glass.

In the lot on the corner, reached by marble steps and walking along a short path, was a sculpture garden with the types of pieces you see in sculpture gardens everywhere: reclining nudes with distorted features, geometric shapes, art disguised as an oversized chair. Those, you could see from the street, but viewing is always more enjoyable up close than through a fence.

The entry fee was a dollar.

> <

The easily amused can always find a laugh on English menus in non-English speaking countries. At the Cohiba, the options included "French fries ration," "curd Spanish ham" and "smocked salmon," all of which have potential of a sort not associated with fine dining. The listing also included an offering of "piquillo pepper and tuna croquettes," which was more stomach-churning than anything else, especially knowing the Cuban love of canned tuna. The French Union had a listed item that wasn't available when I tried to order it: "fried pork masses."

I also discovered, again at the Cohiba, that the "American breakfast" was designed to prove the gluttony of America: ham and cheese omelet, six slices of toast, a plate of fresh fruit, juice and coffee, and a small cookie with the bill. Decadent, perhaps, but absent rice and beans, it quickly developed a certain appeal. An executive version, with no eggs and less fruit, was a suitable substitute.

><

I'm always surprised to find signs of life so near places so obviously crafted for tourism. The Cohiba and the Riveria, the mobster-era relic that sits next door, are tourist hotels with sweeping views of the Atlantic Ocean and lines of taxis awaiting the tourist trade. But they aren't alone in commanding the scene: very Communist-looking apartment buildings—all square and drab and covered with the draped laundry of a people who clean in the kitchen sink—share space there, too. And one block back, the pre-revolution homes still sit, guarding the edge of the Vedado neighborhood, a place full of schools and children whose cacophony sings out the day long.

><

My next English speaker of the day was Pepe, the head of the diocesan mission program. He was responsible for creating self-sustaining projects in as many of the church's four dozen parishes as he could. Most of the projects involved agriculture and using land the church already owned to grow food for an occasionally hungry congregation. And, hopefully, to grow extra food to sell to locals to generate income to keep the operation going. There were other projects, too: daycare centers and seamstress shops that turned out baby clothes for the *ninas* and keepsakes for the tourists who came through.

He earned his doctorate in education, then taught economics at the University of Havana before joining the church staff in 2013. He was hired to create the mission and outreach program.

"I have to teach people about the mission of development," he told me. "This is all new for them."

New for them, he said, and new for the church and the country, too. Five decades of socialism taught people what to expect from their government, he said, "but it didn't teach ambition."

Teaching self-reliance is not an easy task. "No country that is socialist has figured it out," he said. "Venezuela is having the same issues right now."

Pepe's office was focused on food security and sustainable development. Any parish could propose a project, and Pepe would consider it. He preferred well-written plans that included multiple levels of accountability. He was not running a handout program, he said, and the money was an investment, not a gift.

He repeated what he told applicants: "That's not your money. People gave it to you for a project, and you're responsible for it."

He talked about different projects people wanted to start and how those pitches usually came up short of being complete. The ideas, he said, were never a problem. What confounded people was having to think beyond immediate needs.

He said he had seen several requests for money to raise chickens and rabbits. Both animals are easy to raise and easy to turn into profit, but they're also prone to all manner of predator, disease and natural forces that can quickly destroy them.

"We're an island. Every two or three years, a hurricane comes," he said. "What's your plan for risk management? If you have chickens and rabbits, are you taking them in your room with you? You can't just leave them out there."

In solving problems, he said, "you have to be creative."

In Santiago, the wife of the priest proposed opening a daycare center in space the church already had. She and a paid staff would care for 15 children, whose families would pay for the service. The fees would cover the cost of the operation and generate a small stipend that would go back to the church. And the parents, mostly single mothers, would be free from seven in the morning until five in the evening, five days a week, to pursue work they hadn't been able to before because they were home watching their children.

Some of those mothers, Pepe said, were using their time to make clothes, which they could then sell in markets. They were learning skills they could use to ensure that they would be able to continue earning money "so they have more money so they can feed themselves better or buy a DVD player or whatever they want."

But setting up those programs could be a tricky issue in a country where the government long had absolute control over everything. It had made efforts to loosen state control and allow people some say in how they earned money, and it was easy to find family restaurants and food stands and other small businesses that were run for profit. People rented rooms in their homes and used their family cars as taxis with the approval of the government.

But Pepe said there was a limit to how far the church could go, and his intention was to stay well inside that limit.

He helped set up 10 projects by the end of 2014 and had plans to add another five or six in 2015.

Pepe also proved to be a great conversationalist on a wide range of topics. In two hours, he moved easily from the widening of the Panama Canal (a potential windfall for Cuba, which was already building a new port just west of Havana, at Mariel, to handle the jumbo-sized ships that will one day sail this way) to the disappearance of an American college student (thoughts of a serial killer in Virginia) to the Ebola outbreak in Africa (Cuba was the first nation to send doctors and nurses to help heal the sick and work to stop the epidemic) to the global threat of extreme Islam.

"Four months ago, I'd never heard of ISIS, no one talked about Ebola," he said. "Two years ago, no one talked about food security or sustainable development."

He urged President Obama to end, or at least ease, the embargo, an idea that would take surprising shape in the weeks after we spoke.

He also lamented the reality of chickens and other livestock wandering around Havana, including from yards within a block of his office at the Cathedral. Technically, he said, the animals were prohibited within city limits because of the threat of disease, but the law was not strictly enforced.

A rooster crowed around the clock just down the street, in a yard that may have been the picture definition of "shade tree mechanic."

More than anything, Pepe talked about the possibilities to come.

"Things are going to change," he said. "You're invited back for it."

><

A solo trip by motorcycle taxi into Old Havana proved to be

the worst idea of the whole trip. It may have been the worst idea of all my trips to Cuba combined, even worse than thinking I could speak French to that girl all those years ago.

It seemed necessary, though, at least once, to ride in one of those orangeish-yellow, three-wheeled bubbles that you see in photographs. The "coco taxi," it's called. Go to Cuba, you'll see them. Find a crowd of tourists, there's a fleet of cocos nearby.

I'd been in a "tap tap" in Haiti, one of those beat-to-shit old pickup trucks that had turned into part rolling folk art exhibit, part exercise in exploring the physics of how many people could be crammed under the canopy of one vehicle. I'd taken a bicycle taxi in Peru and watched in amusement and with respect as the driver struggled up and down the streets of Puno for a sum of money that would not have yielded a candy bar at home. I'd been on a water taxi that zigzagged along the shores of the Bosphorus Strait in Istanbul all the way to the Black Sea. I've taken double-decker bus tours everywhere I've been able to find them, joyfully playing the role of tourist as I scoped out the sights to which I might return on foot for better inspection some other time.

Travel can be fun, and getting about in taxis and buses and boats is part of the adventure. I figured I could handle a few miles in an underpowered bubble that was putt-putting through Havana. But almost immediately, I noticed two things.

One, the driver had to wear a helmet but the passenger did not. If nothing else, that was peculiar, and it certainly seemed to imply a lack of trust in a safe journey on the part of the driver. I'm not sure I'd want to wear a loaner helmet on a coco taxi, but the offer was never made.

Two, because of the design of the bubble, you can't actually see much of anything except what's right in front of you, which is mostly the back side of the driver. The cocos I'd seen scooting along the *Malecon* looked so picturesque from the sidewalk with the driver gripping the handlebars and the people in the back smiling their little tourist smiles. But from inside one of them, I could hardly see the sidewalk, and my little tourist smile was more a sneer in the making, the look of bewilderment at something seemingly so good gone so wrong.

The limited view proved especially troublesome when the driver pulled up alongside the small park that separates two museums—*Museo de la Revolucion* and *Museo Nacional de la Belles Arts de la Habana*—from two tourist hotels.

I paid the fee and climbed out of the bubble and onto the sidewalk, and the woman driving it sped off. She probably knew what was coming and didn't want to be there to see it.

If I'd have emerged with a sandwich board that read "Fuck with me, I'm a naïve tourist" front and back, I would have attracted less attention. Every step, there was another person tugging at my arm with a sob story.

One man skipped the usual pleasantries of "where you from?"—unnecessary, I guess, from a coco passenger—and dove into a story about his father in Washington and how I needed to write down a telephone number so I could call when I got home and let dad know that his son was still alive back in Havana. Only he didn't have the phone number. He'd been waiting 30 years for someone to come along and offer to make the call, and he never thought to write down the number. That was in the possession of his sister, who he said worked in a restaurant in a hotel nearby, to which he assumed we would go. He grabbed my arm and wanted to lead me off, only he was headed in the direction from which I'd come, back down *Agramonte* toward the tunnel that goes under the harbor, and there was no hotel there, only a construction site and an alley and the promise of who-knows-what.

I broke free from him and walked briskly toward the art museum. Before I could get to the door, I was greeted, such as it was, by someone else beckoning me over to hear her woes. I waved her off as best I could and made for the door. She was saying something about baby formula.

Perhaps they were all legitimate woes, and I, the rare lone American to wander by that day, had been a true beacon of hope, their one chance of getting a message off the island. But the neighborhood was crawling with Americans, whole groups of them, many of them with name cards on lanyards and fanny packs strapped around their waists and much more likely to take pity than me. I was in no mood to play the sap.

I'm the American who has heard so many sob stories in so many places, I'm gleefully numb to them all and not so interested in involving myself in someone else's quest for a long-lost whoever. A few pesos, I can spare. Gladly. That's my kind of help, the 20-peso handshake. But involvement in your scheme, I don't want.

So I ducked instead into the lobby of Havana's National Museum of Fine Art's modern gallery (the older pieces are housed in a separate building a few blocks away). The building looks like an ugly square from the outside, but inside, you notice that its center is a courtyard and it is actually a hollowed-out square, the glass walls of the four sides looking inward. It's vaguely reminiscent of an arts building on the campus of Virginia Commonwealth University, both dedicated to creativity and featuring ugly, if surprisingly user-friendly, architecture.

The open space on the first floor was used for sculpture and benches, a fine piece of furniture the Cubans have been kind enough to place nearly everywhere, island-wide, except, of course, along the outside of the Cohiba. A people who spend their days waiting need a place to sit, and Cubans seem to prefer a good bench.

The galleries held a lot of angst and aggression, some of which predated Castro. Americans tend to have a view of Cuba as a great playground, forever waiting to be reopened for their rapacious longings—*Godfather IV*, waiting to be shot—but Cuban artists have apparently seen something else entirely: from their brushes emerged a dangerous, duplicitous world of stark, abrupt images. If there was fun or playfulness anywhere in sight, it was hidden somewhere else.

The emphasis was on the abstract or overtly political. In one gallery, a life-size Jesus stood with three sabers thrust through his torso. In another spot, a puppet house was mounted to the wall, and museumgoers had their choice of dozens of puppets and the freedom to stage their own shows. The moment I walked in and saw it, Joseph Stalin shared the stage with Charlie Chaplin, much to the amusement of a small group of German tourists. They stood and exchanged what I imagined were lines from a dialogue of their own creation. Maybe not. I don't speak German, and I couldn't really tell what they were saying. Whatever it was, they found it funny.

A gallery or two away, there were lines of block prints and pencil drawings that looked to me like German Expressionist art from the early 20th century. The German tourists had disappeared by then, so I'm not sure if they saw the resemblance too, or if I was just projecting my love of the particular form onto someone else's work.

The most interesting sculpture was a small castle, perhaps six feet high, made entirely of hundreds of tin espresso pots, which may explain why I wasn't able to find one for sale in my neighborhood market. I thought about trying to pry one loose but thought better of it.

As I circled back around toward the entrance, I thought of the people I'd spurned on my way in. I tried leaving by a side exit in hopes of avoiding the sob stories on the main steps, but a young guard shooed me away from the open door.

"Your exit is that way," he said, pointing all the way across the courtyard to the door through which I had entered. He was more friendly than officious.

"Do I have to?" I asked, looking over his shoulder toward the crowd by the main door.

He missed my point, or chose to ignore it, and either way, he looked at his watch instead and pointed and said I still had 15 minutes. He was trying to be helpful.

I spent most of that time in the gift shop, thumbing through well-worn gallery catalogs and trying to convince myself of the beauty of the posters hanging in a rack, which I never could. I finally gave up and left.

Approaching the exit, I saw my sob-story man still on the steps, so I waited until he turned his attention away, then walked out in the opposite direction at a brisk pace. I kept my head down and my eyes focused on the sidewalk right in front of me. If he was looking, I'd never know.

I rounded a corner, then another, crossed the street, walked another block and ducked around yet a third corner. I slipped into the arcade that leads to the lobby of the Hotel Sevilla, a grand old hotel whose sweeping, open first floor includes couches and soft chairs along the street side, backed with small café tables and then an interior courtyard, where a band was quickly running through a playlist recognizable to anyone who has been subjected to what's supposed to be Cuban music. I'm not convinced that anyone really likes the song "Guantanamera" after hearing it two or three times, but it's always playing somewhere.

I'd spent much time in the lobby on previous trips, and the area has become one of my favorite places in Havana. I've never actually stayed there, but it's a block from a hotel where I once spent a week and it offered the comfort and respite the other place lacked. There's a window where you can exchange money, the bathrooms are easy to find and no one asks questions if you just appear and make yourself at home in any of the many places to sit and watch, even if you're not a guest.

I ordered a coffee from the short end of the bar, next to the reception desk, and took a seat far from the band, obstructed from its view by a pillar. I still had to listen, but at least I didn't have to see.

But that didn't spare me the sales pitch from the singer, who used the set break to make the rounds of the few people there to hawk her CDs. I'm usually inclined to buy the music, whatever the music is, but theirs had been lifeless and I wasn't interested. When I declined, the girl switched tactics and strongly suggested that I needed to make a donation to her band.

I declined that, too, being an American who doesn't like being told what to do, and she left mad.

I finished my coffee and left, too, and was quickly accosted by a man with a lame arm who asked if I needed a taxi.

"In fact I do," I said, trying to put out of my mind how he was going to be driving with just the one good arm.

"Wait right here," he said. Then he walked away. I could see him approach a taxi on the street and start talking to the driver, and it occurred to me that he was a taxi *getter,* not a taxi *driver.*

And I thought, "Why would I ever need that service? I'm standing in front of a huge tourist hotel, half a block from another tourist hotel and across the street from two museums. How hard can it be to get a taxi?"

Harder than you'd imagine, it turned out. There were no coco taxis in sight, and the woman standing by her more conventional cab refused to take me back uptown to the Cohiba. So did the next driver. Neither would say why, though both seemed rather put out just to have been asked.

I walked away, confused and agitated. I don't live in a taxi city back home, and I'm not used to the world of hailing taxis like someone from New York might be, but I was sure I was being played a fool of some sort.

The taxi getter was in close pursuit, promising better results soon, but I waved him off without turning around. If he couldn't succeed with the best of odds, what hope did he have on a block without a taxi?

Being a hard-headed American, I decided I could walk back uptown to my apartment, covering the four miles or so between here and there in the heat of the afternoon wearing flipflops with no problem. So I turned the corner away from the Sevilla onto *Paseo de Marti*, the wide boulevard dissected by the *Paseo del Prado* promenade, and headed to the *Malecon*.

Two blocks away, an old black guy in a yellow 1954 Plymouth convertible pulled alongside me.

"You need a taxi," he said, his words falling somewhere between question and command. He sounded friendly enough.

My mind said "no" but the word never came out of my mouth. I must have stared at him, the vacant look of someone who does need a taxi but is too tired and pissed off to articulate that simplest of things.

When he leaned over and opened the door, I stepped in.

He was chatty and gregarious, and hungry, too, biting through an ice cream sandwich, a drip behind the liquid running down his hand. He talked all the way back, except when he was licking ice cream juice off his hand.

He kept one hand wrapped around the food and the other occasionally, but not always, on the steering wheel, as he explained how he'd had the top removed so the car would appeal to tourists. He pointed to the spot where the roof had been cut free, and I could see the ragged edge where someone had tried to file away the most dangerous spots. A little rough, but it worked.

I couldn't enjoy a bit of the scenery because he talked the whole way. But he was nice enough, and I enjoyed the quick getaway from the hell of Old Havana and not having to walk four miles in the afternoon sun. It's important, at some point in a trip to Cuba, to hop into an old American car, so when you're asked later—and you will be asked, the presence of American cars being of great concern to everyone back home—you can dismiss it with a cursory, "Of course I did."

><

 Walking back to my apartment, up *Calle 13* toward *Calle 6*, I saw my first Cuban woman with a yoga mat tucked under her arm. From behind, she could have passed for a tourist, but I caught up and decided, based on my keen observation, that she was a local who had discovered the secret of American serenity or had fallen for the even more American lure of tight leggings and a rolled foam mat with a convenient strap for easy carrying. Toss it over your shoulder, and away you go.
 She was obviously no novice. She had that look you see outside yoga classes, where people are so relaxed and at ease with their incredible ability to be flexible and bend in the most inhuman way, they almost look pissed off at having to walk upright and normally among the masses of people who can't do what they can.
 She kept her sneer to herself and ducked up a driveway and into a small apartment building, and I didn't see her, or any proof of yoga, again.

><

 The king of the two-dollar calzone turned out to be a budding artist in search of colored pencils. Adriano Rodriguez, who worked at the pizza and calzone stand two blocks from the cathedral, offered an easy familiarity the first time I walked onto the patio separating the sidewalk from the window where he was selling Italian food to Cubans.
 He talked to me in English, then he taught his coworker to greet me in English. Another night, he quizzed me about the cost of pencils.
 "Where you from?" he told his co-worker to ask when he discovered that neither the cook nor I spoke a language the other could understand.
 "Where you from?" the cook asked me.
 "The United States," I replied.
 The cook offered a knowing nod and an equally knowing smile before walking back into the kitchen to make my dinner. Perhaps he'd taken the same self-study course in language skills I'd tried.

I went back two nights later and tried the approach myself.

"Where you from?" I asked Rodriguez as soon as I walked up.

He just laughed and said, "Calzone? For to go?" My second time there, and he already knew my order. I loved it.

The second of the two questions was important: "for to go" meant I would need a box, and that meant I had to pay an extra quarter. Most customers got their food on metal trays and ate standing up along a chest-high counter by the patio.

I placed my order and sat on the short wall that wrapped across the front and down one side, dangling my feet over and watching the little patio fill and empty as passerby stopped for a cup of fresh fruit juice or a coffee. I saw eight to ten people coming and going, all laughing and enjoying their brief respite before resuming whatever their journeys were.

The crowd cleared for a minute and Rodriguez left the counter and joined me. He looked at my notebook and pointed at my pen and asked about my work. He listened long enough to be polite, then he turned the conversation his way.

"In the U.S., how much for a colored pencil?" he asked.

"A colored pencil? For drawing pictures?" I said.

"Yes. I'm an artist, but just pencils. No paints. How much in the U.S.?"

"I don't know, maybe three or four dollars for a box of two dozen."

"Here, two dollars and fifty for one."

So I played the role of American and offered to bring him a box the next time I came through town, an offer that excited him enough to offer to write his name in my notebook.

It was a nice moment, and all was well until I got home and bit into my calzone. The first night, my calzone was stuffed with cheese; the second, they loaded me up with onions and peppers, an unpleasant surprise. But for two dollars, plus the quarter for the box, there wasn't much to complain about. I picked through and found enough to eat.

A few months later, when I went back to Havana, he got his pencils and a couple of sketch pads.

><

By the second day, I figured out the street grid in Vedado,

which greatly satiated my desire to always know where I was in relation to where I wanted to be.

The *Avenida Paseo* runs south to north, bisecting the neighborhood. To the west, until the neighborhood ends at the *Rio Almendares*, odd numbered streets run east and west, perpendicular to *Paseo*. Even numbers run north-south, parallel to *Paseo*, down to the *Malecon*.

You can be at the corner of Fourth and Fifth. If you are, you'll see two houses, a school and a *supermercardo*, which appeared to be super in quantity, not variety: the building was nearly empty except for hundreds of eggs and 50-pound bags of rice and beans.

To the east of *Paseo*, all the way to the *Avenida de los Presidentes* and beyond, the even numbers are replaced by the alphabet. *The corner of Fifth and B* doesn't have the same ring to it.

><

Clueless but still hopefully affable I showed up in the church office again, hoping yesterday's meeting with the bishop might happen today. I waited two hours, from 10:30 until lunch was served at 12:30.

By the fourth day, some of the staff had worked up the nerve to try their limited English, for which they apologized. I apologized too, for still not knowing Spanish, and we all smiled at each other a bit, then the woman in the first office invited me to see pictures of her daughter and grandson. I learned about her trip to the U.S., when she visited Dallas, Denver and Florida. She liked Denver, because of the snow, and didn't say much about Dallas, though you can imagine the shock of going from the privations of Cuba to the largesse that is anything Texas. On Florida, she just shrugged.

"We're Cubans," she said. "Florida? That's nothing special."

The priest from Santa Cruz stopped by and waved and then slipped into an office, from which he was quickly brought back out and introduced to me. The office manager, Say, was not going to waste an English speaker.

He stayed long enough to tell me about his 100-year-old church full of fishermen and oil and gas workers and how the long-ago bishop from Richmond, Hugo Blankingship, was a god in Cuba.

"He was bishop for 30 years!" he said.

The number was off by a decade, but I didn't correct him.

After Blankingship left and the revolution became a way of life, the church slipped away, the priest said, because there was no will and no money. But now, with some money coming back in, things were changing.

Then he ran out of things he knew how to say in English. He looked to make sure Say wasn't paying attention so he could escape. He apologized for not knowing more, and he started to leave, but not before walking to the television, mounted from the ceiling in one corner, and turning the channel away from a soap opera.

"You like baseball?" he said, changing the channel.

Doesn't everyone?

><

I spent part of the morning trying to read *Granma*, and I discovered that I had a better grasp of written Spanish than spoken Spanish.

The blockade, or *el bloqueo*, was the subject of much coverage every day I looked in the small, thin newspaper. One day, there was a story about Cuban diplomats at the United Nations, in New York, asking that the blockade be ended. The next day, the blockade story was about the impact on the arts community, which was apparently huge, what with keeping cash-dispensing Americans away from the chance to buy Cuban art.

There was also news of the U.S.'s love for deporting Mexicans, particularly minors—that had been in the news at home before I left—and the need to be prepared for pathogens and other biological disasters.

After four days of waiting, I was finally to have my meeting with the bishop, I was told one morning. We were going to meet over lunch in the dining hall of the cathedral.

Say looked at me and smiled and would have given me a conspiratorial big thumbs-up, if that was the kind of person she was. I could see it in her eyes.

She led us all out of the office and through the open hallway and down the airy corridor to the dining room, at the far end of the cathedral's block-long building. She sat me next to the bishop and went to get our trays.

The bishop was brief but to the point. She was sending me to Camagüey and Santiago to speak with priests and parishioners there.

"That's good, yes?" she said.

That seemed like a detail that could have been worked out in her absence, but what little I know of church hierarchy is that you don't question the bishop, especially when she's so nice and accommodating about everything.

"Of course," I said.

But I would have said yes to anything at that point, especially if the bishop were doing the asking. She was the kind of person you wanted to do things for.

So with the help of Daliana, the flighty girl from the office, and Lautaro, one of two church drivers, we hopped a three-wheel motorbike contraption—kind of like a coco taxi, but with a better view—and headed toward the bus station so I could discover another peculiarity of Cuban life: the bus voucher.

For the following day's trip to Camagüey, I spent $31 for what sounded like a ticket but was actually a voucher printed on a dot matrix printer, which do still exist in Cuba. The following morning, I would need to exchange the voucher for the actual ticket, also to come whirring off a dot matrix printer. And then I'd have to repeat the process later in Camagüey to purchase my ticket to Santiago.

The hopeful news for this occasionally timid, still language-ignorant traveler was that there would be someone to meet me at both stops.

And the bishop gave me an envelope for each, into one of which I saw her place a check. So it wasn't just lackeys picking me up, it was people awaiting official news, and perhaps money, from the bishop.

> <

Before leaving on my trip out of town, I allowed myself one more opportunity to pay the price for not completely understanding the language.

I trooped back to the French Union for another meal. Instead of the customary pizza upstairs, I sat on the first-floor veranda and took the longer menu with more traditional meals.

I ordered the six-dollar chicken with pineapple, and nodded and said yes as the waitress ran through the details about the salads and rice and plantains that would be served with it. There was more food than I could eat, but luckily a cat found its way to me and stayed closed enough to help me.

I ordered a coffee at the end and asked for the check and was a bit shocked to see $16 across the bottom. All of the options I thought came with the meal were extras, and the waitress had done a stellar job of upselling me.

I paid the bill and left a tip, even though one was already included.

The six-hour bus ride from Havana to Camagüey turned into a nine-hour one because the two drivers showed no abandon in their pursuit of coffee or cigarettes. They stopped first for a break for the whole bus a couple of hours into the trip, everyone getting off at a little roadside bar and souvenir market for a quick shot and the chance to buy straw hats and T-shirts and Pringles, which are very popular in Cuba. They later made numerous shorter stops to reload themselves.

Outside of Havana, which took more than 20 minutes to clear even without much traffic with which to contend, the scenery changed from urban decrepitude to rural blandness. There were occasional towns, including Santa Clara, which is rather large, but mostly the drive was through farmland. Whether it was bananas or rice or sugarcane or cattle, which looked quite plump, something was growing near the road nearly the entire trip.

It was uneventful, mostly, except I had trouble understanding the order to disembark in Santa Clara, where we had a layover that lasted more than an hour.

I've taken long bus trips in the U.S., but I've never been forced from my seat on a bus I would keep riding.

"The bus is closed," one of the drivers finally said in his final attempt to pry me from my seat. Then he pointed at his watch and told me when to return. He was off by an hour, but I wouldn't have strayed far even if I'd know how much time I had to kill.

The station had slips for six buses, two waiting rooms, a small café and a bathroom guarded by an attendant, who politely collected tips from users. There was a manually operated gate guarding the entrance to the lot. Every time a bus pulled in or out, as happened every 10 minutes or so, someone had to open the gate and then close it. It didn't seem the most efficient of operations, but perhaps there are different expectations of efficiency in Communist countries. It did make for good busy work, and the guard looked sharp and official in her uniform.

While waiting for the crew to return, I noticed a few American touches in the exterior of the Chinese-made bus: little stickers meant to look like bullet holes covered one corner of the door, and there were several stickers on the windows, including the Rolling Stones tongue and another of a hooligan with his middle finger thrust forward. Inside, there were two toy dogs dangling from their tails above the driver's seat, a touch of playfulness you might not appreciate from someone commanding a full-size motor coach.

CHAPTER 3

CAMAGÜEY

THE BUS FROM Havana to Camagüey was three hours late, mostly because the drivers found it impossible to go more than a few miles without stopping for something. When they weren't pulling over to trade seats, which they did every hour or so, they were stopping for coffee, mostly, but also for cigarettes, a kiss on the cheek from a pretty woman on the street—I would have stopped for her too, though I'm not sure I would have gotten back on the bus afterward—to pick up a work crew whose own bus had broken down and sometimes just to chat with people walking by. I should have hired those two as guides; they seemed to know everyone in Cuba.

Entertaining as it was, getting to see the country by bus at such a contemplative pace, by the time we rolled in, I was feeling a bit anxious. I was afraid my ride would have long since given up, and the idea of getting stranded in the station wasn't sitting too well. The only thing I knew of Camagüey came from a friend whose father was raised there. But he'd fled after the revolution and then was part of the failed Bay of Pigs invasion. He survived that only to flee back to the U.S., where has long since been a used car salesman. What information my friend could offer was way out of date, and his father's name wasn't likely to endear me to anyone.

But Cuba is Cuba, and the people who live there know better than to rely on printed schedules, especially when they're headed to the bus station to pick up strangers. People who visit don't always know that, of course, and I stepped off the bus and into a shoulder-to-shoulder mass of people without the faintest idea who was getting me, if he were still there or what he looked like, or how worried I should be about not knowing any of those things.

I stood clueless looking around the rectangular room. There were benches in the middle, a few offices lining one of the long walls and what would have been windows lining the other, overlooking the bays for the buses, if the station had been in America. Only it was Cuba and it never gets too cold and I guess windows are an expensive luxury in such conditions, so nothing had ever been placed in the large openings. A canopy over the bus slips would keep out the rain. A man in a uniform guarded the door leading out, and two others in uniforms worked at a small desk by the doorway that led back to where the buses parked. They kept a close watch on their door and checked the paperwork of all who tried to pass, though you could easily dodge them by stepping through the wall, the absence of windows making it easy and expedient to avoid their scrutiny.

I circled the lobby slowly, then stepped past the guard, through the out door and into a sea of taxi drivers, each of whom seemed personally invested in my welfare and ready to whisk me off to god-knows-where. The more I said "I'm looking for someone," the more offers I had.

The drivers seemed to be shills for hotels, and all convinced they knew the place I needed to be. Each offered to take me somewhere different. Maybe. Like I said, I don't speak so much Spanish, and it could be they all had their own code names for the same places, or were particularly brazen sharing the same shakedown.

"Let me take you, you clueless American schmuck, around the corner and rob you," they could have been saying. They didn't look like that kind of crowd, but what did I know? It didn't sound threatening, so I smiled and did my best to not agree to anything while I scanned the crowd for a friendly face.

I finally snuck back into the station, past the suspicious guard at the door, who wasn't keen on the idea of someone coming in through the exit, especially not without a voucher. But I obviously wasn't a local, and I obviously had no idea what I was doing, so he let me pass in that way security people have of letting you pass with the tacit understanding that if they pretend to not see you, you won't ask them for help.

I started to make another round of the open, packed room, when I stumbled into a tall, skinny man wearing a short-sleeve shirt with the familiar logo of the Episcopal church.

"Zacharie?" he asked, softening the "ch," unpronounceable to all the Cubans I've met, into a more pleasant "sh." It sounded nice, and I thought I should do that, too, whenever I introduce myself.

"My savior?" I said, somewhat but not completely in jest, when we made eye contact.

The Right Rev. Evelio Perez did not argue. Though in fairness to him, I tend to mumble, and the crowded room was loud, and he might not have heard what I said.

"This way," he said.

He turned his back and led the way out, as eager as I was to escape.

He led me back through the taxi drivers, who wanted to help him as much as they had wanted to help me a few minutes before, and toward the part of the parking lot that should have been full of cars, except that so few people drive in Cuba, there are always plenty of empty spaces. He stepped toward a Russian-made SUV and began apologizing before we even stopped walking.

"It's Russian," he said, by way of explaining any number of faults that might impair my comfort or keep us from reaching our destination.

I tried sitting in the back, but he wouldn't allow it. He pointed to the front passenger door as he gently pushed me forward. He climbed in the back.

I sat in the front with Tico, a 19-year-old friend of the family whose questionable command of a manual transmission didn't impede his willingness to drive. We lurched from corner to corner, making our way through a town intentionally designed centuries ago as a maze to thwart intruders. That it would also forever confuse the residents was overlooked or deemed a necessary price for safety. Either way, it was no place for a Russian SUV.

We could have gone a mile, maybe five—I'm not sure, we were going so slow and so many directions through those winding streets—before arriving at the door of the rectory.

Pulling into the gated driveway, I considered the possibility that Tico, not the Russians, was the cause of the problems with the SUV. He'd put the clutch through a workout.

Then I started to roll up the window on my door and the plastic handle came off in my hand.

Perez had anticipated that. "It goes back on," he said, barely giving it notice. Then he muttered another "It's Russian," spoken with an air of resignation, to emphasize the source of the failure.

It was like a theater class exercise, watching Perez. "Give me a happy face. A sad face. An 'It's Russian' face."

We stood on the driveway for a moment without speaking, my bag at my feet, then Perez offered two choices: stay with him or rent a room several blocks away.

His room, next to the kitchen, included two beds, a fan, its own bathroom and a pleasing mix of privacy and proximity to everyone else. It was also about 10 feet from where we were standing and wouldn't require another trip in the Russian SUV.

The rental room offered air conditioning and a caution from Perez to stay inside after dark because of the neighborhood.

"It's maybe not always so safe," he said.

Tico nodded in agreement. Perez looked at his house and pointed toward the single room that opened onto the patio by the kitchen door.

"Here, it's free," he said.

I stayed with Perez, but not because of the money. The $25 a night at the other place, I could afford. I would have paid it to Perez, if only he would have accepted it. (He wouldn't.) After four days alone in Havana, where my daily morning ration of English speakers offered my best chance at conversation, I was ready for company. I'm chatty and it drives me nutty not being able to talk and listen and generally be in the midst of people saying things I might understand, and the Perez family offered the chance to fill my mind with things I'd remember, or at least the chance to talk out loud to others instead of just myself.

Plus, they had a nice looking house, a two-story stucco, with a yard wrapping around all four sides in a country where most people live in apartments or row houses. I wanted to go inside and see what they'd allow me to see.

Their house, I learned from Perez, once belong to Paul Alexander Tate, the headmaster of the town's Episcopal school and the American consular agent for Camagüey Province before he was forced to leave in 1961 after the U.S. and Cuba cut off diplomatic relations. When he left, he gave his house to the Episcopal Church. The house and the church, unlike the school and the old rooming house for students, still belonged to the church. The consular business was long gone.

By the time Perez moved there in 2012, the house, like the church four blocks away, was well into a period of neglect and decay. It had been built solid and didn't require much attention, but it did need some.

The Perez family, Evelio and his wife and their daughter, Claudia, patched ceilings, painted walls and were rebuilding the wood-louvered windows one at a time. There were treating it like a home they might have for years to come.

Perez showed me the first floor, which included a long, rectangular living room along the side that ran parallel to the cross street. There was a couch and chairs and television at one end, a dining room table at the other. A small, square dining room and a large foyer with steps that wrapped toward the second floor were in the middle of the house, and the square kitchen was at the other end. Just outside the kitchen was a breezeway separating the house from the garage. My room was a few steps off the breezeway in the front. It backed up to the kitchen and the foyer but was only accessible from the outside. It had the placement and feel of a room that had once been for the help, though I'm not sure that was the case.

He told me I was welcome to anything in the refrigerator, which he opened and showed off like a game show host. It was full of bottles and bowls and all the stuff that makes you know a house is a home, the leftovers and pieces and condiments of a people who will be there a while, the little pieces you'd throw away before offering to a guest but keep because you'll eat them when no one is watching.

He introduced me to Claudia, a 21-year-old medical student who spoke good English and was game for talking to the middle-aged American her father was hosting as a favor to his boss. She, too, apologized for her English, but I think it was a precursory thing in case I really stumped her later with some odd word or phrase; for the most part, she sounded as fluent as I was, and didn't mumble nearly as much.

The family was still settling in after coming from Esmeralda, a small town to the northwest where Perez had served for 20 years before being asked to replace the priest in Camagüey, who had died rather suddenly. Perez was the archdeacon of the area, in charge of all the churches, and he couldn't say no to the bishop's request.

Seated in the living room, Perez began by talking about Bishop Hugo Blankingship, the lone American to have led the Cuban church and a native of Richmond, the town in which I live.

The current bishop signed off on my trip and helped arrange my travels on the presumption that I was writing about Blankingship—that had been the idea, anyway, though every day in Cuba seemed to yield something else that was just as interesting—and Perez accepted the challenge of sharing what he knew with me.

As would be the case on several trips, and all over the island, anyone quizzed on Blankingship opened with a plaudit and went from there.

Perez started with a general overview of Blankingship's greatness. The bishop had been well-regarded throughout Cuba, Perez said, though he did invoke the ire of some older priests when he helped move the cathedral from a working class neighborhood in Central Havana to its current home in the then-posh Vedado neighborhood in the 1940s. The new location included a church, separate houses for the dean and the bishop, a carriage house for the bishop, an administrative building, a central kitchen and a long building with offices and classroom space on the first floor and dormitories on the second. It was a substantial compound, and it took up the length and half the width of an entire block.

The move, I later learned, came against the advice of Blankingship, who wanted to stay in the older, poorer neighborhood, which needed the service of the church. He ultimately bowed to his benefactors—wealthy Americans had a substantial presence in Cuba at the time—because they were paying the bills and they wanted to feel safe in their church, or perhaps just didn't want to travel so far to get there.

That aside, Blankingship was revered partly for his willingness to add to the church's land holdings, which he apparently did whenever and wherever he could. Traveling around Cuba, you got the idea that Blankingship had been one of those guys who couldn't see a "for sale" without at least stopping to ask.

Much of that land was lost in the revolution, when the new Communist state took it, but some had remained in church possession.

"Here, they took the school and the (rooming) house and gave us a house next to the church," Perez told me my first night there.

The next day, he showed me the house the church had received as compensation: all that remained was most of the front door and the frame from which it hung. The rest had collapsed years ago. The lot on which it once sat was used by neighborhood children as a soccer field, an activity that occurred with much vigor and enthusiasm and volume a day later while Perez was conducting a baptism.

But more than buying land, Blankenship's magic touch had been organization. He built the church into what it still was decades later when I visited: four dozen or more parishes spread across the island. There were clusters in some towns, particularly Santiago, and single parishes elsewhere, all aligned with the main office in Havana. Some areas were stronger than others. Parishes in the east were stronger than those in the west, as they always had been.

At the time of the revolution, the site of the rectory in Camagüey was a block-long complex that included the house, the school and a sports center. All the church had been allowed to keep was the house, though the wide corner lot did stretch the depth of the block. The back half was closed off by a fence and included chickens and turkeys and fruit trees, which Perez planted. The yard also had avocado trees, which produced fruit three or four times the size of avocados found in the U.S.

> <

The life of a priest in Cuba hasn't been easy since the revolution.

It has been worse, perhaps, for Catholics than Episcopals, especially after Pope John XXIII excommunicated Castro in 1962 for his treatment of the church and the Catholic community took up the mantle of resistance. But it was bad for all, and when the Communist Party outlawed Christmas in 1969, the country sank into a spiritual rut that would last decades.

People stopped going to church, and the churches missed out on generations of people growing up thinking that going to church was a normal thing to do. The loss is still felt deeply today.

Things began to ease some in the early 1990s, when Castro changed the country from being atheist to secular and began allowing Christians into the Communist Party. The big turning point came in 1998, when Pope John Paul II visited. It was the first time a pope had ever been to Cuba. He stayed five days and visited Havana, Santa Clara and Santiago.

By the end of that year, Castro had reinstated Christmas as an official state holiday, and the island's religious community began to slowly and cautiously reemerge into public view.

Before all that happened, Perez decided to become a priest. It was into an environment of great caution and risk that he willingly placed himself. He entered the seminary in the late 1980s, before anyone suspected that the life of a priest would ever become anything less than arduous. He was born after the revolution, but old enough to have heard the stories from those who lived through that time. Priests and others active in the church were persecuted. Those who didn't slip away were often sent to work camps. Even free, they were denied seats in the universities and the better jobs.

Perez shrugged off the idea that he'd given himself a stiff occupational challenge at an early age. He was called to serve, he said, and serve he would.

He preferred to talk about the church.

"People started to be afraid of the church," he said of the years after Castro took power. Another problem, he said, came from the pulpit. "Left-leaning priests emptied churches. Particularly here, it was not a good match. People don't want to talk about politics in church. They want to hear about God."

Those in line with the revolution weren't shy, either, about enforcing their way. As a child, Perez learned to play the saxophone. One day, he was playing a new song, enjoying the feeling of being able to create a melody. The trance of creation was broken when he was approached by party loyalists and told to stop playing.

"They thought the song sounded religious," he said.

He had stopped playing then, and wasn't sure if he could when I talked to him. It had been a long time since he had last picked up a saxophone.

Things have changed some, but not completely. Claudia said in her high school philosophy classes, the teachers would "attack the church. We were told church doesn't let people grow like a person."

She was allowed to express her opinion in her college medical courses, but didn't often find many sympathetic ears. Her class of 14 included herself as the lone Episcopal, plus one Catholic, one Seventh Day Adventist and 11 non-believers.

Her father said the numbers did not surprise him. "They don't have the habit to go to church," he said of the young students. "It's not normal for the people."

The habit was broken fast in the 1960s, when people quickly realized that their Sunday ritual was costing them the rest of the week. So they stopped going.

"The church is not like it was before," he said. "In the time of Blankingship, a church like this would have had 50 kids in youth programs. Today, there are three or four."

And there was a gap between the very old and the very young. The most passion, Perez said, came from the oldest in the congregation. "You can't find that emotion right now" from younger people, he said.

Claudia agreed but couldn't offer an answer, or hope.

"The church used to be very dynamic," Perez said a little while later, eyes showing the wistful look of someone who knows the problem but can't quite figure out the solution.

><

The physical business of fixing a church was a complicated process in Cuba.

Materials were hard to find and expensive to buy, and getting permission to do the work was even harder.

Perez spoke of a church that had been damaged in a hurricane. Even with money in hand, it took seven years of haggling with the government to get the proper permits for the work.

Starting a new church in a new place was even more difficult. The best bet was to do it in a private home, he said, provided you could find a homeowner willing to submit himself to the government permit process.

If successful, a home-based congregation was limited to 30 parishioners, Perez said. And, of course, the government knew who was friendly to church people. That wasn't the concern it once was in Cuba, but it still was not a path lightly taken, because the neighborhood watch was still a real thing there. The Committees for the Defense of the Revolution, the CDR, exists to this day, and the membership lists of the neighborhood-based groups include a solid majority of the population. The little signs with the logo were easy to spot on houses everywhere.

Perez tried to keep to the business of running his church and preparing as best he could for whatever came his way. In St. Paul's, he stockpiled lumber. When you walked in, the left side of the sanctuary was piled high with pieces of mahogany. There was no plan for the wood, Perez said. But it was there, and the church would find a use.

He wanted to repair the roof, which he said leaked, but he didn't have the money and he wasn't certain he could find enough skilled craftsmen to do it. He pointed up to the intricately detailed wood beams and talked about the gaps between the roof and the walls.

"I don't know who can fix that," he said. "A concrete roof is better."

St. Paul's wasn't likely to ever have a concrete roof, but not for the reasons that would keep it from happening in the U.S. In Cuba, they might overlook the architectural significance of the roof and rip it off anyway, but the pitch was too high and the cost to replace it too great.

> <

Claudia taught me what she said was the true meaning of coffee in Cuba while we were sipping a cup in the living room.

"We spell it c-a-f-e. That's *caliente, amargo, fuerte, esporadicamente*. That's hot, bitter, strong, occasionally. That's how Cubans like their coffee."

My experience taught me that the "e" should really be a *menudo*, meaning *often*. And truthfully, by the time Cubans finish pouring spoon after spoon of sugar into those little espresso cups, so much sugar you're convinced it's a magic trick to make everything fit, the "a" for *amargo*, or *bitter*, was more of a "d" for *dulce*, or *sweet*. But maybe something was lost in the translation. Anyway, the first and third letters were true enough, and any excuse to talk about coffee usually led to an excuse to drink coffee, and that was cause for celebration, even if it was loaded with enough sugar to send the healthiest person into a diabetic shock.

><

In 2012, when Perez moved to Camagüey, the congregation of St. Paul's numbered fewer than 10 people. By the fall of 2014, there were 30 or 40 who regularly attended.

Before the revolution, the church ranked second (to one in Guantanamo) in attendance in the whole diocese, and second (to the cathedral in Havana) in the amount of money raised, Perez told me.

But that was a long time ago, and now no church draws particularly well, and only eight, of more than 40, bring in enough money to pay their priests. The others get by on money from the diocese or from partner churches overseas, mostly in the state of Florida and from Canada, which has been the Cuban church's lifeline since it was abandoned by the American Episcopal church in the 1960s.

Not that the church has more than 40 priests to pay. The number was closer to 20 in 2014 when I visited, with most priests responsible for multiple churches. Perez, the archdeacon of Camagüey Province, had three.

"There aren't enough priests," he said matter-of-factly. Five more were ordained the following summer, but that left just one in seminary.

The diocese had three kinds of churches: regular parishes that generated income; organized missions, which relied on other churches; and unorganized missions, which could be any number of things in the formative stage.

The churches that did raise money didn't always raise much. St. Paul's, Perez said, might generate 1,000 pesos a month, the equivalent of about $40.

"It's no money, because you need to buy things," he said.

At that time, he had been trying to paint his church, under the theory that people don't want to walk into an ugly building. But the paint cost about 16 dollars a gallon, so he was stockpiling when he could.

"You have to buy as much as you can, because you never know if they'll have the color again when you go back," he said.

I helped him load eight gallons of yellow paint into a closet in his house. He had 20 gallons there already.

He had painted the front of the church but didn't have enough paint for the sides. The old concrete walls soak up so much paint, it's hard to tell how much is needed, and he didn't want to start if he couldn't finish.

And St. Paul's was his well-heeled parish. Another of his churches, in a more rural part of the province, also attracted 30 or 40 people a week but generated no money.

"Those people are very poor," he said. "When you open the refrigerator, all there is is water." He wasn't trying to be funny.

> <

Perez showed off the water heater in the shower in my room and promised that I could take a hot shower whenever I wanted, which was nice even in the heat of the Caribbean.

But the water heater was actually in the shower, a development of some concern for an American accustomed to having his hot water piped in and available at the turn of a knob. The little heater was mounted to the shower head itself and appeared to have been installed by a moderately skilled do-it-yourselfer. The wires that powered it were twisted to the wires from the shower head and left loose.

It worked fine, but I never quite felt comfortable standing under it, with exposed wires just above the water flow. The lights dimmed and a spark was visible from within if I turned the dial to adjust the temperature, and so I kept it on one setting the whole time and showered as fast as I could.

><

Camagüey had more of a country feel than Havana, even though it was a city of more than 300,000 people. Roosters were crowing all morning, and the bread salesman was trying his best to peddle his wares. He was up and working long before I'd planned to be up and working. He'd wake me, his incessant calls from the street easily penetrating the louvered windows, and I'd rise early to complain about it. But both acts were solitary, and I'm certain he never knew I was trying to sleep 20 feet away. I didn't know what to say to him.

But the city wasn't too rural. The Perez home was on a corner lot, and there was enough truck traffic throughout the night to remind me how close a street could be. The rumble of a heavy truck is the same in Spanish as it is in English: familiar, annoying and a little threatening for someone whose childhood home was once invaded by a pickup truck driven by a drunk. A wall was no barrier to motorized momentum.

><

The family kept a row of bright green avocados lined up on a table in the breezeway next to the kitchen, sharing space with pieces of yucca, an open tub of white rice and loaves of bread, somewhere between fresh and stale in the thick air. A cookie sheet on a counter nearby held homegrown coffee, picked from a tree in the yard and sundried in the driveway.

In the kitchen, a small water purification system was on the counter. It was a filter-based process but still required drops of chlorine.

"We have to be careful," Claudia said, allowing tiny drops from the small brown bottle to fall into the pitcher. "There's cholera in Cuba now."

In the refrigerator, there were fresh eggs from the chickens in the yard, a pitcher of thick milk and a slab of butter, which the family purchased in anticipation of my visit.

"We got butter for you," Perez told me the night before, hinting at the treat to come the next time we dined. Because Americans require butter, I suppose. I don't eat much of it at home, but I availed myself liberally the days I was with the family, spreading it on the bread we had with every meal.

> <

A chair that once belonged to Bishop Blankingship was in the dining room, in a corner just inside the door to the living room, which also had a dining room table. The chair was a low, slung-back piece with wide arms, perfect for holding a cup of coffee and a book.

When Perez moved to town, the chair, minus one arm, had been on the trash heap. He had rescued it and found a carpenter to make a new arm. It was one of those chairs that looks plain and uncomfortable, but then you sit in it and you don't want to get back up.

I stayed there for more than an hour, first drinking my coffee and reading my book, then scribbling notes in my journal and finally just staring at the walls, not wanting to get up. But I forced myself up when Perez passed through the room a third time.

"That's a comfortable chair," I said.

"It is," he replied.

And then we went back to talking about the church in Cuba.

In his early 50s, Perez was one of the older Episcopal priests in Cuba, one of the few who'd made the commitment to serve during the anti-church years.

He had definite ideas about what did and what did not help the church, and he shared them openly.

He told me that I needed to speak with the Rev. Ivan Gonzalez, not Juan Ramon, when I returned to Havana, if I really wanted to know about the church. Gonzalez is the rector of a small Episcopal church on the outskirts of Havana, the second, and by far smaller, of the two churches in the city.

I'd visited the church on a previous visit and spent an afternoon in the company of Gonzalez, who was in the process of moving his congregation from his living room, where 20 or 30 people would crowd in on Sundays, to an actual church that had been built on the lot next to his home.

Gonzalez, Perez told me, knew the real history of the Cuban church. He said it as a statement of fact, not an opinion, though a fact he knew I might not believe.

"Juan Ramon, he has changed the history," Perez said. "He's a good man, passionate, but he talks too much politics."

In the 25 years Ramon led the Camagüey church, Perez said, attendance dropped by more than half. Some people kept going to church but changed allegiance and took up with the Catholics down the street, which may have been worse than if they'd just stopped going altogether.

Later, in Havana, Ramon wouldn't refute Perez's claim about talking politics from the pulpit. He would argue that it had been an important part of fitting into the new Cuba and that doing anything less would have been even more harmful.

Perez felt differently. "In Cuba, you turn on the radio, politics is there. Turn on the television, politics is there. You don't need that in church."

Or in the Perez household most of the time. The family preferred laughter, good-hearted humor at each other's expense. We sat in the living room that night for more than an hour, and the three Perezes and their friend Tico took turns poking fun at each other. They did it mostly in Spanish, with Evilio or Claudia occasionally translating something that had caused a particularly prolonged bout of laughter. The translation was for their benefit, not mine: people enjoying each other's company.

><

We went back to the bus station my second day there to repeat the business of acquiring a voucher for future travel. The lobby was nearly empty, but we still had to wait. The clerk was in her office with the door closed. We opened it and found her sitting at her desk, but we couldn't reach her because a woman with a mop was swabbing the floor in wide arcs around the desk. We had to wait for it to dry before we were allowed to step in.

"This is Cuba," Perez said in disgust as we seated ourselves on a bench outside the office, facing the opaque door. His words carried the same tone as his apology for his Russian SUV, a simple declaration of disgust and resignation. It could have been another of the theater faces: "Give me a 'This is Cuba.'"

"Why this couldn't have been done last night?" he asked to no one in particular, not that anyone would have answered. The lobby was nearly empty, and the few people there were in no hurry to do anything, including listening to the grumblings of a man who had his own car.

The woman with the mop worked at a deliberate pace but finally finished and opened the door and beckoned us back into the office with a smile, a friendly worker doing us the favor of opening for the day.

To produce the voucher for my trip, the clerk went through a lengthy process of punching in names and numbers, transcribing information from my passport and generally busying herself with the duties that keep state-employed bureaucrats busy.

It was all very official and officious and involved the use of the type of ledgers that went out of style elsewhere with the rise of the computer age. If carbon paper still exists anywhere in the world, it's in Cuba somewhere, stuck between the pages of a legal-sized ledger, held sideways and perched between desk and lap as a clerk jots numbers into small squares. What any of it meant, only she knew.

The amount of time it took, and the frequency with which the woman flipped through my passport, front to back and back to front and sometimes at random in between, I wouldn't be surprised if she'd recorded the details of the six years' worth of travel stamped on the pages.

The woman with the mop reappeared in search of her coffee cup, which she'd left next to the computer on the clerk's desk. The cup was nearly empty, which apparently won't do in the Camagüey bus station clerk's office, so she walked around us and filled the cup from a thermos in the windowsill, then sat on the couch and enjoyed her espresso.

She sat and sipped and stared vacantly sort of at us but also off into the distance of whatever lay behind the wall, then she finished and grabbed her mop and disappeared through the door.

The clerk smiled and exchanged pleasantries and never once complained to the woman with the mop or apologized to us for the delays.

The clerk took my money and turned on her dot-matrix printer, which then whirled through its belt-action printing and produced the voucher that I would have to exchange for the actual ticket the next day, in the exact same office.

The whole process would have to be repeated for each of the dozens of seats on each of the dozens of buses every day, year-round.

><

Perez took me to meet some of his flock after he'd made sure I'd be able to get out of town. It was the work part of my visit that the bishop had asked him to arrange.

We stopped first to pick up Albert Springer Howard, a 73-year-old retired welder. His very English-sounding name and impeccable command of the English language came from his parents, natives of Barbados who had settled in Cuba in the 1930s. Howard told me that he was allowed to speak Spanish only on the streets with his friends. At home, his parents insisted that he speak English.

He was a lifelong member of the church who was spending his retirement in a nice home at the end of a dirt street, which looked more incomplete than rural. The street was neatly lined with houses, each set back to allow room for modest front yards. Sidewalks came from the front doors and comfortable patios, lined with potted plants, toward where the street should have been, but no one ever got around to actually putting the street in place. So it was mostly dirt, except after a rain, which was the case the day I visited. Then it was a muddy mess.

Perez pulled up in front, but after a brief talk with Howard, he pulled away slowly. We drove down the block and circled back around and pulled in front again, only this time with the driver's side nearest the house. That way Howard could get into the seat behind the driver without stepping into the mud. The board from his sidewalk into the street only went so far.

From his home, we went to a home shared by Alfredo Gonzalez, a 67-year-old retired surgeon and medical professor, and his mother, the 97-year-old Mariella Carmen Marino Gonzalez.

Carmen was a lifelong member of St. Paul's. She had a photo album full of images of the church from the 1920s, when a wood-frame building housed an overflow crowd, onward. She was there the day the current church opened in 1931.

The Gonzalezes welcomed us with hugs and handshakes into

their comfortable home. In the living room, where we sat, there was a dark leather couch and matching chairs in a room with deep, beautiful wood paneling. The front door was open, and we enjoyed something of a breeze and the sight of an odd array of horse-drawn and motor-powered traffic.

Aflredo brought out his laptop, on which he had been writing his mother's story—for what, he wasn't quite sure; posterity, at least, and perhaps publication—and the photographs.

Carmen said her parents, who were Spanish, had helped found the church in Cespedes, a small town east of Havana and near the main highway. There were 11 Episcopal churches then, each with its own school. She had attended through the sixth grade, which was the customary age to stop at the time.

"The church was alive then," she said. "It was full of members."

There, she had met her husband, and there, she had raised two sons: Alfredo, the surgeon, and another, who would become a dentist. (Both men would marry women who shared their professions, and Alfredo's daughter is a doctor, too, now living in Syracuse, New York.)

Alfredo pulled a matte-print, black-and-white 8-by-10 photograph out of an envelope and showed me the image from his wedding day. He and his bride, handsome and beautiful side by side, he in a well-tailored suit, she in a stylishly short white gown with a long veil—think a Cuban Jackie Kennedy—stood at the altar. They were married by Bishop Gonzalez.

The church started to change in the mid-'60s, Alfredo said. In 1964, he decided to study medicine, and he realized then that he would have to distance himself, at least in public, from his church. To get into medical school, he said, "I could not say I was a Christian."

He still went to church, but he did it hours away in Santiago. And even there, he was careful.

"I looked this way, then I looked that way to make sure no one from the school was looking," he said. "Then I had to hide in the church."

Carmen said she never stopped going.

A short woman with large glasses, she offered a firm handshake and a steadiness in her voice that made you know few people questioned her now when she was pushing 100, or had decades ago, when she was in her prime. She had been the mother children obeyed.

"After the revolution, I kept going," she said. And that was that. She was always ready, she said, to give her head and hands to the church.

In the years immediately after the revolution, she said, she and others in the church worked to make pajamas for poor children. They would sew and sew and sew until they couldn't sew anymore.

She also taught Sunday school up through 1970, when she quit because there were no more children to teach.

"At the time of the revolution, there were many children in Sunday school," she said, asking her son to find photographs of her old Sunday school classes. "It was beautiful to see those children."

She started teaching again, in November 2014, picking up after the 44-year hiatus. "I think there's a need now," she said. The children had not immediately returned in great numbers, but she said she hoped that offering activities, such as Sunday school, would help bring them back.

Her son said the children weren't the only ones to leave the church.

"After all those years pass, you don't have that relation with the church anymore," he said.

The congregation dwindled to three or four people some Sundays.

"It was losing strength," he said. "People did not feel secure."

Howard said the visit of Pope John Paul II in 1998 helped. After then, all Christians, not just Catholics, had more liberty in their faith. If something good happened, he said, you could again say "thanks be to God" without fear.

Howard knew well the price of faith. In 1975, he was offered a job in a bank but stumbled in the interview.

"I was asked, 'Do you believe in God?' I said, 'Yes.' I can't say no to what I believe. I was limited because of that. But I always believe in God." He was never interested in being part of the Communist Party. "I wasn't looking to get high places by denying God, because (if I did), one day, God would deny me, too," he said.

Repeating what Perez had been telling me, Gonzalez said

politics hurt the church. "People go to church for church, not for politics," he said.

The Episcopal Church, he said, fell in line with the revolution, and the few people who remained were loyal to the state first. Before then, in its strongest days, the Episcopal Church had drawn members from all walks of life, black and white, young and old.

"It was a spirited environment," Gonzalez said. "But because of politics, people left the church."

Still, he was never tempted to quit entirely. For a long time, he said, going was difficult. Sometimes because he was assigned to work away from his home. Others times, just because.

"I was separated from church activities," he said. "It was difficult to be in the church, but I never left."

The difficulty manifested itself in the church, too, and the cost is evident today. As people left, money for the church dwindled, and as the money dwindled, there was less available to maintain the building. Then the people who were left started feeling uncomfortable in a crumbling, ugly building, Perez said. "You fix the church, it's more inviting, people will want to come," he said.

After Perez had dropped me off and gone somewhere else, Gonzalez was generous in his praise for Perez and his presence. "This reverend here is a worth a lot," he said. "He'll go out and find where the people are and ask what they want."

><

They all remembered Bishop Blankingship fondly. Howard and Gonzalez both said he confirmed them. When he retired and left for the United States in 1961, there was a farewell service in the town of Morón, northwest of Camagüey.

"I was only 14 years old. At that age, you don't give great value to those things," Gonzalez said. But 53 years later, he still remembered the day with clarity.

Both knew that Blankingship wanted to build a camp. "It never progressed," Gonzalez said. "It didn't have the opportunity to continue."

Howard said the problem was that nobody went. "They did not have the good will to continue that work."

Or the means to get there, perhaps, the camp being in a central location on the island, yet removed from nearly everything. If you find yourself in the middle of nowhere in Cuba, you'll be at Camp Blankingship.

><

Out the front door of the Gonzalez home, the street was alive with horse-drawn carts, motorcycles, trucks and bicycles. A small market across the street attracted steady business.

Something settled into Howard's mind, and he started to smile. He asked Carmen if she remembered the song that was playing when the bishop would walk in. She shook her head "no."

"It was 'Onward Christian Soldiers,' in English," he said. Then he started to sing it in hopes of getting Carmen to join in. But she didn't. Howard petered out after a verse, his voice falling to a whisper then disappearing altogether.

Carmen let the room sit silent for a moment, then she began speaking about an old friend who had recently returned to the church after decades away.

"I asked her why, and she said because she had an emptiness in herself: 'What I have in my house is not significant.' Her inside was empty," she said

Howard listened, then began quoting scripture, but neither Gonzalez paid him much attention at that point. As with the singing, he quickly lost enthusiasm.

The younger Gonzalez said the problem with the church in Cuba was that for many years, there was no companionship between churches in the country and no friendship with people from the rest of the world. What they knew at the time was what was in front of them.

I'd heard similar versions of that sentiment on several trips: how hard it was to expect people to rise up when they don't know they needed to or to fight back against an enemy they didn't know existed. Isolation had worked magic like denial never could. People just didn't know what they didn't know.

Gonzalez sat silently for a moment, thinking about something, looking for the words to articulate his thoughts on an idea he was forming. After a moment, he spoke.

"We are very glad to have you in our midst," he said.

> <

Retirement has not been easy for either Howard the welder or Gonzalez the surgeon. Howard said he received 10 convertible dollars a month in his pension; Gonzalez received 40. Ten a month, Howard said, wasn't enough money to keep him in Sweet Tarts, his candy of choice.

"You retire to enjoy retirement. But your life is tied up" in the pursuit of money, he said.

None, it seemed, had been available for watch repair. After nearly two hours in the Gonzalez home, I finally realized that the watch on Howard's arm wasn't working. It was stuck on 11:35. I don't wear a watch, and I hadn't been able to check the time against anything, but 11:35 it was not, anymore.

Gonzalez didn't talk about his pension. He said life had been good, even when life had been tough. The world had come to him through the years.

Castro's Cuba has long been a medical leader in the Caribbean and throughout Latin America, and aspiring doctors had traveled there to train for generations. As a medical professor, Alfredo helped teach students from Colombia, Peru and Angola. Even in retirement, he marveled at the opportunity he once had to shape minds at home and abroad.

> <

As we sat in the living room, Howard and Gonzalez reminiscing as we looked through the stack of photographs, a familiar song wafted in from the radio playing in the yard next door. It took a minute, but it didn't take great or deep knowledge of Spanish to recognize the tune.

"*Si vas a San Francisco/*
Asegúrate de llevar algunas flores en el pelo."
"If you're going to San Francisco/
Be sure to wear some flowers in your hair."

A touch more melodic in Spanish, perhaps, but no less grating. And a little odd, a hippie-era mantra casually playing in a country that fought so hard in the hippie era to keep everything American at bay. Five decades of Communism seemed a failure with the broadcast of that one song. Perez had once had to put down his saxophone because the music he was playing offended the state. Now "San Francisco" had not only been translated and accepted, it had been relegated to background music.

No one else paid the song any attention.

Gonzalez said times were changing in even more obvious ways. "They allow a stranger to visit," he said, sitting on a couch 10 feet from an open door, through which anyone on the street could have peered in and seen, or heard, our conversation.

If he'd had any reservations about allowing me into his home, or about speaking openly about a part of life his government long tried to stifle, he didn't show it.

> <

Camagüey is a large city, but it seemed to have more bicycles than cars. Many of those bicycles carried two people: one on the seat, as you'd expect, and the other, usually a woman, sitting side-saddle on a special, long narrow seat mounted over the rear wheel. It didn't look comfortable, but in a country where you sweat just walking in the shade, I guess any ride is better than none at all.

On some streets, horse-drawn carriages also outnumbered cars. They were not the Central Park carriages, either: there was no romance in Camagüey that day. Hard metal wheels, slab seats and the makeshift poop bag opened toward the back greeted the passengers. Each carriage I saw was carrying a full load, a dozen or more people sitting quietly, and patiently, as they clomped their way to wherever they were going.

> <

Lunch was time for the Perez family to shine in the kitchen.

The night before, for dinner, there had been sliced ham and cheese, rolls and my slab of butter. It had been filling, for sure, but also austere, a humble meal in a country where humble meals were still the norm.

For lunch, there was a plate of boneless chicken breasts (at least I think so: the next day, Claudia referred to it as beef, and I can't say for certain that either of us was right), white rice, black beans, avocado and cucumber salad and the tastiest fried plantains I've ever had. I was offered the butter, too, though it wasn't on the table.

Tico was gone by then, back to his duty as a soldier, and the absence of a growing boy meant it was too much food for the four people left. We tried hard to work our way through, but didn't come close to finishing.

Some of the food had come from the yard, where the family has six avocado trees. They also grow coffee, papaya, guava, bananas, peaches (per Claudia; I didn't actually see those myself), and raise chickens and turkeys. If Cuba were the kind of country where they wrote newspaper stories about people who are quirky in good ways, the Perez family would have had a framed page on the wall with the story about their garden.

><

The city had a train station, with six sets of tracks spreading out. It offered service to Havana, to the northwest, and to Santiago, to the southeast, and to points in between. For someone raised in the U.S. in the Amtrak era, with bland cars shuttling passengers about like bus service on rails, there was great appeal in hopping aboard rolling stock from the days when trains were the means of proper travel. But a quick glance at the yard dismissed thoughts of "proper travel," and everyone I asked greatly discouraged me from riding.

The train was the cheapest way to travel in Cuba but also the least reliable and least comfortable. It apparently stopped in towns too small or inconsequential for bus service—hard to believe, based on the bus trip I'd taken to Camagüey; we'd stopped everywhere there had been a person—and it supposedly had a tendency to meander its way to the next stop. Plus, I was told, the seats were just benches, and the bathrooms weren't fit for humans.

The small engines pulled rusted, weathered cars. It looked nice, in a picturesque way, but not like something on which you'd want to rely for transportation.

I passed by the station half a dozen times in my two days there, and every time the platform was crowded. I never actually saw a train moving, though I did once see one idling.

I'd ignore the advice and ride the train anyway, but I never had the opportunity.

><

The town had an old world feel: narrow, winding streets, with buildings coming right up to sidewalks so narrow you'd have to step in the street to pass another person walking by. Everywhere, the doors were open. In some, there was evidence of homes: couches and chairs, televisions, people lounging right up next to the door, inches from what traffic came by. In others, there was commerce: small shops, barbers, an eyeglass repairman, anything you might need, as long as the need didn't require a consumer good beyond the most basic necessity, because those were always scarce. Discolored, disfigured fruit was in great supply.

Most of the roads were hard to navigate by car: there were so many ruts, dips and potholes. And because of that, the infrequent clear, straight sections were crowded with every form of transportation imaginable. Throw in a Russian car and a directionally challenged driver—Perez found his calling in the pulpit; he wouldn't have made much of a cabbie—and the shortest of trips became winding journeys.

But there was always something to see.

Cubans love art, and Camagüey, like all the other towns I'd visited, was dotted with small parks that always had benches and sculptures, and not always busts of Jose Marti, though those were everywhere. And like parks everywhere, these were full of people lounging. Mostly men, but also couples, and people young and old. Some were playing dominoes, others just talking. Unlike American parks, there was little evidence of vagrancy, but perhaps Cubans have more ingenious ways of drinking during the day than sitting on benches clutching paper bags.

> <

After the large lunch and an afternoon nap, Perez again led me by car to the home of a parishioner. And as had been the case earlier in the day, the late afternoon session included the bonus of a second, English-speaking parishioner who augmented his translations with stories of his own.

The modest home belonged to 91-year-old Jose Benito Gonzalez, a retired warehouse clerk, and his wife, Georgeina Serni. They were not related to the Gonzalez family I'd seen earlier.

They lived in the traditional Cuban home with a living room in the front, spanning the width of the house, and three bedrooms and a bathroom, one after the other, leading to the back, where the house again spread out for the kitchen. Running parallel to the bedrooms, but not under a roof, was a long, narrow interior courtyard.

The living room had a red leather couch and two matching chairs. Along one wall was a tall bookcase, every shelf full, including the complete works of Jose Marti, 27 volumes with matching white covers embossed with the image of the long-dead national hero. Nowhere in the world has a journalist been more venerated than in Cuba, but few journalists have ever been quite like Marti.

Marti had special relevance to Gonzalez.

He said he vividly remembered his first English teacher, Miss Newell, and how she would speak about Marti, whom she had once met.

So there I was, in October of 2014, one person removed from Marti, who had died in 1895, 119 years before. I've spent most of my life in the American South, where you're never too far removed from someone with a tie to the Civil War, so such lineage isn't uncommon, but it was still kind of cool, and it lent importance to a shelf of dusty books.

The street, just feet from the front door, included the usual variety of traffic, closer here than earlier in the day because this home opened right to the road while the other home had had a small porch.

The translator was Jose Hidalgo, a 64-year-old computer network administrator who looked like someone you'd know back home, no matter where back home was. He would have been at home in any number of countries. If you saw him in Starbucks reading the paper, you wouldn't blink. He had graying hair and a matching mustache, blue jeans and a blue-and-white striped oxford cloth shirt, untucked, and dark boots. He wasn't shy with an opinion, but was not obnoxious about it. He liked to talk, and he had a certainty about his thoughts, that was all.

Both Joses joined the church years ago, Gonzalez in 1929 and Hidalgo in 1955. Their paths diverged greatly for decades, particularly when Hidalgo left the church to pursue a career free of the stigma of Christianity, but had come back together.

Gonzalez finished his formal schooling in 1941, when he was 18, and went to work as a teacher in the St. Paul's Episcopal School in Camagüey. He stayed there until 1961, when the government nationalized all of the church schools and hired its own teachers.

Gonzalez was nearing 40 then, and he'd spent nearly his entire life in classrooms, as a student and then as a teacher. He was sent to work in a warehouse as a clerk.

After the revolution, he said, he could begin to see "misorganization" of the church. And he could begin to see what being part of a church meant to his life outside of the church. For many years, he said, "working with the government, we couldn't talk about our belief in the church. It wasn't possible to be a manager and to be a Christian."

He could have lost his job because of his beliefs, "but I was very careful." In the end, he said, he believes that his coworkers respected his decisions. He continued going to church, but with less regularity than before.

Hidalgo said church membership would have cut off his access to a wide range of jobs, including journalist, doctor, lawyer and university professor, and he wasn't willing to make that sacrifice. He studied economics in school, weighed the reality of life in the new Cuba and stopped going to church altogether in 1965.

"I almost forgot what it was," he said.

He worked, he married, he raised a family, he did whatever like-minded Cubans did in those years when Castro was asserting his authority over the country. Mostly, he kept his mouth shut and tried to avoid notice.

But then Hidalgo reached that stage in life when people start thinking about what they are and what they want to be. It was then he started thinking about church again.

"In the '90s, I turned back to the church," he said. Then he paused for a moment before finishing the thought. "I needed to be where my origins were."

During the same era, in 1994, Gonzalez traveled to Miami for a vacation. While there, he visited a priest who had once been one of his students in Camagüey. The priest encouraged him to find other former students who had left the church and try to get them back together. Gonzalez tried.

Now, every December, the group meets. "We're trying to make our revival, but many are dead now," he said.

Gonzalez is part of a vanishing breed in Cuba: old-line churchgoers. He started at St. Paul's in 1930, the year before the current building opened. Like Mariella Carmen Marino Gonzalez, he said he was there the day it opened in 1931, though neither seemed to remember the other.

> <

Gonzalez and Hidalgo talked at length, often in animated tones, about Tate.

Both had distinct memories of the long-gone American, drawn from their own experiences and from stories they'd heard through the years. Their stories converged on occasion, but the two men had different ideas about what was worth remembering and what wasn't and what was worth laughing about and what was worth scorn, even all those years later.

"He was a well-known man," Hidalgo said, opening with a casual understatement. Tate once cut quite the figure in Camagüey. He was an American, to be sure, a 1928 graduate of Sewanee College, in Nashville, Tennessee. But he moved to Cuba the following year and stayed for more than three decades.

"He was seen here like a citizen, a normal person," Hidalgo said. "He believed in Jose Marti's ideas."

For all his work with the church and at the school, Hidalgo said, Tate's heyday came between the first of January 1959, when Castro's forces took control of the country, and January 3, 1961, when the U.S. broke off consular relations with Cuba.

Those two years, Hidalgo said, saw church attendance rise dramatically because people wanted to meet Tate and earn his favor. He was the one who had the power to issue exit visas.

He laughed at the thought, evoking the intrigue of the movie *Casablanca*, where everyone was holed up in the Moroccan city in the early days of World War II, trying to flee the Nazis and find passage to America.

In Hidalgo's version of history, Tate's home was the Camagüey version of *Rick's Café Americaine*, without the drinking and gambling.

"You'd go to his house, and he'd invited you in, and he'd take the passport and stamp stamp and say 'good travels,'" Hidalgo said, mimicking the motion of stamping a passport.

He smiled at the thought, but Gonzalez didn't see the humor in it.

He had a stern look on his face the whole time Hidalgo was talking, and when it was his turn to speak, he offered quick words about that era.

"I didn't like that period," he said, his disgust cutting through the years. He didn't like sharing his church with people more interested in escaping their country than in believing in God.

But after 1961, when the American was gone and Cubans were in control of everything, there were worse changes.

"Things were absolutely different," Gonzalez said. "Priests more closely followed politics, not the church." He kept ties to the church, but the conduct of the men in the pulpit was contrary to what he thought a church should be. "Many friends, parishioners, brothers in Christ didn't attend anymore."

Still, he stayed, and in 1967, risking his ability to work peacefully, he baptized his children in the Episcopal Church. It worked out, he said, "because the fellows at work respected the wish of mine. But I spent much time with discomfort."

His attendance finally began to wane, he said, because the Episcopal priests aligned themselves, as best religious men could, with the government.

"I believe in separation of my religious beliefs and political ideas," he said. And that was the end of that part of the conversation. Gonzalez rubbed his hands together and stood up.

His wife, who hadn't said a word the whole time, also stood and smiled at us.

Hidalgo and I conferred and determined that it was time for Perez to come get me. The end had been abrupt but not unpleasant. Gonzalez had said what he wanted to say, and that was that.

Hidalgo made the call, and we all stood up and stepped toward the door. But we were still in Cuba, and a quick end to a conversation did not mean a quick exit. We waited on the narrow sidewalk and continued talking until Perez came, and then when he joined us, we talked for a while longer afterward.

><

The Episcopal Church lost some parishioners to the Catholic Church in the early 1960s, Hidalgo said. The Catholics "were preaching against the Revolution." The Episcopals fell in line with the new government.

"It was sad," Gonzalez said of watching his church decline.

He stuck with it, though. "I am not a perfect person. But always, I have been a member of the church. My Christian belief is the same."

These days, he said, the church is getting stronger, particularly since Perez came to town. The attitude of the priests has changed, he said, and that has made it stronger.

Both Gonzalez and Hidalgo said they have seen glimmers of hope of late, particularly since Raul Castro assumed the presidency from his brother Fidel in 2008. "(Raul) said government must be more respectful and tolerant with churches," Hidalgo said.

It has been a glimmer of hope, though, not a bright beacon: Gonzalez said so much time passed, it's hard for people to remember what being part of a church is.

"There is a change in the culture of the people, a very important change," he said on the sidewalk in front of his house. "For my grandchildren, church is not very important."

The years of political teaching by the government, the years without a church presence, will take generations to overcome, he said. If it ever happens.

Hidalgo agreed, sort of. "My children, they don't know anything about the church," he said. He didn't raise them in church, and they didn't learn on their own from their friends, because there was nothing to learn.

Yet his 35-year-old daughter found religion on her own as an adult and joined the Catholic Church. He might have preferred she join him with the Episcopal Church, but he wasn't too worried about it.

"It's her choice," he said. "That's where she feels at home."

> <

Hidalgo said leaving the church in 1965 was hard, but that he had to be realistic. He was young and wanted to raise a family and he knew that he had to make a sacrifice. He kept his copies of the Book of Common Prayer and the Bible but stopped going to church.

"It would have cost me many, many opportunities," he said. "I had to sacrifice for a future."

Thirty years later, in 1995, he walked back into church.

"I just went one day," he said, still a little surprised, even nearly 20 years later. "It was like the first day."

He kept going and became a member of the vestry, involving himself in the business of the church.

"People need belief," he said.

><

Hidalgo and I then discussed 1968, the year I was born.

"That's when Bobby (Kennedy) died, and Martin Luther King, Jr. The Vietnam War got worse," he said, running through a partial list of American disasters from that year. He did it without sympathy or malice; he was simply reciting facts. "It was a bad year here, too. That was the year of the radicalization when the government took all of the private businesses."

By 1962, Castro's government had full control of wholesale and foreign trade, banking and education.

But by 1968, a decade after the revolution, there were more than 55,000 private businesses conducting trade in retail, transportation, construction and other industry. Many of those businesses had begun *after* the revolution, selling food and other consumer goods to a population that couldn't get what it needed from its government.

Castro took them all that year.

Some of the former owners were allowed to stay in place to run their former businesses, but most of the workers were shipped off to collective farms to work in agricultural jobs.

Life would change from bad to surreal the next year, when Cuba's Communist Party outlawed Christmas. It was not only no longer a holiday; people weren't even allowed to celebrate it on their own in their homes. Not that they could have found, or afforded, much to give each other.

After a decade of warming up to the task, fending off the U.S. and dispatching his internal enemies and consolidating everything he could put his hands on, Castro entered the 1970s in full control.

> <

While we were on the sidewalk waiting for Perez to lurch up in his Russian SUV, I asked Gonzalez and Hidalgo one more question.

"Is the world better, worse or just different from before?" I asked

Gonzalez didn't hesitate.

"It's not better," he said with the sad certainty of a man who has seen more than he'll ever share. He did not elaborate.

Hidalgo countered the point.

"Much better," he said as he reached his hand into a pocket of his jeans. He pulled out his cell phone and pointed to it.

"Computers," he said. "I can call China right now with this. It used to be, you wrote someone a note and went to the post office and waited and waited. Now, at home, on my computer, I have the whole world."

Then he offered two pieces of Cuban history before we parted ways.

"You know, all of Marti's papers, his handwritten papers, they are in the New York Public Library," he said. "Our government has never tried to get them back."

Marti lived just 42 years, but into them he crammed enough literary and revolutionary accomplishment to make him a hero Cubans still worship to this day. Go anywhere in Cuba, and you won't have to look far for a white bust, bleached in the sun, sitting on a pedestal. They're in front of homes and stores, government offices and churches. Everywhere you go, there's Marti. His image is the commanding presence even in Havana, lording over the complex where the government is run.

He was the ideal hero, in many ways: he fought for a righteous cause, died for it and preached a message that has held its resonance for more than a century.

He pushed for independence from Spain and wrote of the coming evils of U.S. expansion at a time when the U.S. was deeply into its Manifest Destiny phase.

He was killed by the Spanish after initiating an ill-advised two-man charge on May 19, 1895. He was trying to dispel the notion that he was more talk than action. Dressed in black, riding a white horse, he was an easy target in the Battle of Dos Rios. He died where the *Rio Contramaestre* and the *Rio Cauto* met, not far from the city of Santiago.

He had spent many years in exile, including large parts of the 1880s and early 1890s in the U.S., where he wrote about independence—and other things, too.

"He once wrote an article on the Brooklyn Bridge," Hidalgo said. "It's a beautiful thing. You should go read it."

His other piece of history was about Calixto Garcia, also a war hero from the same era as Marti. There's an imposing statue of Garcia on the *Malecon* in Havana, at the point where the *Avenida de los Presidentes* ends at the ocean. At the other end of the avenue, up the hill, is a hospital named in his honor.

He died on December 11, 1898, at the Raleigh Hotel in Washington, D.C., while awaiting a response from U.S. officials to a Cuban diplomatic request. Manifest Destiny was for export, not import, and foreign diplomats weren't at the top of anyone's list of must-see visitors.

"They say Spanish bullets couldn't kill him, but pneumonia could," Hidalgo said.

The point being, the ties between in the U.S. and Cuba run deep, for better and worse, and never go away, no matter the politics involved, he said. It wasn't so funny as ironic, and that's something Cubans know well, the irony of their own history.

><

Winter was coming to Camagüey.

Perez said it was already too cold for him. Claudia said the walking bread salesman had moved his delivery back from between five and six in the morning until between seven to eight because of the weather. She, too, complained of the chill in the air.

The whole conversation amused me, seeing as how I was sweating while we talked.

I asked if they were expecting snow, and they both laughed.

"Only in pictures," Claudia said.

The winter chill had little adverse effect on me. We were standing still in the shade, and I still felt hot.

Winter there was when the highs rarely topped 90 and the

lows dipped toward 70.

I made it through the night without a blanket.

> <

Sunday was baptism day at St. Paul's Episcopal Church in Camagüey. The family with the baby was coming from Esmeralda, a small town northwest of the city of Camagüey but still in the province of the same name. That's where Perez served for 20 years before the bishop moved him.

Perez knew the mother, the grandmother and even the great-grandmother. The only piece of information he could not easily recall was the name of the baby. No one in the house could remember.

Seated at the table for breakfast, father, mother and daughter all spoke in a fast Spanish, the conversation going around in the circles, everyone looking amused.

Then they all stopped and laughed at each other. Perez told me they had been discussing the possibility of naming the baby *El Nino*, the child.

They laughed again, then stopped for the pre-meal prayer.

> <

About two dozen people showed up for church that morning, less than half the normal turnout. Perez and several of his parishioners apologized for the small size of the crowd.

"I think it's because of transportation issues," Claudia told me later in the day. "Sometimes the buses don't run like they're supposed to."

I waved off the apologies as best I could.

My thought, which I kept to myself at the time, was that maybe Cubans are like Americans in their churchgoing habits, too: when they see a baptism listed in the bulletin, they stay home for fear of being caught all day watching someone else's crying baby get sprinkled with holy water.

The service went off well, with Perez offering his sermon in an easy manner from the front of the altar, not behind the lectern. He was animated and engaging, and he earned and kept the attention of his small flock. He was talking to friends, it seemed, not strangers, and the whole thing made me feel right at home. It was kind of like the breakfast table; a few more people, but just as much laughter.

During the baptism, the little girl mostly behaved, and Perez and the grandfather were seen sharing wide smiles as the holy water fell from Perez's cupped hand and landed on the child's head. She was dressed in a traditional white gown, with a white flower on a wide white headband stretched across her brown hair. She was the kind of the baby who would make people coo and say things like "she's adorable" and "you should have more" and, if they knew the parents really well, "who's the father?"

One relative scooped holy water from the font into a plastic soda bottle, but no one paid him much attention. He filled the container, capped it and stowed it away for use of some sort.

Only once did Perez trip himself up.

The family had brought along a second child, a year or so older than the one being baptized.

I could see Perez talking to them and looking at the second child. And I could tell the parents weren't following along.

"I asked when I was going to baptize the other child," Perez told me later in the day. "They told me I already had." He laughed off his forgetfulness.

During the baptism, a crazed-looking man wandered in off the street and through the open doors at the back of the sanctuary. He made his way up front to the ceremony, where he joined the crowd around Perez. He stopped briefly to stare. He looked confused, then turned around and left.

No one paid him much attention, though when he was gone, two of the men made a quick check of the security of the side doors.

At the end of the service, Perez came a few steps closer to the congregation and did as priests the world over do: he made announcements of interest to him and the congregation, spreading the news of church while the flock was there to hear it. Among other things, he spoke about the cost of repairing the leaky roof. When he mentioned the sum of one million pesos, laughter filled the room. It seemed a congregation as comfortable with its needs as with its limitations.

><

There was a beautiful, deeply colored wood pulpit off to the left side of the altar. Perez didn't use it, but it was hard to miss.

A worn brass plaque was attached to one side. It read: *In Loving Memory of Caroline Helena Webster Storey, 1824-1869, Given By Her Daughters.*

No one in the church knew much about the pulpit, and no one knew who Storey had been or why her daughters had dedicated the piece in her honor. Her death predated the arrival of the Episcopal Church in Cuba by a year or two. Like so much in Cuba, it was just there, where it had always been.

I later found a mention online about Storey, who was born in Cuba and died in New York City, shortly after the birth of her seventh child. But I couldn't find anything else.

><

On the way back home, still apologizing for the small turnout, Perez said the Episcopals can't match the Pentecostals when it comes to filling a church, but he's confident that the people he does attract will stay.

"If you go back (to a Pentecostal church) in a year, it's all different people," he said. "Our growth is much slower, but the people who come stay."

It was something I would hear again several times before my trip was over, always about the Pentecostals.

We returned to the rectory after the service. We had tea with three members of the parish who had come to bring sweets to Perez's wife, who had been relegated to the indoors after eye surgery. Her bandages had come off, but she couldn't handle the sun, so she stayed indoors. Even there, she often wore dark glasses.

The women spoke of youth groups, diet plans and the difficulty of making tea that appeals to people who live in Florida. (Like the Pentecostals, tea and Floridians were a topic of mystery to several Cuban Episcopalians I met.)

One of the women, a chemistry professor at the local university, finally stopped and looked my way. She was beautiful like a middle-aged woman who had worked hard to stay beautiful, with the air of nonchalance those women always use to make sure you know how beautiful they are without having to say a word themselves. A tight skirt and leopard-print blouse didn't hurt.

"You know nothing?" she asked me, smiling, politely. I think.

"You can't imagine what I don't know," I said.

She laughed and returned her attention to the women.

The group finished its visit in short order and left, and Claudia retreated to the kitchen to pack me a lunch for the road. I didn't protest.

"It's too early for lunch now," she said. "You'll want this later."

She packed me two sandwiches: one with ham and cheese, the other with a slice of what she called beef but that I thought was chicken. Either way, it was bread wrapped around a thin slice of meat of some origin, as identifiable as a piece of jerky. It was what we'd had the day before.

I also refilled my water bottle, then Perez drove me back to the bus station.

><

I traded my voucher for a ticket and took a seat in the lobby, where I was quickly joined by a family of flies. I tried several other seats, but they followed me and I finally gave up and returned to where I'd started: at the end of a row of four seats nearest the opening in the wall through which I could see buses come and go. One of the other seats had the evidence of an ice cream cone gone awry, an orange, sticky liquid hardening in the heat of the afternoon.

The station was shared by all of Cuba's bus companies, and while I waited, several of the well-worn Astro and Nacionale buses came and went with their loads of locals. Some had been headed my direction, but I either wasn't allowed aboard or didn't know any better.

My Viazul bus pulled in mostly on time, a pleasant surprise, and we boarded and pulled out without delay and began the seven-hour, back-and-forth drive to Santiago.

Taken straight, the drive could be done in four hours. But buses the world over work on their own schedules and maps, and Cuba's are no exception.

We headed first for Las Tunas, an easy, straight shot east on the main highway. But then we were also supposed to stop in Holguin and Bayamo before making our way to Santiago. Those cities are north and south of Las Tunas, and the three form a triangle of highway, before the road heads east again toward Santiago. One way or the other, it meant a long detour.

We also stopped at half a dozen other places I couldn't identify. At one, we picked up a man and drove him across town, then dropped him off in a seemingly random spot. He was happy, though, and waved as we pulled away.

At another place, we pulled up to an intersection, where one of the drivers hopped off and had a casual conversation with a woman who appeared to be a close friend. She kissed him on the cheek, and then he hopped back on, and the bus moved on down the road.

Unlike the drive from Havana to Camagüey, the ride into Santiago was not to be interrupted by a waiting session in a station parking lot, no "is closed" admonition from a weary driver trying to dislodge the last passenger. But I didn't know that at the time, so I was nervous most of the way anyway.

We trucked through the whole thing with no need for me to relinquish my seat. I did think about doing so on once, when the couple across the aisle, in seats to which I had an unobstructed view because the way the rows were staggered, became somewhat amorous. But they rolled toward the window on their side of the bus, and I diverted my attention to the scenery through the window on my side.

The trip was not completely without uncertainty. At one point, we were on a solid, paved, sparsely used highway, and I saw a sign pointing in the direction of Santiago. But the driver went another way, pulling the bus onto a narrow, winding road that crossed train tracks and snaked its way through an industrial park of some sort. When we rounded a corner and went back over the train tracks and onto what appeared to be a dirt road, I began having doubts about the itinerary and whether or not I would see Santiago, or anything else I knew, ever again.

But I was in a poor position to do more than sit still and wait it out, so that's what I did. I pulled out the first of my two sandwiches and a Payday candy bar and tried to make the most of what looked like a ride straight into doom. Which was hard, what with my love of knowing where I am. But I hadn't been able to find a street map, and I reluctantly resigned myself to ignorance.

After a while, we rounded more corners, pulled back onto a regular looking road and made our way to the Holguin International Airport, which offered some relief. I saw signs promising the arrival and departure of flights to and from Toronto and Barcelona, and I felt a little better knowing I was near an emergency escape plan, should the need for such arise at that very moment.

By then, the sun was beginning its descent behind us and a heavy rain set in. The driver tried to outrun it, pushing the bus faster than he had all day.

Cuba has not mastered roadside drainage in a deluge, and I could look out the window and see swiftly moving streams expanding from the pavement deep into the fields. It was fine sitting high in the bus, dry and safely removed from the consequences of bad driving, but most people in Cuba don't share that luxury. The streams were dotted with the lucky people on horseback trotting over the water and the not-so-lucky on bicycles or foot, trying to find steady footing on a ground they could no longer see, all the while avoiding the wake caused by the bus.

The driver tried at first to spare those people an outright spray of water, but the effort was short-lived. At one point, I could see a boy looking on in terror as we approached. The bus didn't slow, and the boy was last seen covering his head with his hands as he was drenched by a wave we'd just created.

After a while, the rain stopped. Then the sun disappeared completely and we rolled on in darkness, oblivious to what life may have existed roadside the rest of the way.

Being American and somewhat accustomed to schedules, I grew excited as we began our descent from a hill and I could see lights spread far and wide in the distance. I checked the time on my iPod, and it matched the general timeframe of my scheduled arrival, so I was certain it was Santiago.

I held tight to that belief all the way into town.

I lost grip as we passed through.

We didn't stop, and I couldn't see a sign, and I resigned myself, again, to the hope that things were going to work out as planned. Eventually.

There wasn't much of the island left anyway, I knew, and if we overshot Santiago, we were certain to wind up in Guantanamo, where the main highway ended.

We finally made our way to Santiago and slowly crawled through town as the driver approached the station.

I was determined to avoid the fiasco with eager taxi drivers into which I'd thrust myself in Camagüey, but I failed. They got me before we even pulled to a complete stop.

My side of the bus was closest to the station as we pulled in. Only it was a Cuban bus station, so there was a gate that had to be raised, which meant the bus had to idle as the gate raiser got into place.

As we waited for the guard to raise the gate, several of the taxi drivers made eye contact with me. Those whose gaze I avoided got my attention anyway by tapping on the window. I was like a squirrel with a piece of shiny foil: I couldn't help but look.

"You need a taxi," I kept hearing, not sure if it were a request or a command. Either way, I knew what was coming.

I took my time disembarking, then waited patiently as the bags were unloaded onto the sidewalk between the bus and the building. All the while, I scanned the nearly empty waiting room for someone who looked like a priest, but I couldn't find a good match.

After all of the other passengers went into the terminal, I did, too. They wouldn't let me stay outside.

CHAPTER 4

SANTIAGO DE CUBA

THE LOBBY OF the Santiago bus station was nearly empty. A few scattered people lingered about, looking like they were settling in for the night, and it was obvious that whoever was meeting me wasn't in the room. But I wasn't ready to give up the peaceful desperation of having been forgotten for the chaos I could see on the streets.

I wasn't ready to go because I didn't know where it was I was going, and I'm the kind of guy who likes to have a plan in mind before heading out with his too-heavy bags slung over his weak, tired shoulders. And I wasn't ready to step outside because there were a lot of people, thousands and thousands of people, and they were engulfing the bus station the way crowds do in those television news clips just before something really bad happens. One minute, it's a big crowd, moving all nice like, almost hypnotic in its unison, then before you know what's happening, someone does something stupid and it all goes to hell.

So I stayed inside. I dropped my bags on an empty seat and looked around again, thinking maybe my guy might have emerged, all Harry Potter-like, from a secret entrance no one else could see.

Barring that, I'd have to be patient. Somewhere in that crowd out on the streets, I knew, someone was probably looking for me. He was stuck in traffic, and he'd probably be there as soon as he could. The American in me wanted to believe he'd apologize for being late as he hurried in and whisked me away to safety, far from the masses, but I knew better. In Cuba, no one ever promises you an exact time they'll be there so there's never a need to apologize. They come when they come, and you smile and get a cup of coffee and move from the conversation you were having with the person over there to the conversation you're now having with the person over here.

And if none of that worked out, if no one in that crowd was there to find me, I'd be all right, because I had a trump card I hadn't had in Camagüey: a name and phone number.

Somewhere in Santiago, there was a trumpet player from Finland who spoke English, owned a house and had a room for rent. He was a friend of a college music professor I'd once written about. A tenuous connection, perhaps, but still, he was someone. He had a stepdaughter and two telephone numbers and a street address, all of which I knew. It had been a pleasant enough story, and the connection was offered, not yielded on request.

The trumpet player and I traded email before I'd left home, and I had his information tucked into a secret pocket in the generic looking black journal I kept in my bag. I had an in, if I needed an in.

I wasn't certain I could figure out how to use a Cuban pay phone, but I could see one in the lobby, and if nothing else, I could start pointing and hope the guard would help.

But the whole thing was an exercise in American-style anxiety, and I was out of there in less than five minutes.

Before the bench had stopped shaking from the jolt of my bag landing hard, the Rev. Halbert Pons stuck his head in the door of the station, looked straight at me and said the magic words.

My name.

He spoke it with the sound of a hope of relief that he'd succeeded in finding the man his boss had sent to him. On a bus, in the dark, late on a Sunday night, just as the entire population of town was headed home from a rally.

"I'm glad to see you," I said as he whisked me past a gaggle of taxi drivers on one side of the street and the approaching populace of Santiago on the other.

"Yes," he said, pushing forward.

I'd come to find him as chatty as me, but not just yet. We had a crowd to beat. We went down the block and ducked around a corner and into a wide alley, where he had parked his car.

He deposited my too-heavy bag into the too-small cargo hold of his Korean sedan, then directed me to the front seat.

The Most Rev. Ulises Agüero Prendes, a lifelong resident of Santiago and the supposedly retired bishop suffragan of Cuba, was there, too, waiting by the car in that way Cubans have of letting you know that they just happened to be waiting, and not for you. If you hadn't come along, they'd be fine, just the same. I saw that all over the country. One day, I saw a pot-bellied middle-aged man leaning against a fence in Havana, the Rick James song "Super Freak" playing on the radio you could hear through the open door of his car. He had his white tank top rolled up over his belly—a peculiar, but common, fashion statement among men in Cuba; the women don't seem to do it—and was standing there, enjoying the shade and waiting for who-knows-what. He didn't even look when I passed by.

Ulises, who had his shirt on the normal way, insisted upon taking the back seat. He shook off my protests, so I leaned in to pull up the seat so he could get in. But it turned out that the car had four doors, not two. There had been an entire row I'd passed by so quickly that I hadn't even noticed. It was a small car.

My surprise at the size wasn't lost on Halbert.

"This model is so small, they don't sell it in the U.S.," he said when he noticed me tucking my knees under my chin as we pulled away. "I was in Florida and I went to a dealership to get a part, and they didn't even know it existed. I had to show them on the Internet." He was talking about the car, not the part.

He didn't say anything about the crowd he was driving into, so I asked.

There had been a celebration that night in the town's revolution plaza, which was across the street from the bus station, and that's why the streets were full. But it was an easy drive past the crowd. Cuba's the kind of place where you can be in a car in the middle of a crowd of people in the street, and no one seems to mind. You just drive slow, and eventually there's an opening and you head off down a side street and you're on your way. Back home, in that situation, some self-righteous prick with a bad beard and a snug T-shirt and skinny jeans would be pounding on your hood telling you what an asshole you were while he was telling his free-range kid why it was all right to hate people like me.

No one seemed to hate us, though, and we quickly wound our way to Halbert's neighborhood and pulled to a stop in front of his house, where a dozen or so people were lingering about on the curb, enjoying the pleasant evening in the glow of the street light.

I met his wife, Yeleni, his boys Jose and Juan, and members of the church who lived nearby. At dark, on the street, it looked like a larger crowd than I'd seen that morning in church in Camagüey, but Halbert's estimate of attracting 50 or 60 regulars on Sundays wasn't much more than what Perez, the priest in Camagüey, said he saw most weeks.

The church, St. Luke's, takes up most of the front half of an entire block. The rectory is at one end and a daycare center at the other. Lining the back of the rectangle is the church itself. There's also a large courtyard and a two-story building with a kitchen and living room on the first floor and dormitory-style rooms on the second. It was built so visiting groups would have a place to stay. Business had been moderate.

Inside St. Luke's, there was a modest rectangle of a sanctuary with a high ceiling. It had a small balcony in the rear, facing toward the altar, but no one went up there. Halbert said access was restricted because work hasn't been finished.

Ulises said the space wasn't needed at the moment anyway.

"The choir is not very good," he said.

The church was one of two the Episcopals still had in Santiago. There were once five, but after the revolution, one was turned into a clinic and another into a home. The other was left in place, but the congregation drifted away and the church fell into disrepair, and then it actually fell, crumbling down on itself. Today, an empty lot is all that remains, though Halbert planted a cross in the front and planned to rebuild.

In the St. Luke's courtyard, Halbert dreamed of building a school and a library.

Bishop Griselda wanted to use some of the space for agricultural projects, which was her passion, but Halbert was holding out for the buildings.

Ulises said he understood Bishop Griselda's thinking. "She's Bolivian. They like their farms."

The space once held a school, but when the government began taking church schools after the revolution, the bishop at the time ordered the building demolished. A standing school, the government would have taken and used itself. An empty lot, the church was more likely to be allowed to keep. The strategy worked.

(A few months after I visited, Halbert paved the courtyard with stones and built open-air rooms in part of the space. He was moving in the direction he wanted. There was no word about the bishop's urban farm.)

> <

Santiago de Cuba is the country's second-largest city, with more than 500,000 people. It calls itself the city of heroes. It and the surrounding province of the same name are the homeland of Jose Marti, the 19th century freedom fighter who to this day is the most revered man in Cuban history.

The area also claims, or at least accepts responsibility for, Fulgencio Bautista, the mid-20th century strongman and president.

Fidel Castro, the guerilla fighter who overthrew Bautista and who remained in power for 50 years, also hails from that part of the country. But the story goes back way before those guys and starts with someone who makes the mob-connected strongman Bautista look like a lightweight. The city's first mayor was Hernán Cortés, the Spanish conquistador better known for toppling the Aztec Empire in Mexico. Before killing off an entire people in the name of greed, he'd lived in Cuba from 1511 until 1518. There were fewer people and less gold in Cuba, so he moved on.

Centuries later, the city's San Juan Hill would play a role in the making of the reputation of future U.S. President Teddy Roosevelt. His charge to the top with his Rough Riders helped topple the Spanish, ostensibly freeing the country of its colonial lord in favor of Cuban independence.

The presence of American troops apparently tempered the locals' enthusiasm for claiming complete victory, but the accolades for Roosevelt continued for more than a century. In 2001, he was awarded a U.S. Medal of Honor for his action in Cuba.

Today, there's little sign of Cortés in Santiago, and San Juan Hill boasts a Ferris wheel and motel in addition to memorials to the war. Time goes on, even after the history is written.

The town also boasts a seemingly endless parade of youth with access to the latest fashions and an indifference to traffic that would make them the envy of any American college campus. The side street on which I found myself late that night boasted what could have been, and maybe was, a cast of extras from a hip-hop video. Loud and brash, but not particularly threatening, they flowed through the way groups of young people always do, tightly woven into their own worlds and completely oblivious to anything a foot or two either direction.

The young men wore tight white jeans and matching shirts and baseball caps slightly askew, and the women wore as little as possible, a lack of modesty that looked more like South Beach, in Miami, than the Cuba I'd seen so far. For nine o'clock on a Sunday night, it was an impressive sight. It made me wonder what Santiago was like on a Friday.

> <

Halbert said he grew up in the city of Camagüey as a Catholic, and he pursued a career in that church first. The Catholic bishop sent him to Rome for two years to study in a seminary there. The bishop told him the school wasn't the best but that the experience would make it worthwhile.

"I think people need to see more of the world to really understand it," Halbert said, repeating the lesson he'd learned years before.

He could have studied in a seminary in Cuba, he said, but then all he would have known in life would have been what he'd seen in Cuba. His future line of work specialized in the big picture. So he got his passport and hopped the plane and went out in search of something new to see.

The seminary in Rome claimed to offer courses in Italian, English, Spanish and two other languages, so Halbert said he arrived with an air of comfort and confidence. But that quickly dissipated.

The school's promise did not translate into a promise from his professors of adhering to it. In his first class, his first professor told him that while the school had five languages, his class had one, Italian, and that lectures and exams would be given in it.

"If I wanted to succeed, I needed to learn Italian," he said, with his easy smile and little laugh.

Halbert is a man who knows how to embrace life, and something like a language barrier wasn't going to stop him for long. "I learned Italian. Fast."

He said he was fluent enough to get by in class within two months.

He said he enjoyed his two years. He got to travel throughout Western Europe and developed a particular fondness for Spain. Along the way, he also became fluent in English.

He said he particularly enjoyed the ease with which he could travel. Europe's rail network offered transportation the likes of which a Cuban couldn't imagine, and border crossings were easy. But he never thought about staying behind.

When he finished his studies, he returned to Cuba with the eagerness of a homesick man finally on his way back. He'd seen Western-style freedom, but he longed for what he knew.

Once back home, he was ordained and settled into his home church for what could have been a lifetime of service. But he didn't take to the life of a Catholic priest. He lasted a year, then quit.

"I didn't want to be alone."

The congregation was "very dry," he said, the type of parishioners who kept a cordial but firm distance between themselves and their priests.

After mass, the flock went one way and the priest, reluctantly, another. For someone as outwardly social as Halbert, it was a sad sight, and it was repeated every week.

But it wasn't all solitude, and he did make friends in his year of service. When he left the pulpit, he kept some of those friends, including a young woman from a rural part of the province. When he left the church, their friendship evolved into a courtship, and then they married.

He still felt called to preach, though, and the Episcopal Church accepted him. He had been in Santiago for five years when I came through town.

><

In Santiago, I stayed in a rooming house on a side street that was about halfway between Halbert's home and that of the retired bishop. It was the usual corridor design, though everything was under roof and the space that should have been the courtyard was the kitchen instead.

There were swinging doors on either end of the kitchen, giving the place the feel of an Old West saloon, especially when the Italian couple staying in the room next to mine burst through late that night. It sounded like they'd been pushed through, the prelude to a brawl. But they were laughing, not running, and they settled in fast and kept up their loud, conspiratorial tone for an hour as they cooked pasta in an exaggerated manner. Then they retired to their room, separated from mine by the thinnest of walls, and engaged in a different kind of loud, exaggerated activity. They seemed to live large.

In the morning, I discovered I hadn't been given a towel and there wasn't one in the bathroom across the hall from my room. I went to inquire, but before I could ask, I was offered coffee by the mother of the couple who owned the house.

She didn't speak English any better than I spoke Spanish, but coffee is a customary greeting, an offer so universal it answers any questions. Poured from a worn plastic thermos into a small cup, it was lukewarm and super sweet and not very good. Super strong as a way to drink less coffee, I can appreciate, but the sugar took some getting used to. And the thermos with the pump on top is never good; it can ruin coffee in any language.

After I finished, she handed me a small piece of cloth that approximated a dish towel, and I retreated to my room, which backed up to a school. By half past seven in the morning, the students were in full riot mode. Each new voice was layered over the last one, giving the roar the din of an angry crowd awaiting action.

But they were just students, and the occasional screeching of a desk being drug over a concrete floor reminded me that students are loud in any language. At some point, the noise stopped and, I imagine, lessons commenced.

> <

I spent nearly an hour on the front stoop waiting for Halbert. The night before, he'd slyly added a "more or less" to the time he said he'd pick me up. I hadn't paid it much attention then, but the next morning, I was reminded that no one keeps an exact schedule in Cuba.

"What time should I be ready tomorrow?" I'd asked as I pulled myself out of his car.

"Nine o'clock," he'd said. "More or less."

I didn't give it much thought at the time. It sounded like an "about," a little window that in the U.S. covers five or 10 minutes either way.

The next morning, the meaning became more "more" than "less."

"Maybe 10, probably closer to 11, but don't worry; we're not in a hurry. Enjoy your coffee," he could have said.

I had time to enjoy the parade of passers-by from behind the locked bars of the front porch. I could see clearly, but no one could reach me without the key, which I clutched tightly in my hand.

Many who passed by ignored the sweltering heat and ambled by in blue jeans. I never would have guessed a Caribbean island as quite the market for denim that Cuba proved to be, but there it was, everywhere: basic jeans on the men, denim jeans and jumpers and blouses and skirts on the women.

A street sweeper worked the block from one end to the other and back, all the while pushing a garbage can and carrying a satchel over one shoulder. Other than the wheeled pail of garbage and the wide push broom in his hand, he looked quite official with that satchel, and I wondered for a while what it was that a garbage sweeper carried that was important enough to warrant such a nice bag.

Cuba is still a land of officious bureaucracy, and I ran through any number of things that might have been in the satchel: paperwork, permits, notes on the neighbors and their suspicious abundance, or lack, of garbage in the street.

Finally, he answered my question by stopping and swinging the satchel around to his front and opening it. From inside, he pulled out a small tarp. I don't know if that's how all Cubans carry their tarps, when their tarps need to be carried, or if he were just a touch eccentric.

He stretched the tarp over the garbage, then turned his attention to the women walking by. He called to several, most of whom wisely ignored him. In a fit of misplaced curiosity, one woman turned toward him long enough to make eye contact, which she quickly identified as a mistake. He began blowing kisses her way and saying something in the manner of a man who may actually have been a threat. She moved along quickly without looking back.

Even with the nice satchel, he had a creepy demeanor, and most people gave him a wide berth.

><

I was there to work, though, not ruminate on the satchel or the street sweeper, and I had two interviews lined up for Monday, and I checked and rechecked to make sure I had enough notebooks and pens. I'm nervous that way, always. I learned somewhere how stupid it'd be for a writer to want to write and not have the simplest of tools, so I've always been kind of neurotic about it. I once went out to cover a school board meeting for my newspaper and looked in my bag and counted 19 ink pens. If someone had asked to borrow one, I would have said no, for fear of being caught empty-handed myself. And I wasn't even using one of them by that point; I'd moved on to taking notes on my laptop by then. But I'd still pull out a pen and jot notes or make little doodles on a printed copy of the agenda.

I had my supplies, and I was at ease because I'd already met the people on the list for the day.

The first up was Halbert. He and I were going to talk over breakfast at his house, assuming it was still breakfast time when he came to get me.

The second was Ulises, who'd invited me over for lunch, or who had at least agreed to the idea.

I wasn't sure if I was going to get to talk to any parishioners, as I had in Camagüey, but spending time with the guys in charge seemed a good way to start.

Halbert was 38 by the time I met him, but he could have passed for a man a decade younger. A hint of gray was starting to appear in his hair, but he was in good shape, physically and emotionally. He neither seemed nor looked his age. He had an ease about him that made him seem timeless.

He was the rector of three churches and two missions, and he was hopeful of adding a sixth location to his workload. In Santiago, he presided over two churches.

St. Luke's, which I had seen the night before, looked in daylight to be a middle class neighborhood. It had wide, clean, nearly empty streets—there were fewer cars there than I had seen in Havana—and little foot traffic.

It was also the site of the rectory, so it could have been Halbert's home church. But he doesn't sit still very well, so he's not content just tending to the church that happens to be on his block. He kept his car closer than he kept the church, and from the Kia, he could get anywhere.

A ways across town, in a poorer neighborhood, was St. Mary's. That was the livelier of the two churches. Halbert held a weekly Sunday school at nine in the morning, followed by a mass at 10. That church was home to a high-energy, singing and dancing congregation, he said. The people there traced their roots mostly through African lineage.

When he finished there, he crossed back across town to St. Luke's, where he held Sunday school at four in the afternoon and mass at five. That crowd there was Anglo by blood. It was a more European-based place, which explained the bishop's remark from the day before about the choir. Those were not singing and dancing Episcopalians. Traditional chants and recitation work better there.

Halbert was also responsible for San Juan Bautista church in Palma Soriano, a small town about 45 minutes away by car. And he had missions in Bayamo and Holguin. Both are large cities, each the capital of its province, but neither has had a strong Episcopal presence. Halbert had high hopes for both.

Bayamo is the capital of the Granma Province and is home to more than 150,000 people. It was founded in the early 16th century and is older than either Havana or Santiago. These days, it's known for its abundance of horse-drawn carts, love of chess and weekly festivals.

Holguin is the capital of a province of the same name, to the north of Granma and west of Santiago. Its airport is a popular stop for tourists headed for the beach resorts on the northeast part of the island.

Somewhere among those nearly half a million people, Halbert said, should be enough people to support two new Episcopal churches. Fewer than a hundred, total, would do. At that point, the congregations in those towns met in homes.

He was also trying to rebuild St. Peter's, the church that had fallen down, and for three months, he had been in charge of the church in Guantanamo, one province to the east. The bishop sent someone else there.

"I can only handle so much," he said.

He tried a laugh, but it sounded more like resignation and relief.

The church in Guantanamo, he said, suffered because he couldn't get there often enough. It had once been among the largest and strongest on the whole island, and it deserved its own rector.

><

Both of the churches in Santiago host chapters of Alcoholics Anonymous. The door of St. Mary's has a small sign saying so. There's no outward proof at St. Luke's, but Halbert said it was so.

"It's a big problem here," he said. "People drink at the festivals, and in Santiago, there's a festival every day."

Part of the mission of church, he said, was helping those who needed it most, and he could think of few who needed it more than those struggling with substance abuse. So he opened the doors and let them in.

><

Halbert said the church is different in Cuba from the church in America, particularly the relationship between the vestry and the priest. In the U.S., the vestry is called on to make, or at least approve, the business decisions of the church. The vestry also gets to hire its own priests, or call them to serve, as

Episcopalians like to say. The diocese ordains the candidates, but the individual parishes chose who they want. Not so in Cuba, on any count.

"It's very different here," Halbert said. "The priests make every decision. They call and say, 'Father, the lamp is burned out.'"

He rolled his eyes, then said, in the patient, measured voice of a seasoned priest, "Well, fix it! I'm trying to get them to make more decisions." The experiment was showing mixed results.

Nor was the vestry particularly engaged in the process of choosing its leaders. The bishop assigned the priests, a necessity in a church that struggled to train enough priests to go around.

> <

The church in Santiago has had as uneasy a history as the rest of Cuba the past five decades. From five parishes, it shrank to two. For years, the care of the buildings was entrusted to Ulises, who was an electrical engineer until becoming a priest in his 50s.

His predecessors had tested the limits of Castro's patience, one to a fatal extreme. Alonzo Gonzalez left the pulpit of St. Luke's to fight against the Castro regime in the early 1960s. Twice, he was caught, and twice he escaped. The third time he was caught, in Havana and executed.

"They weren't taking any more chances," Ulises said.

The Right Rev. Emilio Hernandez, who would become bishop in the 1980s, also ran afoul of the Castro government early on, and was imprisoned for a decade as an enemy of the state.

By the time I visited, the fervor had long since died and the church and the state had settled into a somewhat predictable, though still somewhat uneasy, truce of sorts.

"This moment, it's very different," Halbert said. "I think the government has learned it's good to let people participate in church. Things are very different. They know we are important. We know they are important. But we are not friends."

> <

Halbert kept a picture of Bishop Henry Benjamin Whipple in his kitchen. The very stern-looking Whipple, the picture of 19th-century church seriousness in his heavy frock coat, is credited with starting the first Episcopal mission in Cuba.

Whipple was the bishop of the diocese of Minnesota for 42 years, from 1859 until his death in 1901. He was known as a champion for the poor and oppressed, particularly Native Americans. In his later years, he took a winter home in Florida.

He was credited with holding the first Protestant service in Cuba, in 1871. Later that year, he assigned a resident missionary to the country. It's hard to tell if Whipple himself ever returned to Cuba, but his memory lives on for Halbert and his family.

"He's the one who made it possible," Halbert said.

Halbert follows Whipple's lead in spirit, though not in dress. He laughed at the suggestion that he don a heavy frock coat.

"That wouldn't be so good here," he said, looking at the picture.

The priests these days favor slacks and short-sleeve shirts. I've seen robes in services but I've yet to see a coat and tie.

> <

Halbert's home is the two-bedroom version of the standard Cuban layout. The living room in the front and the dining room in the back stretch the width of the house. Two bedrooms, a bathroom and the kitchen run in a row in between, and there's an open-air courtyard just outside those rooms. There's also a single room on the second floor, in the back.

"That's my office," Halbert said. "I don't like it up there. But sometimes I need quiet so I can write, and that's where I can go."

On a wall in the living room, there are several photographs of the family, and several more from the couple's wedding day. The room has a television, a couch and a couple of chairs.

> <

Halbert invited me over for breakfast: coffee, café con leche, espresso, bread and cheese, all spread out on the square wood table in the dining room. I was offered mayonnaise from a large tub Halbert pulled from the refrigerator, but I didn't take any.

Halbert's wife was at work, in the daycare center at the other end of the block, and the boys were at school, so we had the place to ourselves. We spent an hour or so eating and talking, neither of us in a rush. Mostly, it was me asking questions and Halbert patiently answering them.

After we ate, he drove me to the bishop's house, where I was to spend the rest of the morning and part of the afternoon.

The house was a larger version of Halbert's, and Ulises had made it larger still in the 55 years he had lived there. It's of the same design, but with the dining room and living room connected in the front, and a third bedroom on the run to the back. There was also a full second floor, which Ulises, a bachelor, added to accommodate a growing assortment of siblings and cousins and nieces and nephews who also call it home.

He and his sister have bedrooms on the first room; the rest of the family lives upstairs.

In the living room, there was a large fish tank, and the tile of the floor was cut into a fish pattern. In the small, narrow courtyard, there's an open-air tank of goldfish.

"My nephew loves fish," Ulises said. "He has them everywhere."

><

Ulises followed an unusual path to his spot near the top of the Episcopal church.

He grew up in the church in Santiago. After college in Havana, he went home and served as a lay reader for many years. But then came the revolution and the 1960s, and the importance of church life went into a sharp, fast decline across Cuba, and young people with an eye on their future considered other options. He pursued a career as best he could without completely turning away from the church.

He and Bishop Emilio Hernandez worked closely, and the bishop encouraged Ulises to study in the seminary.

"He knew I was a faithful member," Ulises said, trying to explain his call to serve in a more formal role.

He was ordained a deacon in 1992 and worked in that position for nearly two years before becoming a priest. For five years, he worked with Nerva Cot, the wife of Juan Ramon, the long-time priest in Camagüey who had been installed as the dean of the cathedral in Havana. Then she went to Guantanamo, and he took over.

He kept working as an electrical engineer for another five years after becoming a priest, because that job paid him and the church did not.

In 2007, Ulises and Cot were appointed bishop suffragans. Ulises was 70 at the time, so he was able to serve just two years before being forced to retire because Cuba mandates it at age 72. But he kept working, doing what he could, and what he wanted, to help Halbert. In a country with a chronic shortage of priests, no one really retires, anyway.

When he started in the church, Cubans were closely aligned with the Episcopals in the U.S., but that relationship ended in 1966, when the Americans cut their ties and the Cuban diocese became an extra-provincial, or non-aligned, diocese. It is not formally attached to either the Episcopal Church, based in New York, or the Anglican Communion, based in England. A Metropolitan Council, consisting of the leaders of the Canadian, U.S. and West Indies churches, offers oversight and guidance. (In the summer of 2015, the church in the U.S. began talking about reestablishing formal ties with the Cuban church, but no action was taken.)

"After the Revolution, the American church said, 'You are independent,'" Ulises said. "There were bad years in the beginning."

All of the changes, internal and external, took a great toll on the church. Membership declined and so did the flow of money. For years, the priests who remained weren't paid, and that included Ulises, which is why he kept his other job.

Things have improved, he said. "The church is now alive. People are more interested."

In June 2014, four people graduated from the seminary, a bumper crop in a country with only two dozen priests spread across four dozen churches, "so we are growing."

And there's money, too, to pay priests, "so now the donations (from overseas) are for projects."

But that took a long time. Ulises said he worked for 13 years without being paid once. When he started thinking about retiring, he said he demanded that the diocese find money to pay the priest who would replace him.

"And I told them, 'You will start now by paying me so you will get in the habit.'" The statement was proof of his pragmatism, not a playful boast. He wanted to make sure the next priest—Halbert, as it turned out—could afford to take, and keep, the job.

The interesting change, he said, had been watching the way people regarded the church after the government began to ease restrictions. The buildings had always been there. As the taboo of attending faded, the curiosity of what lay inside increased.

"There was a sense of, 'What's in the church that the government doesn't want us to know?'" he said. "Cubans are very religious. Not just us, but Catholics, Protestants, Presbyterians."

He clarified, saying the Presbyterians weren't so big in Santiago but had a foothold, of sorts, further west in the country.

Ulises said Griselda brought a new approach the church needed.

After spending her career as a parish priest in a small town, she was appointed bishop in 2010 by the Metropolitan Council after the country's priests failed to pull off a conclusive election of their own.

"She has changed everything," Ulises said. "She has many good ideas. We have a plan for three years. She likes projects."

Some of the projects involve agriculture, including a large farm attached to her old parish in the town of Itabo. Her husband, Gerardo, one of the five new priests who were ordained in June 2015, is now in charge there.

But there are other ideas, too. In Santiago, Halbert's wife pitched the idea of opening a daycare center. She had an idea, created a plan and presented it to the office in Havana.

Griselda found money for projects, but in exchange for it, she did something foreign to Cubans: she demanded operating plans and measures of accountability. Anyone could pitch a project, but anyone hoping to succeed had to prove that their idea was sustainable and able to operate within a set budget.

Doing something different wasn't out of the ordinary for her. That she had become bishop was something of a shock.

Three years before, Nerva Cot had become the first woman appointed bishop suffragan in a Latin American country. Then Griselda became the first woman to be named a full bishop.

"People were astonished, because she had only attained the level of priest in Itabo," Ulises said. "And some people said, 'Oh, a woman.' But it worked."

And anyway, the church in Cuba has many more women than men, in attendance if not in the pulpit. And the government,

Ulises said, had always had an easier time influencing men.

"Our tradition is very machista. 'Church is for women,' men say. The philosophy of our government works more on the minds of men than women."

While the men talked about their politics, he said, it was the women, mostly, who had kept alive the traditions of the church.

I'd seen the same in Haiti, where the extreme prevailed: the macho culture there made men too proud to do much of anything, especially work, while the women toiled away at keeping everything in motion.

> <

Ulises said the Episcopals lagged behind more outwardly dynamic faiths in attracting new members.

The Pentecostals, he said, knew how to pack a house, at least for a night, repeating what I'd heard from Perez, the archdeacon in Camagüey.

"They are very excited. There's a lot of singing, but the people don't stay," he said. "They say, 'We have 400, 500 members.' but really, they have maybe 50."

All religions are benefitting from the expanding openness, with more churches and more open services and more people willing to attend. Ulises credited the growth to clergy who had figured out how to work within the Communist system.

"Many priests sympathized with the government," he said. "They said, 'The people fill your plazas and hear your speeches, they are the same people who go to our churches. Don't discriminate against us because we're *open*."

Not all Cuban religions are open. Santeria, like voodoo in Haiti, mixes African tribal beliefs with elements of Catholicism. It has long been popular for certain parts of the population, but, also like voodoo, has typically been practiced far from public view, or at least not in traditional cathedrals. Its roots were in the slave culture of the Caribbean, and the secrecy developed as a necessity, then stayed as a tradition. But it was secrecy nonetheless, and Ulises did not approve. "The African religions are OK because they meet in private?"

In the beginning, he said, the government was inflexible. "But now they realize life is different. Different doesn't make us an enemy."

Early on, the Catholic church led the charge against Castro—excommunicating him was a decisive step—and decades later, through the visits of two popes, John Paul II in 1998 and Benedict in 2012, the Catholic church had opened the door to more freedom.

"Now Cubans are anxious to attend church. I would tell people, the church of Cuba is alive and working and spreading the gospel," Ulises said.

In the past, people were afraid for their jobs. Not that they would lose them but that they would have to do them in different places.

"You're trouble here, maybe you won't be trouble there," Ulises said, reciting the once common divide-and-conquer ploy of moving workers to different parts of the island and into different types of work whenever they threatened trouble. The threat of working in hot fields with rudimentary hand tools was enough to keep many people in line.

For Ulises, the cost was occasionally subtle but always clear. "The government sold cars to some engineers, but not to me. The government sent some engineers to study for two or three months in Russia, Czechoslovakia, East Germany. But not me.

"I could not be in charge of a section. It was very hard to know a vacancy belongs to you but goes to someone who is younger and has less experience.

"But God provides."

Ulises would get his chance to see the world after all.

In the early 1990s, the government began granting tourist visas for those who wanted to, and could afford to, visit other socialist countries. Ulises applied twice, and, surprisingly, he was accepted twice. He visited most of the Eastern Bloc: East Germany, Poland, Romania, Hungary, Czechoslovakia, Russia and Bulgaria.

"Europe is Europe," he said, sounding like a weary world traveler. "It was less developed then but very interesting."

And church is church, only more so in a free society. Ulises said it's not uncommon now to see people in their 30s and 40s being baptized.

"They didn't have the chance as children," he said.

> <

The Episcopal Church in Santiago traces its roots to 1905, when it was founded by Juan Bautista Mancebo, a native son who had studied in the U.S. and returned with a fervor for building churches. He is credited with starting all five parishes that once existed.

He was not as prescient when it came to the details of running them. While he purchased the buildings and the land they were on with church funds, he kept the titles in his name. When he died, his daughter discovered that fact and took everything, Ulises said. The church had to buy back its churches.

The only church spared was in nearby Palma Soriano, because the deed for that land specifically said the transfer was for the sole purpose of building a church.

><

Ulises said the Revolution was a good thing for the poor but not for the rich or middle class. The confiscation of private business and the redistribution of wealth worked in one direction.

His father once rented the house in which Ulises has now lived for decades. After the revolution, the government credited renters with making payments, and if the payments were enough, the renters assumed title to their homes. Ulises's father had, and did, and to this day, the family owns the house.

It didn't work out as well for St. Luke's Church, which had rented out a house it owned between the rectory and the church. Its ownership, too, passed hands, and to this day that is a sticking point for the church. The house separates the one in which Halbert lives from the rest of the church property on the block.

><

Life is different in Santiago.

Havana is the face of Cuba, what people in the U.S. think of when they think of the country: cigars, showgirls, old American cars driven along the *Malecon*. It's waves splashing over the seawall near the *Hotel Nacional* and *Castillo de los Tres Reyes Magos del Morro,* the Morro Castle, guarding the entrance to the harbor as it has since it was built in the late 16th century.

It's more than that, of course, a vibrant world that goes on even when the tourists stop paying attention, but the Cuba known casually by the rest of the world is Havana.

Way down at the other end of the island, more than 12 hours by car if you drive straight through, is Santiago. It's the heart and soul of Cuba, the place that has produced revolutionaries and rebels, freedom fighters and, for that matter, the rum: Bacardi hailed from the city.

"It's different in Santiago," Ulises told me while we sitting in his dining room, finishing our lunch. I'd stumbled into one of his areas of passion, telling people about what makes his hometown the best city in Cuba.

"We have our own accent, different words for things," he said. "A rocking chair here is a 'balanzes'; in Havana, it's a 'sillon.' Fruits have different names, too. The rest of the island is different. Maybe because this area is the most isolated."

He sounded like someone from New York trying to describe the pointlessness of life anywhere else, except he wasn't enamored with the big city.

Havana, he said, "is very different, very dirty."

> <

At St. Mary's Episcopal Church, the cornerstone is dated 1921 and reputedly includes coins from the countries that donated money for the construction. At the consecration, the national anthems of Cuba and England were played.

The church today is the more vibrant of Santiago's two Episcopal outposts, Halbert said. The congregation is drawn from its somewhat poor working class neighborhood, and the members more easily trace their roots to Africa than to Europe.

On Sundays, Halbert said, the place comes alive with song and dance.

The chapel can hold maybe a hundred people. When Halbert began, it was a dark room, but he was able to rebuild the windows to allow in more natural light. An electric, backlit sign that says "Peace on Earth" and includes images of the Virgin Mary dominates the wall behind the altar.

The only space that's not used in the room is the old wooden balcony that spans the width of the chapel along the back side, just above the door to the street.

"Everyone's afraid to go up there, it's so old," Halbert said. "They think it might fall down."

There's also a large meeting room that is used, at different times, for a daycare center and Alcoholics Anonymous meetings.

A small hallway connecting the two large spaces has two other doors. Through one is a small office, which includes a desk and several pictures: there's a black-and-white portrait of Mancebo, who brought the church to Santiago, and another old image of the original Cathedral in Havana, with its formal, ornate sanctuary, which was torn down in the 1950s after the church moved across town.

Through another door is a courtyard that is dominated by a towering palm tree, which Halbert would like to have removed because of the threat it poses during storms. Even on a pleasant day, it sways far and wide in a breeze; during storms, he said, it threatens to crash into the church. He wants to use the space for basketball and volleyball courts in an effort to attract more young people to church.

Running alongside the courtyard is a building the church does not own: a wood-sided, barn-like structure that is apparently a home. It looked like it would fall over in a stiff breeze. I thought it posed more of a threat to the courtyard than the palm trees, but Halbert ignored it.

"It's not ours. We can't do anything about it."

The weathered wood and open windows give it the appearance of an abandoned barn. In the United States, someone would demolish it and sell the siding to one of those companies that turn old barns into expensive tables and chairs.

On the steps outside the church there was a small collection of broken African religious icons. By tradition, practitioners of those religious leave their broken goods on the steps of Christian churches. How they break so many icons, and what they expect the priests to do with them, is a matter of conjecture.

Ulises and Halbert both scoop them up and toss them out. Neither was particularly sentimental about it.

Halfway down the block that spanned the side of the church, a family had the obligatory bust of Jose Marti, but the customary bright white had been painted dark black. It's the only black

Marti I've seen on the island; there could be others, but I haven't found them.

><

We also visited the site of St. Peter's Episcopal Church. The long, narrow, steep corner lot once had a church, but it crumbled long ago. When I visited, the front portion was overgrown and uneven. It had become a neighborhood dumping ground, and home to anthills every few steps. A dead turtle, left to rest upside down, emitted a stench that protected one spot from human intruders.

The upper portion, protected behind a makeshift steel fence and heavy vegetation, had a garden that was tended by a neighbor.

Across the street, in a home reminiscent of the television show *Sanford and Son,* the church was paying the owner to store building materials that could one day be used to rebuild the church. There was a stack of steel beams and a pile of lumber. It hardly looked like enough to build a small shed, but Halbert said it was the beginning of a rebirth for his church.

Halbert knocked on the door, and the potbellied, shirtless owner came out. He smiled and shook hands and let me look into the yard. He and Halbert chatted some, then we left.

><

The reverends were keen on sightseeing, ready to prove that their "city of heroes" deserved its title.

The first visit was to San Juan Hill, one of those history-class places of which everyone is aware but that few can actually pinpoint on a map. It's part of the great American timeline, just before the annexation of Hawaii.

It's also part of the greater Santiago metropolitan area. It rises not far from the part of town in which I was staying. The spot shares space with a zoological park, which prides itself on having a mix between a donkey and a zebra, a biological perversity that would have amused the world-traveling, big-game-hunting Roosevelt, who cemented part of his fame not far from where the animal would one day be caged.

At the bottom of the hill was the spot at which the Spaniards signed a peace accord with the Americans and, presumably, the Cubans. There was a ringed, fenced monument with large tablets listing participants by regiment. In the middle was a peace tree; the one that day was the second, having replaced the original after it died. Outside the fence, lining the sidewalk, was the requisite collection of cannons.

Across the street was a monument to Calixto Garcia. Like Marti, Garcia was one of the lasting heroes in Cuban history. It had the cold feel that marble and bronze monuments often do, but near the base were a used condom and an empty liquor bottle, so it's possible the spot also offered a place of romantic respite in a crowded city. Just what the guys had been fighting for, I'm sure.

San Juan Hill itself was up a winding road, just past the children's zoo on the left and the San Juan Motel on the right. Circle around to the back, and you'd find the San Juan Ferris Wheel, a brightly painted circle with enclosed cars, giving it the look of a miniature London Eye, only painted in circus colors.

It was not open the day we visited, but the priests said it was a popular attraction, particularly with children.

On the hill, there was a fort-like lookout that was two stories high, individual monuments to the three armies, another fine collection of cannons and shells, and concrete-enforced trenchworks reputedly dug by American troops.

If not for the trees that have grown up through the years, the hill would provide a sweeping view of parts of Santiago. But I couldn't see the water, and what was then and still is now the central part of town wasn't in easy sight, and it was hard to imagine how that particular hill had become so pivotal in the history of the island. It seemed but a blip in a town full of hills.

Still, the monuments were tasteful, each country apparently having been given permission to create its own in accord with respect for the others.

I tried to go into the tower so I could see the view from above, but Halbert and Ulises stopped me before I stepped through the doorway. They conferred in Spanish, trying to figure out how to explain to me why the short ascent was a bad idea. They settled on a description of the building's common use.

"It's a piss house now," Ulises said.

> <

The bishop led me on a walk of the neighborhood in which he had lived for most of the past 55 years. We passed small businesses that government has begun allowing people to operate: there were fruit and vegetable stands, a shoe repair stand, a man selling ugly ceramic pieces that reminded me of items my grandfather bought on a trip to Russia in the late 1970s, music and movie peddlers, and barbers, among others. The guy selling liquor did brisk business.

We crossed a busy street and walked through a small park, then rounded a corner and came upon the Melia Santiago, a tourist hotel that towers over its surroundings. It's run by the same Spanish company that runs the Cohiba, in Havana, an equally unappealing tower. (But it's also the company that operates the Melia Habana, which is sleek and cosmopolitan, on the beach a few miles west of the Cohiba.)

Other than a quad of apartment buildings, a few blocks the other direction, Santiago is not a tall city: most people live within four floors of the ground, but the Melia rose 15 stories in a red-and-blue rectangle with glass-enclosed exterior stairwells. It had the appeal of a resort hotel built in the era before the resort had come back into fashion. It served a function with little apparent joy.

><

Halbert picked us up in his little Korean car, and we, along with Ulises's grandniece, took an extensive driving tour of Santiago and its environs.

We began with the cemetery, *Cementerio Santa Ilfigenia*, a 19th century memorial park with the grandeur and scale from a time when no one considered the possibility of running out of space. There were wide, open, spacious plots, and nearly everything was the brilliant white that comes in the Caribbean. It was laid out in an orderly grid.

We snuck in a side entrance, and Halbert talked our way past a guard by passing me off as a visitor of more esteem than I'd seem to possess based on appearance. If she and I had been able to speak, my esteem would have diminished further, but I just smiled and nodded my head and kept my hand on my camera. She didn't fuss much, and we walked down an aisle with head-high mausoleums on one side and beautifully engraved and appointed marble markers on the other.

Halbert showed me the highlights that proved the bishop's earlier contention that Santiago was the true home of the Cuban spirit. We passed a memorial for Carlos Cespedes, who started the 19th-century revolution that led to the ouster of the Spanish; several graves for members of the Bacardi family, including Emilio, the son of company founder Facundo (and a great benefactor of the arts, I heard on several occasions, in several towns), whose dark granite, pyramid-shaped marker was unique in design and stood out in the sea of otherwise bleached white markers.

There were markers for the Maceo brothers, also of the revolutionary movement, and hundreds of others whose names would roll off the tongues of well-informed Cubans.

The grandest of all was the mausoleum for Marti. His flag-draped remains rested on the lowest level, protected by an honor guard. The walls of the circular room were lined with the official seals of more than a dozen countries that each contributed a scoop of dirt to the project. In life, Marti had been a man of his world, and in death, that world was brought to him.

The upper level, reached by stairs on either side, included a huge statue of Marti, seen seemingly staring in concentration at his own remains, visible through the cut-out in the floor. The walls in that room include the emblems of the six original provinces of Cuba. (The number had grown to 15, plus the special municipality of the Isle de la Juventud, by 2015.)

The square, open-air mausoleum rose another two stories or so and was topped with openings for natural light. Each corner on the outside included a larger-than-life statue.

We walked out as the cemetery was closing for the day and were allowed to stand, some distance away, behind a yellow line in the middle of an access road, and watch the changing of the honor guard. I'm not sure why we were kept so far back. Two priests, a guy in shorts and a little girl... how much trouble were we going to cause? But back we were, because the people with the guns said so. But no one complained when I took pictures.

The team of three high-stepped it in impossible fashion—one leg perfectly straight, thrust to the point of being perpendicular with the body, then switched and repeated, step for step—and relieved another team of three, which in turn repeated the march on its way out.

To the right of, and somewhat in front of, the Marti memorial was a fenced-off work site that some believed would one day hold the remains of Fidel Castro. There was no official designation as such, and one person there said "our government loves to act in mystery" but few doubted the ultimate purpose of a grave given so prominent, and large, a placement. It later turned out to be a memorial for soldiers

><

The tour continued past the train station, which looked much more fantastical than the service it provided, and onto a street that ran roughly parallel with the harbor. But Santiago's not the kind of town where you just walk down and enjoy the view; it's a working harbor, and much of the frontage was covered with warehouses and blocked by fences and gates.

From there, the town proceeded uphill at various angles and widths, the streets giving the town a colonial feel no one would duplicate from scratch these days.

We made our way through town and back out, then up a wide but deserted highway into the low hills closest to town. The bishop wanted to show off the high view so I could see how large Santiago was and how far it spread out. But the obvious route was blocked by a military installation, and we retreated through a block of apartments houses that made me realize that the one-for-all and all-for-one mantra of Communism wasn't always applied in the most fair of manners. The people in those buildings, set away from town and neglected, hadn't been afforded the same opportunity as some of those in town, who were allowed to live steps away from all life could offer.

When we cleared the small ghetto, we wound back down the road toward the highway, but stopped short of where we had to make a turn. We pulled alongside the curb and got out of the car. On one side of the road, perched on a ledge, was the Hotel Versalles. Across the road was a field that offered most of the view the bishop wanted. In the distance, you could see the few tall buildings: the Melia hotel, the twin spires of the Catholic cathedral, the four green-and-tan high rise apartments clustered together, but it was still hard to get a feel for the town without being able to see the water.

Walking back to the car, Ulises stopped for a moment and said he remembered going to the Hotel Versalles when it opened, right after the revolution. He had steak and lobster that night. He couldn't remember the occasion, other than that the hotel had opened.

Construction began during what would be the waning days of the Bautista regime. The optimism of that era, of the town spreading out and catching up to the hotel, never played out, and the Versalles sits today somewhat distant from everything else except the ghetto, a touch of luxury just down the hill from the village for the forgotten.

><

We dropped off the bishop and his grandniece on the curb by their house, then returned to Halbert's house for dinner with his family.

Halbert's family is the kind you'd like to claim as your own, if you could. Or at least the kind you'd like to visit again and again. Like Perez in Camagüey, Halbert kept a comfortable home: plenty of laughter, plenty of hospitality, the home of a family at ease with its self and its place in the world.

When we walked in, after I'd kept Halbert away from his work and any chance he'd pitch in at home all day, his wife was in the kitchen. She looked happy to see us. She smiled at me and asked a question or two, her English better than she'd admit. Then she stood by the counter with Halbert and chatted for a while as the dinner cooked. They traded stories about their days the way people do when they care what each other is saying. It was a sweet thing to see, two busy people making time to talk.

She was making a feast: baked chicken breasts, rice and beans, mashed potatoes and slaw. It may have been the most filling meal I'd ever had in Cuba.

The boys sat at the table with Yeleni's sister, who was visiting. They were talking and playing with toys and carrying on the way nephews do when the cool aunt is in town.

Yeleni's sister stood up and said hello then went out front, where her husband was watching television. I took her place at the table.

Juan and Jose, seven and nine, couldn't stand their inability to communicate with me, an apparent imbecile who couldn't understand the most basic Spanish. From playing with the cool aunt, they'd been relegated to entertaining me.

One of them got up and walked over to a bookshelf and came back clutching a copy of the *Oxford English Picture Dictionary*. He proudly spread it open on the table, and the three of us spent a half-hour talking about wild animals, numbers, colors and household furnishings.

They laughed a lot, as they should have, trying to teach a 46-year-old American the basics of basic Spanish by pointing to pictures, but they were good sports the whole time. Then they lost interest and wandered away until they were called back to eat.

After dinner, we cleared the table, and it seemed like the day was about to end, as if we'd reached the part where people start saying things like, "I think we'll retire now so this nice man can get home." Except I was in the company of Halbert, for whom days never end. They keep presenting more opportunities for excitement and adventure.

The five of us squeezed into the family car and went touring again.

"I tell people, 'When you're in Santiago, see. We can rest later,'" Halbert said when I asked him if the family really wanted to take a tour at the end of the day.

No one complained. They told me to sit up front, and Yeleni climbed into the back seat and the boys spread out around her.

We went first to *Cespedes Parque*, the oldest part of one of the oldest towns in the New World. On one side is the *Casa de Diego Velázquez,* which was built in 1522. The first floor was for trading and a gold foundry—the Spanish were nothing if not consistent in their belief that gold poured from the ground everywhere a ship could land west of Europe—and the second floor was for the living quarters of Velazquez, the first Spanish-appointed governor of the island. It's the oldest house in Cuba. Like oldest houses the world over, it's now a museum, the *Museo de Ambiente Histórico Cubano.*

The big Catholic cathedral with the two towers you can see from high points all around town was also on the square. It was undergoing a renovation, and parts, including the left tower, were covered with scaffolding, but it was hard to miss the grandeur it cast over the square. Along the first floor, facing the square and a little ways down either side, were glass-fronted shops. Before the revolution, the church rented the space to generate income. That practice stopped for decades but had recently resumed. Among the businesses there that night was a shop selling wine and liquor.

Next to the cathedral was the *Hotel Casagrande*, which looked like something from a Graham Greene novel. It had a second-floor terrace overlooking the square and enough lattice to offer any manner of intrigue.

Yeleni had her eye on the hotel for a weekend getaway, but Halbert wasn't so sure about the idea. She looked at it and got that wistful look romantic wives get when they want something their husbands aren't ever going to give them, either because they don't pick up on the hints, no matter how obvious, or because doing it just isn't in them. Halbert got the hints, but he looked at it in an entirely different way.

"As a priest, I don't think I can justify the expense," he said. "You can do a lot with that kind of money."

In tourist dollars, a room cost about 200 a night. I'm not sure what the rate was in local currency, or if local currency was even accepted.

Next door was a music hall, and rounding out the square was the city hall, which loomed opposite the cathedral in a juxtaposition that was once common throughout the world. It sat as a reminder that power doesn't always travel in the same direction. The directives that once flowed from the church long ago ceased, replaced by edicts from the bureaucrats across the square.

On that Monday night, the square part of the square was full of unambitious vendors—the man with the paintings called from his seat and lazily thumbed through a roll of images, but he never stood up—and an otherwise sedate crew of mostly adults enjoying a pleasant evening. It was about as nonthreatening a public place as you could find in a large city.

A few blocks away, the family led me through a small concert hall and onto a large terrace overlooking the oldest part of town. In the distance, but not visible at night, was the harbor. Halbert said it was the best view of the city during the day. I could make out a few rooftops, but it was hard to imagine what he was seeing.

We turned our attention inward and watched a woman trying to explain a song to the guitar player, the two of them by a wall off to the side. The band had taken a break and the singer was chatting up front, the way singers do with pretty women between sets. It would have been a nice scene, but the guy's soccer jersey ruined the aesthetic.

We got back in the car and drove to the square dedicated to Marti.

There was a huge crowd and live music there, and I could see dancers in colorful costumes even from a couple of blocks away. But before joining in the fun, we walked downhill a block and stopped at the Chocolate House, a privately run ice cream shop, for dessert.

The boys had chocolate ice cream, which they ate fast and pronounced "bueno" with chocolatey smiles. The *Café American* I ordered was bueno, too: reasonably mild, sugar-free coffee in a quantity that scared my hosts but that at home would qualify as a small. I also had a scoop of chocolate ice cream, for good measure. It cost about a quarter, but Halbert wouldn't let me pay.

"You're a guest," he kept saying.

(Cubans, I've learned, love ice cream. In Havana, they'll line up around the block to buy a scoop. In Camagüey, Alfredo Gonzalez, the retired surgeon, gave me a scoop of strawberry and vanilla with honey drizzled over the top, as casual an offer as a glass of water. In Santiago, the boys just smiled and devoured theirs.)

Back up the hill toward the square, we passed a restaurant called Mama Innes, which looked like a nice enough place. It had a manufactured hip appearance, years of character installed in time for opening day. It should have been full of casual youth, but it was empty and looked closed.

Halbert waved it off without breaking stride.

"It's owned by the government," he said. "And that's the thing about these government businesses. For the first week, it was good. Then after that, horrible."

><

The information age hadn't quite taken hold in Cuba.

Some homes had abbreviated online access that allowed for email but not the entirety of the Internet. Full service, Halbert said, cost about 75 tourist dollars a month, which is more than three times his church salary. He kept busy without the distraction.

"I check my email once a day, and that's it," he said. "I can live without the Internet. We have other things to do… I don't like to be quiet."

He said Bishop Ulises had to remind him that he had to offer guests time to rest when they were in town.

"The bishop tells me I don't let people rest enough," Halbert said. "So I try to remember to ask. That's why I asked you last night if you wanted to rest."

He was satisfied, knowing he had done the right thing.

Granted, he'd asked me that after 10 o'clock on a Sunday night, after I'd had a day-long bus ride. But still, he'd remembered to ask.

> <

Two years before, a group from Virginia had gone through Santiago and stayed in the dorms at St. Luke's for three days. Halbert led them on his tour, and they talked about ways to establish a relationship.

He said he was hopeful that he'd a found a partner who could help him with one of the many projects he wanted to pursue, but it wasn't to be. "After they left, I never heard from them again."

The dormitory space was mostly devoid of visitors, though it did see use for one or another of the youth programs he operated for the diocese. When he wasn't ministering to his five churches or trying to build the sixth, Halbert was in charge of the youth programs in Cuba.

"The bishop likes to give me work," he said, smiling.

He didn't mind the work. The bishop kept a busy schedule, and the least he could do was try to match her pace.

"They don't need to give her a house in Havana. She's never there."

He exchanged text messages with her on a regular basis, and she was always somewhere different from the time before.

"I told her she had to make time for herself. She said, 'You stop, and I'll stop.'"

There was no stopping, though. Everywhere I went with Halbert, he was in demand.

On the walk through *Cespedes Parque*, he ran into two young women from his parish. They stopped and he and Yeleni talked to them about the girls' recent trip to a youth camp in Canada and a visit to Niagara Falls.

In the neighborhood of St. Peter's, the empty lot where Halbert wanted to rebuild, our drive was stopped every couple of blocks as Halbert stopped to talk to someone else on the street. Santiago was a city of half a million people, but Halbert couldn't hide: even on a trip down from the top of the hills, he came across a policeman who had once helped him with a speeding ticket. He gave the man a ride back into town.

"I have a lot of tickets," Halbert said. "One more, and they might take my license."

Having a friend who was a policeman wasn't a bad thing. The two talked like old friends all the way down, then the man hopped out at a bus stop next to the square near the bus station.

><

Halbert and Yeleni honeymooned in Santiago when they were still living in Camagüey. They stayed in a hotel near the old district, not far from *Cespedes Parque*. Each day, they would take a walk, and they kept passing a restaurant across from a small park that was tucked between an alley and the street. There were benches and tables, and the trees offered enough privacy to give it a romantic feel.

"Yeleni kept insisting that we sit out there," he said.

She wore him down, he said, and finally one night, they took their meal to the park and tried to settle in.

At first, everything seemed normal. It was romantic and kind of secluded, especially for being in the middle of a big city. The park was full of men and women. But as they began looking around, they noticed that the women were all with women and the men all with men.

"It was a gay hangout," Halbert said.

They both chuckled at the thought as we walked by.

><

After a long day with Halbert, he dropped me off at the house where I had a room. It was a restless but otherwise non-painful night. The bed had a slick, satin spread and it sloped to one side, and I kept rolling toward the edge. No matter how I tried lying down, I'd wind up clinging to the edge. Every hour or so, I'd wake up and move back to the middle and start again.
    By 10 minutes of eight the next morning, the riot was back on next door. It sounded like a high school gym in the moments before a pep rally begins: allowed the freedom to speak, all do, voices layering upon voices, creating a roar in whose midst only the young can be without screaming or fleeing.
    I packed my bags for the night's departure, but Halbert said there was no need to check out. The house did not run on the American hotel schedule of pushing you out the door as early as possible. He told me to leave my bag and that we could take care of the details later. When it's time to go, you go. No sooner. First, we had to go back to his house for breakfast.
    "The same as yesterday," he said: bread and cheese and coffee.
    It was as good as the day before, and I helped myself to a second slice each of bread and the long, narrow white cheese, and again I said no to the tub of mayonnaise.
    We picked up the bishop and headed to Palma Soriano on the main highway, which ran mostly uninterrupted all the way to Havana. The kilometer markers counted down the distance, more than 750 between the two cities. It was about 45 minutes to Palma, but the drive was easy. Like everywhere else I've been in Cuba, the traffic was light. There had been a few trucks but almost no personal cars.
    The church there was in the hands of Noel Rodriguez, a recent graduate of seminary who had yet to be ordained.
    Several years ago, Halbert and Noel went to Palma Soriano to see what was left of the church. They found the walls but little else. The roof was gone, and so were the doors and windows. Even the tiles had been stripped from the floors.
    They've since rebuilt it, doing most of the work themselves.
    The front door was from St. Luke's, which for reasons unknown had an extra. The pews were from St. Mary's, whose vestry allowed Halbert to move them; Ulises said he thought

they had originally been in St. Peter's and were moved to St. Mary's when the other church collapsed.

The bell that hung from the short tower on the front came from an old American train. Halbert had found it in a secondhand shop.

There were six pews on each side of the small chapel, each of which could hold four adults, but there was room for more and wider pews. Noel said some Sundays, it was standing room only, and that he would like to increase the seating.

Behind the chapel, in the same building, was a small parish hall. It included a table with sewing machines, part of the diocesan effort to create meaningful mission and outreach programs. There, the idea was to teach people to sew so they could make objects that could be sold in the market. Noel pulled out a box with potholders and clothes in various stages of completion to prove the progress.

Of the money that was generated, half went to the person who made the goods, 40 percent went into materials and the last 10 percent went to the person who ran the program. The latter amount could be paid in goods.

Behind the building was a small garden with a bitter orange tree, herbs, vegetables and flowers, plus a cage with rabbits. Noel pointed to a row of sunflowers on the edge of the garden. "They attract bugs, which keeps them from the other plants," he said.

Several of the beds were raised, the borders held in place by lines of inverted wine and liquor bottles. When the sun hit the green, brown and clear glass, it sparkled a little, and the whole thing looked pretty cool.

"Some people look at that say, 'You must have drunk a lot,'" Noel said, laughing. He insisted he'd collected the bottles from others.

No matter the origin, the edge gave the garden a colorful touch and a whimsical feel the likes of which you might have found in an American gardening magazine geared to enthusiastic hobbyists. I tried it back home, but couldn't get it quite right, not having the Caribbean sun in my garden.

Noel had also built a glass-topped case with wire baskets for drying the herbs, including oregano and mint, another idea that would have appealed to a certain demographic in the U.S.

><

Palma Soriano was the second largest city in Santiago Province. Halbert said it had high rates of violence tied to alcoholism, unemployment, teenage pregnancy and lack of education. Too many students, Halbert said, were dropping out of school.

"They have access to education, but they don't want it," he said, sounding mystified.

The town was more primitive than Santiago. It looked weathered and broken down. The water was bad, and the service that brings it—large, dirty tanker trucks—irregular. The roads showed no signs of care or maintenance.

On the drive in, we passed squares and small parks and drove through a small business district with businesses and what looked like government offices. The streets were lined with people, and no one looked particularly happy. They weren't mad; it was more the look of a town that had yet to have its better days. It was the least inviting place I'd seen in Cuba.

Still, or maybe because of this, there was demand for the church.

Noel had programming six days a week, and 25 or so children and 20 adults regularly participated on some level. There were posters on the wall spelling out the daily calendar of events.

The children, Ulises said, offered hope. The idea is to "instill Christian values in them and hope they will take them home with them."

One member from before had come back, and she brought her grandson. They lived in the house next to the church.

The church also had a member in a wheelchair. The young girl, Rosa, had a muscle disorder and struggled to move. At that moment, she had to be lifted into the church, and lifted again if she wanted to go into the garden. She apparently wanted to go everywhere, and she sang in the choir, so Noel and Halbert were working hard to find ways to ease her path.

Noel had plans for a ramp that would run the length of the building, allowing easy access to a side entrance and, further back, to a bathroom that he also hoped to build. He had the materials, in boxes in the chapel, and was trying to figure out the labor and how to tap into the town's sewage system.

> <

Across the street from the church, a shirtless man of some girth sat in the shade of his front porch, running his finger across pages of type. A crowd opposite him offered no disturbance; he kept reading the whole time we were there, an hour or more of uninterrupted study.

"He's Pentecostal," Halbert said. "He's reading the Bible. He's told me that he has read it front to back 15 or 20 times." He made steady, unblinking progress while we stood there.

None of the Episcopal priests seemed excited about the idea of spending their days in a similar pursuit. They had other work to do.

> <

Priests in Cuba were paid 600 pesos a month, plus 30 tourist dollars a month, Halbert said. The latter was a gift from the Canadian church. Money aside, Halbert said he was happy in Cuba.

"I want to be in Cuba," he said. "This is where I am needed. Everybody wants to leave, but not me. We need priests here."

He preferred Cuba's version of church life to what he knew of how it operated in the United States. "U.S. priests, I think, spend too much time in their offices," he said. "I like that I can stop by the home of the people in my church. A priest in Jacksonville told me he only sees his congregation when they come to church."

He said that with a tone of disbelief, as if the man in Florida were missing the real opportunity that came with leading a church, the chance to be among his people every day.

But he would like some help. Ideally, he said, there would be three priests, and each would be responsible for two churches.

> <

We took the old highway back toward Santiago. It dipped due south from Palma Soriano, then cut east. Going that way allowed us a detour to the village of El Cobre, the site of the country's most famous religious shrine.

El Sanctuario de Nuestra Señora de la Caridad del Cobre is a shrine to the Virgin of Charity, a gold-robed black Madonna who has been part of the island's lore for more than four centuries.

She first appeared in the sea, helping three lost fishermen find their way back to shore. She disappeared for a while, then reappeared inland near the site of copper mines. The natives built a shrine on top of the mines. It eventually collapsed as the ground was mined out from underneath, and a replacement was built on a nearby hilltop in 1927. Ever since, it has been a draw for pilgrims.

Those from Camagüey were said to walk 11 days to get there. Along the way, they would pick flowers to offer the virgin. Today, vendors line the roads offering bouquets of sunflowers so vibrant and beautiful, they looked fake. You could also buy idols, icons and other goods depicting the shrine, as well as candles that could be burned on marble tables in the building. It was big business, making sure the pilgrims were properly stocked for the journey.

You started seeing the vendors a few kilometers away. In the last few blocks before driving up and into the property, the vendors were lined up next to each other, crowding out the view of whatever in town was behind them.

At the top of the driveway was the shrine, a parking lot for it and a large hotel, which was used by the pilgrims who still came in a steady flow.

Ernest Hemingway is said to have given his Nobel Prize for Literature to the shrine, but I didn't see it.

I did see a shrine to the miracles attributed to the Virgin Mary: a wall of crutches, braces and other medical devices supposedly rendered unnecessary by the caring presence of Mary. They were mounted high and low, an artful rendition of human malady. There was also a case of sports medals, pictures and mementos, with victory credited to Mary. It looked like a collectibles shop, dusty, slightly disorganized and full of treasures.

The space near the altar was lined on both sides by the sunflowers, and the first few rows of pews were full of people deep in prayer. You could go anywhere and take pictures and generally make yourself at home, but they asked you to stay away from the people up front and respect their prayers.

We shared the shrine with a member of the Cuban Five, the group of Cuban intelligence agents arrested in the U.S. in the late 1990s and charged and convicted of spying.

The men were heroes in Cuba in their absence, and even more so when they began earning their freedom and coming home. (The last three would go home a month after my visit, part of an exchange of prisoners that went hand-in-hand with Obama's announcement to ease restrictions between the countries.)

The one there that day came with a group and a police escort. They commanded attention from some of the other visitors, then left.

On the way down, as Halbert slowly drove through the winding streets of the town, the bishop looked around and spoke of the power of the church, or at least the power of the shrine on top of the hill. All that religion could triumph over all else. "The Communists go to church here," he said.

> <

We dropped off the bishop and went to Halbert's for lunch, then left for one more sightseeing trip before my flight back to Havana. Because we were in Santiago and I could rest later, as Halbert would say.

He was still intent on showing me what Santiago looked like from a proper vantage point, so up we went back into the mountains to a restaurant and park with a mountain-top lookout.

Unlike the scene at the Hotel Versalles, this lookout offered the full panoramic view of the city Ulises had tried showing me. With few exceptions, the city had spread out, not up. From the top of the mountain, there was a view of the harbor off in the distance, so far away the details were soft and the whole thing looked like an Impressionist painting. From there, you could see how the city had grown, going nearly every which way for miles.

It looked a little like Port-au-Prince, Haiti, which has also spread out far and wide but hardly up at all except as it crawled through the foothills. Though in Santiago, there was lush vegetation and much less traffic and nothing was on fire.

Near the base of the hill was a sprawling jail complex. Halbert pointed to one building and said that was where Bautista once kept Castro in the early 1950s, after Castro had been charged with trying to overthrow the government.

Halbert tried ministry work in the jail but gave it up after a single day.

"I told them, I can't go back there," he said. "It was too depressing. Everywhere I looked, it was full of men younger than me. They needed someone else there."

At the top of the hill, on the edge of a sidewalk we'd passed on our way to the lookout, two men were untangling the cords on parasails, much to the delight of a busload of school children who had appeared, seemingly without an adult escort.

It took a while, but first one, and then the other, cleared their lines and hopped a short wall. They spread their chutes across the hillside, grabbed the lines and started a brisk descent down the steep hill, followed by children.

Within a few steps, the wind caught the chutes and the men were airborne.

The first was carried under an orange and white chute; he waved to the kids and sailed away. The second man had a bright yellow chute. As the wind took him away, it looked as if he were floating under a huge banana. The children screamed in delight.

> <

Halbert began talking about taking guests to the airport, and he said Bishop Griselda was the person he knew most likely to stretch the limits of timeliness. Once, she got there so late, the crew had already closed the door to the plane. She had still managed to talk her way aboard.

"Most people are born with a guardian angel," he said. "She has two."

He had made sure I wouldn't need to do any talking.

> <

Halbert had traveled the world, studying in Rome, going to Brazil for church conferences and to the United States to meet with benefactors.

In Jacksonville once, he was caught in front of a congregation without a translator, then later in the day was caught trying to figure out just the right mix of sweetened and unsweetened tea to assuage the peculiar taste of Southerners.

"The day I was supposed to talk to the congregation, the woman who had been translating for me just didn't show up," said Halbert, whose English skills are better than he admits. "I looked at the priest and said, 'I can't do this alone.' He said, 'You have to. These people are expecting a report.'"

So he spoke. He said he's not sure what exactly he reported on but he said the congregation responded enthusiastically. After church, he was entrusted with serving tea during the reception in the parish hall.

"One woman said, give me half sweet tea and half unsweetened," he said. "So I filled a glass half with one and half with the other.

"She sipped it and said, 'This isn't right.' So I did it again, and again she wasn't happy. The third time, I told her, 'Tell me when to stop.' But still she wasn't happy."

So he quickly took to the American spirit and stepped away from the table and offered her his spot. "I told her to try herself." He couldn't remember how successful she had been.

Coming home from one of those U.S. trips, Halbert was once delayed for days because of a visa issue.

"I called Yeleni and explained it to her, and she was so calm," he said. "The next day, with the same problem, I called again, and she was still calm."

So calm, he said, he was surprised and maybe even a little worried. If he'd been on the other end of the call, he would have been a wreck.

"When I got home, I asked her, 'You were so calm. What were you thinking?' She said she thought I'd left her and the boys and was staying in the U.S."

Halbert laughed, sort of, but repeated his contention that Cuba was his home.

><

Yeleni hasn't traveled at all.

She was invited to a conference in Canada for church women younger than 30. Twice she applied for visas, paying the fee both times, and twice she was denied.

The reason?

"They said I can't travel because I haven't traveled before," she said.

How she would overcome that obstacle, she said, was not

clear. She still wanted to travel but she had given up on paying permit fees to a lost cause.

><

The flight from Santiago to Havana cost 140 tourist dollars. For Cubans, it would have been 220 pesos, or a little less than nine dollars. But tourists aren't allowed to use pesos, much less benefit from them.

I got to the airport 90 minutes early for my first Air Cubana flight since 1988, when I had flown the airline from Mexico City to Havana for a fishing trip with my father. Back then, the flight had featured real silverware and warm Polar beer, which had tasted pretty good to a guy who couldn't legally drink at home at the time.

Checking in was easy, but the small departure lounge was a disaster.

There were three gates but not a sign in sight. I'd seen the sign outside the lounge saying it was domestic flights and mistakenly believed it to be true. So when the time for my flight came and people rushed the door, I joined in and was pushed toward the front. I made it through the crowd in short order—traveling alone has its perks—but didn't get any further.

The agent at the gate looked at my ticket and said "not your flight" and sent me reeling back into the densely packed crowd, which was reluctant to allow my retreat.

That flight was bound for Madrid, which wouldn't have been an unpleasant destination. I had all my luggage with me.

My flight was about an hour late, but the plane was there, and it did take off, and I was back in Havana before midnight, spared, thankfully, another 16 hours on the bus.

My bag came off the plane so late, they'd switched baggage carousels, and nearly everyone else had departed. I cursed more under my breath than I had for the entire rest of the trip, and I pulled out my American-style irritation for people who were, at that moment and in that place, too slow and stupid and generally undesirable to share my presence. Not speaking Spanish was a bonus that night. So was mumbling.

Finally, my bag came out, and I grabbed it and went outside for the never-good feeling of stepping into a terminal with no one to greet you. Plenty of travelers live that way, I know, but I prefer a smiling face.

I got one at least, on a taxi driver. He was pleasant enough and offered a cheaper-than-expected fare back into town. He dropped me off at the end of the alley and handed me his card.

Tired and cranky, I dug the key out of my wallet and let myself back into the apartment and dropped my bag onto the most uncomfortable bed in Havana. I was facing a bad, pain-inducing night, but I'd survived my trip across Cuba and back.

CHAPTER 5

BACK IN HAVANA

THERE'S NO LONELY like the lonely of walking into an empty apartment you're renting for a couple of weeks in a city far from home. No one's there, and no one at home even knows where you are. In a hotel, there's the solace of being in a building with other people, the hope of a maid showing up every morning, someone to find you, if you need finding. In the apartment, nothing, no one. The lady upstairs had been there before, but she'd gone out of town to visit her children.

I walked to the end of the dark driveway and stood next to the darkened building and dropped my bags on the ground and took out my key. I squeezed my hand through the rungs of the metal security gate and released the clasp on the inside, then I slid my key into the lock on the front door. I let myself into the pitch black of the foyer and said "hello," as I would at home, even knowing there was no one to say "hello" back to me. No one did.

I stepped back into the apartment after five days and found the light switches hadn't been moved, and the leftovers I'd never eat were where I left them in the fridge, and the torture device of a bed was still there, waiting to be replaced by a bed that was an actual bed and that promised a good night's sleep, not hours of backache-inducing discomfort and restlessness. It had been made up neat and tidy, the satin bedspread pulled taut, the pillows in a line at the head, but it was still nothing more than a slice of thin cushion atop wooden slats.

The only change was my jar of *Colocafe* pure Colombian instant coffee had been moved from the top of the refrigerator, where I'd left it next to the empty water glasses, to the inside, where it shared space on the door with the three cans of fruit-flavored malt liquor I'd mistakenly thought were cola in the grocery store. I realized the mistake before I opened the first can, and I never drank any of it. I'm not sure why I bought it anyway; I don't like fruit-flavored cola.

I survived the night, a bit wistful for company but peaceful nonetheless.

The bed allowed me the one night of ease and comfort it had before, and I woke free of pain. Uninterrupted slumber would not last the week.

I walked the eight blocks downhill toward the Atlantic Ocean for the lobby of the Cohiba hotel, which was as charmless as it had been the week before. Just the same, it offered Internet access—I'd been off the grid for an unimaginable five days—and a menu of American-style breakfast options, and I couldn't resist the promise of fried eggs and a croissant with a little plastic tub of marmalade.

I was surprised, again, when an order of bacon yielded a fistful of thinly sliced ham. For a people who so love pork, Cubans struggle with bacon, the tastiest type of pork.

The Internet was just as disappointing. Five days after my last touch with the modern world, and I didn't have a single message worth reading. My wife would tell me that people knew I'd be out of touch so they hadn't tried, but I'd have preferred an attempt or two. I'm needy that way.

><

I walked back into the church office a little before 10 o'clock that morning and received a welcome befitting the returning hero I most certainly was not: hugs, kisses on the cheek, looks of pleasant surprise from the women there. And coffee, too, in copious amounts, in the American-style cup they'd found for me, filled to the rim. They'd learned to skip the sugar on my account and give me an extra full cup of black sludge, and I'd learned how bitter and nearly undrinkable Cuba coffee can be without a little sweetening, like the last cup from a pot made hours before and left to scold. I kept that thought to myself and said thank you and forced it down with the best imitation of a smile I could muster.

Perhaps Say, the office manager, and the others suspected, the week before, that sending me forth on a bus to explore the country wasn't so promising or wise an idea. They had done it because it was the wish of the bishop, to whom you don't say no, but they had not done it with conviction or a sense of success in the making. In the four days I'd spent on the couch outside their offices before my trip, I had not learned any Spanish and I hadn't been able to divert my attention from the large map of Cuba hanging on the wall opposite the couch. A man who couldn't master that map in a glance, perhaps they thought, was doomed in the country at large, traveling by bus deep into territory tourists rarely see. Cuba is pretty much one highway, running between Havana and Santiago, and some smaller highways connecting the other cities. It wasn't that hard to figure out.

But I had survived, and I had walked in as if I were reporting back to work after my annual vacation, just in time for morning coffee. I had my notebook and my camera with me, as usual, and I stuck my head in the door of Say's office, as I had before. Through her, everything ran.

I asked first about the bishop, hopeful that I'd get back on track and be able to sit down with Griselda and talk about whatever it was we needed to talk about. She'd been worried that I'd reopen old wounds in the church, and this was her chance to pitch the story the way she wanted to hear it told.

"She's not here," Say said. "She's gone to the United States."

It was typical Say: matter-of-fact, pleasant, it just was what it was. We're out of sugar. Can you bring in the mail? The bishop has left the country and flown overseas and won't be around to talk to you anymore on this trip, which you planned months in advance and thought was going to include a lengthy interview.

I tried to take it well.

I probably got a funny look on my face and said "hmm," which is my typical reaction when I hear the wrong answer. And

I'd most definitely heard the wrong answer.

The United States? My home, on the other side of the Atlantic, back through customs, where you can get a burger with blue cheese and bacon whenever you want one, even for breakfast some days, and the bacon on it is really bacon, not leftover ham scraps? Where I could have met her anywhere with relative ease and maybe even offered her coffee, if she had a taste for American coffee?

"She has business," Say said, effectively ending that line of inquiry. She wasn't a woman to linger on hopelessness.

That also effectively signaled that the bishop had ended her business with me the previous week during our short lunch together. Thoughts of a long interview had been dashed. She must have trusted me to get the story right, because our lunch had been about the details of my trip. I never asked her about herself, and she never offered any details. She's actually very humble that way; she likes to talk about the work of the church, not herself. It was a wonderful trait in a person, the ability to be more interested in everyone else over yourself—I did not come from a people with such a trait, by the way, and I still love the novelty—but it's not particularly appealing when you're taking notes and trying to write a story that's based on facts.

I regrouped—without incident, I think; I get a lot of wrong answers in my line of work—and quickly went to the next person on my list.

"Is Juan Ramon here?" I asked, hoping the retired dean of the cathedral and the master storyteller of Cuban Episcopal history would be waiting for me, especially now that I'd heard priests say things about him that weren't so uplifting. I'd hoped that he'd around the week before, too, and it had not worked out so well, that blind acceptance that things would work out right. And the earlier hope had been based on a promise, so there had been reason to hope. Not so anymore.

"I think he's not back yet," Say said, confirming my belief that nothing was going to work out that day. "But I can call."

She sounded helpful but not hopeful. It was a trait I'd learn was particularly strong in Cuba, the ability to be optimistically pessimistic. In the face of certain failure, you try anyway, without complaint. But once you fail, you move on. It's not a place to linger on the what-could-have-beens of life.

She went into her office and picked up the phone, and I settled into the couch to drink my coffee and quietly wallow in misery. That was harder than it may sound. I've never been able to hold a grudge very well, especially not when I'm looking at the person with whom I want to be upset. I can be passive-aggressive, for sure—the double shot of being Southern and Episcopal is a killer on that count—but that works best when there's a place to hide, a safe distance between you and them. And I was in Cuba, a country away from whatever real problems I had, still traveling freely in a place most people will never see. Misery was relative, and it didn't take much to know it. I didn't even have to take out the garbage there. Even if I wanted to be mad or put out, and I wasn't certain I did, it wouldn't have worked.

Less than a minute later, Say was standing in the doorway of her office, clutching the phone and smiling.

"He's home," she said, looking surprised, pushing the phone in my direction. If she'd scored me a second-chance date with that pretty girl from all those years ago, the one in whose company I'd bungled my French and had to slink away, she wouldn't have been any more excited than she was by getting Ramon on the phone.

Optimism yielding optimism, it seemed, was a rarity.

He and I spoke for a few minutes and agreed to meet at 10 o'clock the next morning, in the church office.

I finished my coffee in a gulp and in the exuberance of the moment, I gave Say a hug as best I could. She was about a foot and a half shorter than me, and hugging her was like clutching a big teddy bear, and I had to stoop over a good ways to do it. She hugged me back, a warm embrace from the grandmother you like—not the cold clutch from the fussy one with the white couch and the matching picture frames everywhere—then pushed me out of her office.

"You go now," she said. "Back here tomorrow, yes? It worked out well?"

That was forced optimism, the counterpart to the pessimistic optimism, making yourself happy with the outcome, no matter what. Because you got an outcome, and maybe it wasn't as bad as it could have been.

"Of course," I said.

In a manner, yes, it had worked out well. I'd be talking to someone before my trip was over. And not just anyone; I got the guy who tied it all together, the one whose story had prompted me to get into this in the first place. I didn't get all the pieces in between, but by then, I was pretty sure the story had shifted direction anyway.

I went back across the street thinking about what big plans I could quickly come up with for how I'd spend the day, my last free day in Havana before resuming my interviews and then flying home. I was traveling on a religious visa, and technically I was only supposed to be doing religious things, but I figured that stopping in the church office and drinking coffee near, if not with, everyone else every morning counted, and after that, I had a blessing of some sort to be on my way. I spent more time in churches in Cuba than I ever did back home. I wasn't exactly deep in prayer or meditating on matters of great, or even minor, spiritual importance, but still, there I was.

And it's not like anyone was checking. Every time I've been to Cuba, the person at customs stamped my visa and tucked it back into my passport, and there it stayed until I was back at customs on my way out. I'd seen fewer authority types in Cuba than I'd seen anywhere else I'd ever been. Want to see cops? Go to a U.S. college campus in an urban area. Want to be left alone? Go to Cuba. Those scenes in movies where people get stopped and asked for their papers and hustled off to the kind of scary jails from which no one ever emerges, they didn't exist in whatever version of Cuba I traveled through. They were there for sure, somewhere, maybe even nearby, but that wasn't the world through which I was traveling. Being naïve has its perks.

I took a bus ride from one end of the island to the other and sat by myself the whole way, as obvious an interloper as you could find on those highways. No one looks more suspicious than the middle-aged white guy by himself, carrying cameras and notebooks and pretending he doesn't understand anything. I offered myself up to miles of scrutiny in places my friends would never find me, yet no one bothered to bother me. If I'd been followed, it was so masterful a job of watching, I would never have noticed. But I don't think I was worth that kind of attention.

I felt free to roam everywhere I had been in Cuba, and that day was no different. The whole city was waiting for me to show up and take a look around.

Then it started to rain, so I took a nap instead.

I barely woke up in time for lunch.

><

For someone used to the culinary variety available in the United States, a steady diet of rice and beans can be a hard thing to accept. A first-world problem, no doubt, but I live in the first world, and my life at home typically involved beginning lunch with a menu in my hand. I didn't often stray too far from my favorites, but still, I had options.

I walked back to the cathedral for lunch, and I didn't have to struggle with a menu, or choices, for that matter. I knew what was coming before I'd locked the door behind me and headed across the street. I went anyway.

I was handed a gray metal tray that looked like a prop from a prison movie. It had rice in one compartment, a large piece of potato in another, a vegetable of some sort in yet a third. In the largest of the spaces, where the others were given a scoop of bean soup, on my tray was a *bowl* of bean soup. In that bowl, I was given two scoops, the largesse apparently meant to assuage my American-sized appetite. A guy who can drink that much coffee needs a big bowl of soup.

I'm a polite visitor, and I would eat the whole bowl of soup so none of it would be wasted, as I had done before, and they would take that to mean that I wanted a whole bowl of soup, and the cycle would keep repeating itself. But after 10 days of beans, I'd have happily chosen a tray of rice and nothing else.

I shared the room with two dozen people, a little less than what the room could comfortably hold the way it was set up. There were three rows of tables; the rows on either end had three tables, and the one in the middle, two.

The crowd included office staff and church workers: painters, electricians, bus drivers, a few priests. The church was a big employer. There were also a few neighborhood residents who came every day because the food was free, or because they could join others for a meal; both, perhaps. People sat in groups and talked among themselves, the cliques evident by the second visit, the room as stratified as any school cafeteria back home.

The free lunch, Monday through Friday, Say said, was an outreach program for the cathedral. The doors were open to any who wanted to eat, and no one paid. There wasn't even a way to accept money if anyone had offered.

After we ate, Say scanned the room and found my English-speaking companion for the day. I could see her eyes settle on one table, and I could figure out who was about to be asked to entertain me.

I'd seen the woman every day I'd been there, and she was sitting with several other women I also recognized in the front corner of the table farthest away.

Nieve Oliva Mirable was a 50-year-old, thrice-divorced English teacher who was also a lay minister and occasional assistant to the current dean, Jose. It was in that role that I kept seeing her. She taught English at night, private lessons in her home and in the homes of her students; days were for church work.

She was from a town near Pinar del Rio, on the western end of the island, though it's no longer in the Pinar province because the government redrew the lines and squeezed in a new province.

"I don't know why," she said. "It's just a name. It doesn't make sense."

Making sense, I would come to learn, was Nieve's passion. She was as logical a person as I ever met in Cuba, a country where logic is not always in evidence or demand or even appreciated. She was so logical, she hardly seemed Cuban. She was also the only person I met likely to be on time, which is not a prized quality there, either. She liked order and a schedule and knowing what would happen and when and where. I loved it. If I'd been a 50-year-old, thrice-divorced Cuban woman, I'd have been her.

She studied English in school because she liked the language—that bit of impetuousness was chalked up to youth—then became a university instructor near her home because that was the job available to someone with a degree in English.

In 1994, she moved to Havana and began offering private and small group lessons.

"At first, I didn't like teaching, but now I do," she said. It was a matter of fact, the revelation neither extraordinary nor noteworthy. That's the way she talked.

She never thought about quitting or finding another career. Those options were greatly discouraged by her government, and she didn't have the personality to make that kind of change anyway. She had chosen a path, so that was the path she would follow. How she'd been married and divorced three times, I never learned.

She did not grow up in the church—few did in the 1960s and '70s—and she didn't give church much thought until she was 40. She was recently divorced and sad at the time, she said—again, a matter of fact, nothing more or less—and friends took her to a Methodist church they attended. She liked it, but it was too far from her home.

"I didn't want to travel on Sunday," she said. "I travel every day to teach. So I looked for a church in Vedado," the neighborhood where she lived.

She discovered she lived a short walk from the Episcopal Cathedral, so she chose it without consideration of theology. Juan Ramon was the dean at that time, and he taught her about the church. She proved to be a quick study and an enthusiastic student—she's nothing if not determined—and she became part of the cadre of volunteers who kept the church going.

When I met her, her responsibilities included reading sermons on Sundays for Dean Jose on days when he couldn't because of a lingering problem he was having with his vocal cords. He would write the words, but most days, his voice had been reduced to a gravely whisper and it pained him to talk too much. It sounded cool, all hushed and conspiratorial like Brando in the *Godfather* movies, but his life was real, not a movie set, and he handed off his role when he had to.

She would stand and read his sermons in a careful, deliberate tone. During noon services, which Jose held Tuesdays through Fridays, Nieve sat close by. When he could talk, he would. When he couldn't, she filled in. When I was there, they both would look at me and whisper the page number of the hymn or the reading from the workbook.

"I'm trying to be a good Christian," Nieve said. "But it's hard."

We talked for several hours, mostly on the couch outside Say's office.

When we finished, Nieve stood up and offered a firm handshake and a logical assessment of me before she departed. I hadn't asked for it, but she doled it out anyway.

"You're like a child, you ask so many questions," she said.

"Thank you," I said.

"Why?"

I smiled and hugged her, and we ended there.

> <

I failed in my pursuit of figuring out the appeal of Communism in a country with a dual economy. It worked rather well when you were visiting. I think I could have lived comfortably in Havana on fewer dollars than I lived on at home, and I'd have had the access to the things I'd want, many of which were only available with tourist dollars. Even paying the daily rate of 30 dollars, I could have had my apartment for less than a grand a month, not a bad price for that square footage in a big city. And Cuba being Cuba, I'm certain I could have negotiated a better rate.

But if I were Cuban, earning my living in pesos, life would have been much different. I could only see, but not often access, those things, and I'm not sure I'd have remained content with that arrangement.

But that's me and my context. I know what it's like to live in a world where I get fussy about having to choose between the same 87 restaurants every week, all of which will have available nearly everything on their menus all the time.

Many Cubans find ways to live in both worlds, theirs and the one created for the tourists.

Their state jobs pay them in pesos, increasingly now by debit card, and their citizenship allows them access to the ration cards and their allotments of eggs, milk, coffee, rice and sugar.

The little jobs they can find to do for tourists pay them in the convertible currency. A person I know earns 30 pesos a month from the government, which isn't enough to cover the most basic cell phone service. But she also earns 20 dollars a day or more as a guide, a windfall that leaves her willing to work on her days off. Some weeks, she works all seven days, but she doesn't mind because the tradeoff allows her more comfort.

Such as her cell phone.

Such as it is. Again, a lesson in context.

The last time I saw her, she had an iPhone, same as me, which she bought on the black market. There's a brisk business in Cuba of "jailbreaking" phones, working around the software blocks that are supposed to keep people from using the phones without the approved service plans.

It's not like Cuba had brisk competition for those plans, and anyway, the rules were different there.

But she couldn't do with her iPhone what I could do with mine when I was back home, because the cell phone revolution had yet to find its way to Cuba. Which was refreshing... for visiting Americans, anyway, those of us who couldn't go an hour without checking something on ours, or walking a block without bumping into someone who was not paying attention to the here and now because they were engrossed in the there and then on their phone.

It was probably not so refreshing for the Cubans, who got to have their iPhones but not really use them. And particularly not to those who had traveled off the island and seen what cell phones were like in places where cell phones were ubiquitous. They've yet to enjoy the benefit of being able to check the latest tweets from Taylor Swift (headed to London the day I got back to the States; she missed her cats) or see if that email had come in or text everyone, all the time, about the most mundane of things.

It's an odd thing to see, well into the 21st century, a people without phones.

I spent a good deal of time in Haiti and Cuba in recent years. One was noticeably dysfunctional to the core and the other was not. And in the one that worked the worst, where even simple things didn't happen, like having paved roads in populated areas or clearing the rubble from a major natural disaster, even with the infusion of billions of dollars of humanitarian aid... even there, everyone had a cell phone. People who lived in concrete block buildings so brittle, the walls would crumble in your hands, they had cell phones. People who lived in tents with dirt floors, they had them. People who lived on dirt floors without a tent to cover them, they had cell phones, too. Everywhere I went, everyone had cell phones. And perhaps even more hopeful, all those people had someone to talk to. You couldn't go 10 feet in Haiti without running into someone having a loud, animated conversation on their cell phone.

Haiti's not the place for privacy anyway. It's an outside country; even the people with homes go outside, because it was so hot in those concrete boxes and there was no ventilation and air conditioning took electricity, and no one had that, either, and the only place to really be able to bear life was outside. So everywhere you went in Haiti, there were people. Every street was lined shoulder to shoulder with people, and you heard everything there was to hear. It was all in Creole, so you didn't understand much of it, but you could get enough to know the basics: happy or sad? Getting the grocery list from the missus on your way home, or planning a riot? That happens, and so much easier, and faster, with mobile communication.

So cell phones were perfect there, there being no sense of personal space or discretion. It's like that woman in the grocery store at home and how just by walking into the produce section and standing next to her while you picked out some peppers or grapes or something, you could learn all about the thing that just happened to her daughter and how hopefully it wouldn't leave a scar, because they caught it in time. Haiti's an entire country full of that woman.

Cuba was not.

It's a country where people still actually talked to each other in person, face to face, and even made eye contact. Maybe not on the street with strangers—who could blame them?—but still, with each other. It's a dirty little piece of the past, no doubt, people stuck communicating in person because their government won't allow cell phone towers atop every building or the opening of a modern network to feed the phones.

Cubans do have cell phones. You see young people with iPhones, just like everywhere else in the world. It's just that the capability was limited.

The bishop and her priests had cell phones, too, and they'd call and text each other with regularity. But when you were sitting in church on Sunday and you got to that point where the service was dragging on and you thought no one was paying attention and wouldn't that be a good time to check in on Facebook and see what your old girlfriend Suzy, who had moved to Toledo and was married to some schmuck who worked in the glass factory, had for breakfast, you couldn't, because you couldn't get that kind of signal. And neither could anyone else, so they sat patiently and sang their hymns and stood up and sat down and went through the whole realm of prostrations that Episcopalians so love, and they did it without smart phones to distract them.

My young friend with the phone kept hers handy, in her purse, but other than using it to check the time or take photos or listen to music, she couldn't do much with it.

><

The sight of Cubans talking to each other while the rest of the world was caught up in the digital age wasn't the only anachronism I saw.

When I'm home, especially just after I've returned from Cuba, among the first questions everyone always asks is, "Are there really old American cars all over the place in Cuba?"

Because someone would make that up?

Those gazillion tourist snapshots you see on the Internet all the time, with the old cars in the background? Those cars are real. The occasional television news broadcast from Havana, with the anchor strategically posed somewhere in Old Havana, talking in hushed tones? Those cars rolling by are real, too. They're nothing special, really.

Most of the cars are from the 1940s and 1950s. They're what was there before the revolution, and most are of the type that would have been ordinary in their time: Buicks, Plymouths, Chevrolets, Fords. There are some we consider classic, like the 1957 Chevrolet, and some about which we snicker, like a Studebaker or an Edsel. I've even seen a Model T.

Nearly six decades removed from the factory, few are in pristine condition. Most are what the Rev. Halbert Pons in Santiago called "Frankenstein cars."

"They may have a Russian motor, a Ford part, a Chevy part," he'd told me as we passed a group of men standing curbside, working on an old car.

He drove a Kia, because he prized reliability over style.

The cars were interesting to see, in a theme-park way, but they were not the only cars on the road. Cuba is also full of Ladas, Russian-made sedans that look like little Fiats from the 1970s, small and boxy, and Kias of a size so small, you'd never see them in America. I've also seen a few Mercedes sedans, but those are a rarity, at least where I've been.

Once you get over the novelty of seeing the old American cars, the most noticeable things about cars in Cuba is scarcity. There just aren't that many.

In Santiago, which is home to half a million people, congestion is someone double-parked in the road waiting for their mother to get to the door, not cars waiting to get through a light. It's more common there to see people crowded into the canvas-covered beds of large trucks, which serve as gypsy buses in Cuba. They're not sanctioned by the government, and they compete with the state-owned local bus companies, but I didn't see any effort to shut them down.

In Havana, which is home to more than two million people, I've never seen more than five or six cars backed up at a light, and I've yet to see anyone miss a light. More often, you see people crowded onto the buses. Articulated buses, those where the main bus pulls a trailer and the ends are connected with what look like large accordion folds, are common throughout the city. Rarely do you see one with a free seat. Or much free room, at all. People crowd by the dozens at bus stops, and few risk the wait no matter how crowded the bus is.

><

The respite from the horrors of my bed did not last. My second night back in Havana was the worst yet. Maybe the worst night of sleep I've ever had, anywhere. I woke up at three in the morning with terrible back pain, then slept in fits until six, when I finally gave up and crawled out of bed, slowly and cautiously because it actually hurt to move, and made instant coffee.

After more than a week, I finally perfected the art of pouring boiling water from my makeshift coffee pot, a stainless steel pitcher designed for cream, perhaps, but definitely not heat, into my cup without melting another dishtowel onto the handle: slight grasp on the edge of the handle with a piece of cloth and use a sponge to hold tight while pulling away. (In its wake, I left behind a washcloth with several holes burned through, two partially melted towels and a partially melted sponge. It was not a professional operation.)

I had my coffee but little else to do at that time of the day.

I'd finished my book, I couldn't get an Internet signal and I didn't have a newspaper to read: no baseball scores, no puzzles, no tragedies of the world condensed to single paragraphs. The day was wide open, waiting to expand before me. If only I'd get out of the house.

> <

The Vedado neighborhood must have been grand in its day: grand homes on large lots, beautiful architecture, lush gardens. Across from the dean's house, on *Calle 11* between *Calle 4* and *Calle 6,* was an art deco apartment building that stretched halfway down the block.

Up and down the blocks, the streets were lined with the fortresses of a different time, homes designed to offer an outward display of prosperity and inward comfort and grandeur, all surrounded by the vines and flowers and bushes you get in tropical environments, where there's never a reason to lay dormant.

The streets were lined with banyan trees, fast-growing tropical trees that look like bundles of roots loosely bound, shooting upward, with tendrils reaching from the branches back to earth. Some of those trees spread out so wide, you can't touch the edges, no matter how far you stretched your arms. They're the perfect cover on a hot, steamy island, always a dense shade in which to rest.

But the Communists would have their way, too, and not even the trees could block what the government did. Many of those blocks also held post-revolution construction, lifeless rectangles of blah.

Cuba is home to a depressing array of buildings from the Brutalist school, which isn't what it sounds like but is bad in a whole different way. "Brutalism" comes from *beton brut,* French for "raw concrete"—again, an online translation; my language skills were not enhanced by looking at ugly buildings—and Cuba in the Castro years specialized in raw concrete. Decades into the experiment, all of it, old and less old, looked beat. The paint had faded away, walls had long streaks of that blackish green that oozes over everything where dirt and salt water mix on concrete and no one ever cleans it off.

Many of the older buildings, the ones Americans of a type would adorn with brass markers and restrictive covenants, were crumbling: you could see daylight through porch roofs, windows and doors, and it was not hard to find trees growing from the upper reaches of buildings.

In one building, a block down from the cathedral, you could look through the windows of the top floor and see the sky, evidence that the entire roof gave way and had since rotted into oblivion. But the building was still in use, its first floor apartments obviously occupied, and the ones of the second floor, just below the damage above, also still seemingly open for habitation.

A few blocks away, a mansion with a belvedere cupola sitting atop two stories of grand construction, commanding a view of the park across the street had been retrofitted with an odd mix of cinderblock infill and chain link fencing in place of railings. It didn't take an architectural historian to identify the beauty that once was or the abomination that home had become.

An odd exception to the decay was at the Music Academy, *on Calle 6* between *13* and *15*. It was the Cuban version of ASCAP, the agency that licenses music and pays royalties to artists. From the outside, the colonial mansion looked exquisite, painted a bright pink with white trim. It also had an armed guard, one of the few visible in the area, so I didn't venture too close.

Many of the post-revolution apartment buildings were of the same type: set close to the street, with a shallow parking garage jutting below, leaving the first floors to start at about eye level. Short, steep ramps ducked under them. Above, the openings were largely enclosed by louvered windows, entire parts of Havana looking like massive Florida rooms.

><

Cuba has sponsored an ambitious program of large-scale public art, particularly sculptures. For all of its faults in the past six decades, Cuba seems to have been a good place to have been a sculptor. From one end of the country to the other, from large public squares in Havana and Santiago to villages so small that the bus never slowed, there was art on display.

Some of it was expected: life-size war heroes on their horses, bronzed and lording over spots here and there, reminders of the American-style homages common before the revolution. And the marble and bronze Martis, too: memorial depictions of Jose from the ubiquitous busts to the towering figure in the mausoleum, and many sizes in between. Along the *Malecon,* Marti can be seen clutching a child and pointing out to sea. No doubt warning of the dangers to come.

Some of it was exclusively Cuban: many, many depictions of *Granma,* the boat Castro's rebels used to get from Mexico to Cuba so they could start the revolution. And stories-tall, including the murals of Che Guevara and Camilo Cienfuegos mounted to government buildings next to the *Plaza de la Revolucion.*

And some of it was just art for the sake of art. On the outskirts of Santiago, in a small plot bordered by a highway and onramps, was a field of sugar cubes: dozens of large white cubes, set in neat rows, standing slightly askew atop steel rods.

> <

I walked into the church office at a quarter till 10 on Thursday morning, my last full day there, and found Juan Ramon in place, ready to talk.

We sat on the couch, and I was immediately distracted by the television hanging in the corner, the way people are always distracted by televisions that are on in public places. You don't have to want to watch, but you do anyway. It was on, as usual, but in the place of the daytime soap operas that were so easy to tune out was concert footage featuring Eddy Escobar, Cuba's karaoke machine.

He had the full-on rock star look: jeans, leather jacket, long, flowing hair—a wind machine of his own, center stage, perhaps—and a beautifully crafted guitar.

He sang, in order, Bon Jovi's "Dead or Alive," REM's "Losing my Religion"—perhaps better received than understood—and

Steely Dan's "Reeling in the Years." When the band broke into AC/DC's "You Shook Me All Night Long," Ramon had had enough. He muttered something about the music and stood up and turned off the television.

Daliana, the flirty girl, danced through the office several times as the songs played and told me about Escobar, whom she counted as a friend, or maybe an acquaintance. I don't know, our conversations being stilted because of the language barrier.

She frowned when Ramon turned off the music, but she didn't complain. She danced once more and disappeared into the office.

><

Ramon apologized for his extended absence from Havana. He'd been in Baracoa, on the extreme northeast of the island, further out than even Guantanamo, where someone is trying to establish an Episcopal church. If it works, it'd be the church's first presence there.

Guantanamo, Ramon said, has now and always has had the strongest church in Cuba. Back when the church could operate schools, Guantanamo was tops in that, too. He credited the strength in part to strong priests but also in part to a loyal, strong community of Jamaicans.

><

In 1960, when Ramon was ordained, he was sent east and charged with the upkeep of five to 10 churches. The revolution was still young then, but the impact had hit fast and deep.

The goal, he said, "was keeping a presence. It was the fundamental thing we did. We couldn't do a lot."

The Episcopal Church, he said, "was not a church of conflict. The Jehovah's Witnesses caused a lot of problems. We did not."

After the Revolution, the Episcopal Church went from having 25 or 30 priests to having 10 or 12. "Most scattered away with the change." No one was prepared for what was happening, he said, and leaving was "the easy way."

For those who stayed, there was a single new goal, one thing to determine: What is the role of the church in the new situation?

At one point, the clergy went three years without being paid.

Ramon survived because of the "help of God, and my father, who paid my salary."

His wife, Nerva Cot, was also a priest. She had been a Methodist seminary student, and the Methodists, not pleased with her choice of an Episcopal husband, tried moving her to another part of the island to break her of the habit of Ramon. With the help of Bishop Blankingship, she became an Episcopal instead.

They had three children. Two were now priests: their daughter, in Matanzes, and their son, in Cardenas. The third was a doctor.

Ramon talked about the need to talk about politics in church, a topic that had been of such interest in Camagüey. He did not shy away from it. Figuring out where the church stood in the new order, he said, was not easy.

"The role of the church was to understand the situation," he said. "The context changed. The vision and mission of good Anglicans was to have dialog with society, culture, to support humanity."

He said the revolution helped promote ecumenical unity among churches in Cuba. The days of being able to carve out their own places and push their own ideas was gone; after the revolution, the churches were bound together, whether they liked it or not, opposite the state.

He spoke of the Inquisition and the Crusades and the type of forced dogma that had long defined life in some churches and how it just ceased to be relevant so quickly after Castro's rise to power.

But the coming together of the country's religious communities was not easy. "It was a hard task. There were few people left in all the churches."

> <

Ramon said the church was weaker in 2014 than in the 1960s because of the prevalence of companion relationships with churches, particularly in the United States.

"Spiritually, we were stronger before," he said. "Now, we are not so fluent, rich, deep, full of grace and blessing. When we were smaller, there was a strong sense of brotherhood."

Cut off from the outside world, and access to religious goods and services that had long been imported, Cubans had to improvise. The creativity of the church opened as people began writing their own hymns and masses and creating poems and art.

"We were an incarnate church, with all the troubles and contradictions," he said. "The role of the church is not going to Miami. It is here."

Ramon learned that lesson on the road not long after the revolution. He went to Miami 10 times and was prepared to move in pursuit of his new career.

"I told my mother, if the diocese goes away, I'll go wherever the church sends me," he said, repeating the vow he'd made as a young, though perhaps not yet wise, priest.

She was not happy. And he played the role of smart son and reconsidered.

"She said, 'You forget you have a mother and a family here.' I told her, 'I will remain here with the lightning and thunder.'"

And he did.

><

Before the revolution, the Episcopal Church had the best schools in Cuba, Ramon said, but their role had changed through the years, and not always for the better. Before 1940, the schools were open to all: black, white, mulatto; rich and poor. It was an outreach, a service to the community.

After 1940, the churches "were for the middle classes." They may have ministered to the poor but they didn't often anymore minister *with* the poor.

Ramon was part of that middle class. His father was an optometrist.

As the middle classes took control, the people on the fringes, the blacks and the poor, were cast aside and left with little access to education.

"The priests of that generation were trained to serve the middle class," he said.

Before then, a missionary had trained priests to serve the poor. The switch to serving the rich was with all of the churches and involved an ugly reality, he said.

"If you serve the rich, you'll have a good car," Ramon said. "If you serve the poor, you'll be poor. I think it was a little selfish."

The whole church took a turn for selfish in that era, he said. The cathedral itself was moved, away from the poor and toward the rich. It had been in central Havana, in a working-class neighborhood. But the Anglo-Saxon community felt increasingly uncomfortable there and forced the move. They had the money, so they were able to get what they wanted. Ramon felt that was a mistake.

"That took the church away from the people. Our work was there."

But the poor people didn't have the money or the power to fight back, so they lost their church.

There had always been tension in the church between the leaders and the people, between the priests were their dogma and theology and beliefs, and the prophets with their concerns for the people of the day, he said.

"There will be until the end of the world."

He called himself mixed when it came to finding his place between the priests and the people. "I'm half and half. My heart is with the people. But I did not resign my pension like St. Francis did. I don't have that kind of holiness," he laughed.

After the revolution, the middle class went away. By choice or out of fear, it didn't matter. They were gone. And that created a huge problem: the poor people who were left didn't know how to run anything, much less manage the economy, he said. Not just in the church, but everywhere, across the whole country.

Gone were business and political leaders, the mid-level people who knew how to run a country, no matter who was in charge. And the farmers disappeared, too, leaving their fields to hands that didn't understand.

Ramon said it took 25 years for the country to recover well enough to educate and train a new generation of leaders. "It was a time of foolishness. We had a hard time in many ways."

The transition was difficult but they had the "paternalism of the Soviet Union" in the form of aid: money and equipment came in regularly in exchange for allowing the Soviets proximity to the U.S.

"But we weren't able to manage the riches."

> <

Ramon said he felt born to be a priest but also had a big interest in common culture, particularly that of the African communities in Cuba.

Growing up, Ramon said, he was taught the standard lesson that non-traditional religious beliefs represented the work of the devil. (He said he also learned from a Catholic priest that the Episcopalians were the work of the devil.) He learned otherwise through years of meeting with, talking to and learning from leaders of some of those religious.

"It takes time," he said, to form those bonds. Before, there was much discrimination. "We learned that black religion was witchery." In seminary, he began learning otherwise.

"It was not belonging to the devil," he said. "Afro-Cuba, Hindu, Muslim, it's all another way that God knows us."

> <

It took decades, but Ramon said he had learned how to attract a crowd to church, even in a Communist country.

"Music is the secret to fill the churches," he said, then emphasized, "Good music."

That passion extends to all parts of a service, he said, and it was why the Episcopalians trailed the Pentecostals, Baptists and others in filling their churches on Sundays. "We don't have the gift of evangelism."

Many Episcopal churches in Cuba, he said, were opened to meet the needs of now long-gone Anglo-Saxon communities.

"People try seeing things in black and white, but it's not always that way. Sometimes, you need to grab a little black and a little white."

Little by little, the situation is improving. It takes time, he said, to change the minds of people, two or three generations.

> <

Twice in his lifetime, Ramon has seen a pope visit Cuba. He said they helped the rest of the world recognize the status of the country. Cuba was blessed, he said, and respected after Pope John Paul II came in 1998. Before then, Cuba "was always blamed, rejected, was the devil, an agnostic culture, according to the propaganda in other countries. His visit, I think, helped change the minds in other countries, our image in the world. After the pope's blessing, several other countries—Honduras, Guatemala—opened dialogue with Cuba."

Inside Cuba, he said, it helped bring together the church and the state. But it still left a divide between the church and the people it tried to serve.

"Cuban people don't sympathize with priests," he said. "In a procession, people will follow the spirit of the town but of them, maybe one supports the priest and the others don't."

Because, he said, for a long time priests represented power, and poor people didn't benefit from that power. He called it "anti-clericalism, resistant cultures": people support the image but not the priest.

He said some of that has been slowly changing.

> <

Ramon said Bishop Griselda, like the president of her native Bolivia, represents an ancient culture of knowing minds.

"She is doing good work... She's going in a good direction... She doesn't take decisions too quick. She takes time to study... She has special gifts and wisdom.

"We Cubans act too quick."

> <

I asked Ramon what posed the greatest threat to the church today. He sat silently for a long time before speaking, his eyes lost in thought. Finally, he settled on tension between the institution and the movement of the people it served.

"We are an incarnate church," he said, a church of the people. When leaders forget that, trouble starts.

He said the future of the Cuban church might be on display today in China and Vietnam, which are trying to combine capitalism with socialism. "Little by little, Cuba is going that way."

In China, the Anglican bishop is working with a non-denominational church.

In Cuba, "the challenge is to have new ways, new vision in this new context that is coming little by little."

The challenge may be one of success or another way of failure.

"I believe the holy spirit will guide us in the most difficult time."

Church tradition is good in Cuba. "In some churches, tradition is a bad word. But in Cuba, tradition is a living history, it's not dead. In Cuba, history means new life. We've been here 142 years. It's a very long tradition.

"It's in the hearts of the Cuban people."

> <

Ramon made a point of emphasis in saying that the church remained Episcopal. It did not become Anglican, even when the U.S. Episcopal Church turned away and even though it was the Anglicans from Canada who came back for them. Episcopal "is the history in Cuba."

But no matter who's offering guidance and support from abroad, the important thing is that someone is.

"When a church is isolated, they fall down. But when they feel like they're part of the universal church, they have strength. The universal church is present here."

> <

I finished with Ramon, and I'd finished the books I'd brought with me, so I went in search of entertainment.

I walked into the gift shop of the Cohiba with a pocket full of money but couldn't force myself into buying a single thing. All of the knickknacks looked like junk you could buy in any country. I couldn't imagine anyone at home wearing one of the T-shirts, and the book selection was highly suspect. I'd finished my book by then and desperately wanted something new to read, but I couldn't force myself to buy the kind of history approved for sale in a Cuban hotel gift shop. The rack was full of the true adventures of Fidel Castro and Che Guevera.

> <

I took one final walk around the neighborhood: *Calle 6* to *Calle 17*, where I stopped in the park for yet another picture of the John Lennon statue. A taxi full of tourists jumped out there, too, so I walked along to the other side of the park and came across a sculpture I'd missed before of hands thrust toward the sky. It was sort of abstract, but you could get the idea pretty quick.

I went down *Calle 17*, a busy street that cut across the neighborhood, to *Calle 12*, then headed back downhill toward *Calle 9*. I was going to cut across at *Calle 11* but the block had a military guard and "Do Not Pass" signs, so I just smiled and waved a little and kept going. I get nervous around guys with guns.

I got turned around somewhere, and wound up walking blindly, turning here and there, before finally stumbling back on the cathedral heading north on *Calle 11*, from *8* toward *6*.

I was going to head to dinner, but it started to rain and I retreated to my room. I could miss a meal.

> <

My last night there, and I woke up in the middle of night thinking of ways to turn my notes into newspaper stories. I actually had a dream about being back at work, on deadline, smiling as I was about to file a story. I love working on deadline, even when I'm asleep.

I think that was a sign that it was time to go home.

On my last morning, I had my first experience with impatient Cubans. I was told to be ready to go to the airport by 9:30, and Say was at my door at quarter past, prodding me along. "It's time for you to go," she said. "You don't want to miss your flight."

That didn't seem likely, but she wasn't the kind of woman with whom you argued. When she spoke, you said yes and moved along.

I gave my key back to Marta, the woman who owned the house, left some money under the pillow for the maid, and headed out.

I got to Jose Marti International Airport with five hours to spare. It was so early, in fact, I had to wait more than an hour just to check in. And after I did that, the clerk told me I'd have to wait another hour before going through customs.

I spent most of the time on a bench in front of the airport, between the information stand and the stand with the ice cream and potato chips.

The arrival gate opened not far away, and I watched the entertaining sight of Cubans pouring back into Havana with carts full of cellophane-wrapped bags and boxes and bicycles. No one comes home empty-handed, and few seem to consider the space constraints of the cars that will ferry them home from the airport. I'd seen it before in Miami, but that day was the first time I sat in Havana and watched it unfold there. Every other time, I'd rush away from the airport. That day, I could lean back and relax and marvel at the spectacle.

I watched one man load and reload and reload again as he tried to squeeze a bicycle into the trunk of his small sedan. I'm not sure how he did it, but the bicycle, and the woman who brought it, were finally squeezed into place, and they pulled off.

I also noticed that Cuban women seem to love the most impossible and impractical of shoes, the higher the heel, the better. One group of three women, sisters and a mother it appeared, each towered six inches above the ground in their wedge heels, their legs as impossibly taught as their toes were crammed downward. They stood around looking more comfortable than I could imagine, and they finally found the people they had come to get. They all hugged and laughed and grabbed bags and disappeared into the crowd.

The weather was reasonably pleasant, particularly in the shade, but the flies drove me crazy, then I broke into a sneezing fit before I finally went back inside.

I bought three maps at a kiosk, then headed through customs.

Once clear, I was faced with another three hours of sitting still.

The crew on the return leg was feisty to the point of being hostile, the driver of the airport shuttle back to my hotel was a whiner who wouldn't shut up about the shortcomings of his coworkers and when the door opened to the elevator in the hotel lobby, the two women in front of me just stood and stared as if they were awaiting an official beckoning before stepping into the car. They weren't sure what to do.

And there I was, back in the U.S., every ounce of tolerance and understanding I'd picked up in the past few weeks gone in a second. Cuba was no panacea, for sure; it had problems layered on problems, difficulties I'd never understand. But something there felt right, at least for a while, and I'd come home relaxed and patient and ready to look at things in new ways.

And then I found myself standing in a hotel in Miami, waiting for those women to get in the elevator, and I was American all over again.

"I think I'll take this one," I said, stepping around the women and into the elevator. "You can grab the next one."

They stood there a little startled as the door closed, but they never moved.

CHAPTER 6

EPILOGUE (HAVANA, JUNE 2015)

IN THE FIRST six months after President Barack Obama promised to change the relationship between the United States and Cuba and ease the restrictions that have kept the countries, and their people, apart for decades, I went back twice.

In January, a month after Obama's speech, there was an air of excitement everywhere I went. I didn't see any noticeable changes—you still needed cash to buy whatever you wanted, you still couldn't get a decent Internet connection even in the places that offered the Internet to tourists, Starbucks still hadn't moved into any of the dozens of places in Old Havana that seemed perfect for it—but the anticipation had whetted an appetite for something for which so many people had long hoped. It was what people talked about, especially when those people discovered an American was in their midst.

Everyone in Cuba seems to have a relative in the United States, and in January, those who hadn't made the trip themselves were anticipating the swift arrival of the day when they could, without hassle and without having to keep paying the government the processing fees for the visas they kept denying. They were looking forward to going to Jose Marti International Airport, checking in at the counter and flying out, all civilized like the rest of the free world.

Or at least they were awaiting the arrival of more Americans, who would bring their good cheer and their wads of cash and their soon-to-be-useful credit cards to buy rides in the coco taxis and boxes of cigars and bottles of rum and empty suitcases, which would they would fill with the souvenirs so eagerly sold by the friendly vendors, who all know someone in Chicago or Louisville or Baltimore or some other unlikely place they can't wait to tell you about.

Wherever it is, know this: "It's cold there," you'll hear, as the person wraps his or her arms around his or her chest. Then they'll unwrap their arms and continue their sales pitch. Only with the embargo ending, they were going to have to speed up the routine so they could attend to all the customers.

The words of the president read like a long-sought validation of those thoughts, an admission that so many knew to be true but had long yearned to hear from someone in a position to make change.

"All of this bound America and Cuba in a unique relationship, at once family and foe," Obama had said in December 2014, talking about the effect of Fidel Castro's revolution, which had taken place two years before Obama was even born.

"Proudly, the United States has supported democracy and human rights in Cuba through these five decades. We have done so primarily through policies that aimed to isolate the island, preventing the most basic travel and commerce that Americans can enjoy anyplace else. And though this policy has been rooted in the best of intentions, no other nation joins us in imposing these sanctions, and it has had little effect beyond providing the Cuban government with a rationale for restrictions on its people.

"Today, Cuba is still governed by the Castros and the Communist Party that came to power half a century ago.

"Neither the American nor Cuban people are well served by a rigid policy that is rooted in events that took place before most of us were born. Consider that for more than 35 years, we've had relations with China—a far larger country also governed by a Communist Party. Nearly two decades ago, we reestablished relations with Vietnam, where we fought a war that claimed more Americans than any Cold War confrontation."

On the day of the speech, Obama announced the return of two Americans who had been imprisoned in Cuba, one very publicly for five years, the other quietly for two decades, and the release to Cuban authorities of three men who had been in U.S. prisons. All on both sides had been accused of spying, and the exchange was seen as a gesture of extreme goodwill on the part of two suspicious, weary governments more accustomed to making accusations than working out solutions.

Obama's speech caused a mixture of joy and deep-seated concern in both countries. Many on both sides reveled in the thought of easy travel, with strong demand expected in both directions as people sought what people always seek: to see and know that which has been forbidden.

But old foes also angrily chimed in, keeping up their decades-running battles over ideology, property rights, state sovereignty and all the other issues that mean so much to so few but that have kept so many at bay for so long.

No matter the likely outcome, though, Obama's speech undoubtedly caused a very un-Cuban like outpouring of optimism in Cuba.

But it didn't last.

By June, the moment had passed, and resignation had begun to settle back in that Cuba was still Cuba, and that changing the will and way of the United States would take more than a few words from a president nearing the end of his second and final term in office.

"I think Cubans believe what they see, not what they hear," the Rev. Andreis Díaz, an Episcopal priest from the small town of Bolondron, told me in June.

We were in Havana in the house of his mother-in-law, the Episcopal Bishop Griselda Delgado. Diaz and most of the rest of the nation's two dozen or so Episcopal priests were in town for the momentous occasion of the ordination of five new members to their ranks. In a country that struggles to attract priests—only one likely candidate remained in the pipeline, Diaz said—it had been a big day.

But Diaz is as pragmatic as the next well-informed Cuban,

and he wasn't holding out much hope for a speedy resolution to whatever issues separate his government from the one in the United States.

"The Cuban people are not very excited," he said in a matter-of-fact way that betrayed no hint of discouragement. Cubans can be that way about so much, open and honest and neutral in ways that Americans can't comprehend.

Until they saw evidence to the contrary, he said, the people he knew would keep believing what they'd always believed and living as they'd always lived. Reality is a better indicator of life than wishful thinking in a country that still issues ration cards for essential foods.

"You turn on the news at eight o'clock and it says there's a record harvest of potatoes, but you go to the store and you don't see any," Diaz told me to prove his point. "You hear that Venezuela is shipping another hundred thousand barrels of oil a day, but you go to buy gas and the price is the same, not even 10 cents less."

He said he didn't know if it was propaganda or just an overly ambitious approach to reporting the news, but either way, he said, Cubans knew to believe their eyes over their ears. It was just the way life was there.

And that was when they were at least still hearing positive news. If they'd paid attention to the debate in the U.S. in early July, they may have given up entirely.

Obama was talking about appointing an ambassador to Cuba, the first since 1960, but such a move from the Democrat would require the approval of the U.S. Senate, which was dominated by the Republican Party, and its leadership wasn't in a mood to play along.

The Senate Majority Leader, Mitch McConnell, a Republican from Kentucky, called the Cuban government a "thuggish regime" and said the country was a "police state" and a "haven for criminals" who had escaped the U.S.

"You would think that the normalization of relations with Cuba would be accompanied by some modification of their behavior," he said while talking to a group of businessmen in Lexington, Kentucky.

"I don't see any evidence at all that they are going to change their behavior. So I doubt if we'll confirm an ambassador. They probably don't need one."

He said he had seen "film from down there" and that the presence of old American cars was evidence enough for him that the country was stuck in a time warp and not ready for the goodwill an official U.S. diplomatic presence would convey.

"Some of their restrictions on Cuba would require legislation to lift," he said, "and we're going to resist that."

> <

Not rushing into a big change was maybe not an entirely bad thing, Diaz said. An immediate end to five decades of restrictions would come with a whole new set of problems, as it had across Russia and Eastern Europe when the Soviet bloc faltered, split and fell apart in the 1990s. Two decades later, those issues are still playing out in deadly ways.

The onslaught of Americans expected to flood into the country once the gates opened might not find what they'd expected, Diaz said, and the Cubans certainly wouldn't be in a position to help them.

"Cuba is not ready," he said. "You go to a restaurant and you see 30, 35 people lined up, and they don't know what to do. The waiter is used to 10 people. When the 11th comes in, it's"—Diaz started flailing his hands and arms in mock horror—"they don't know what to do. They don't apologize, they don't entertain you or make you feel welcome. They treat you like they've always treated us."

And that, he said, is not good.

He repeated something I'd heard before, that a lifetime of Communism had robbed the Cuban people of ambition. Proof abounds; it's a country that has perfected the whimsical art of "island time" to a maddening level. I once sat through a six-and-a-half-hour wait for an airplane with a single, vague status update, and the locals just shrugged it off without a word of complaint. In the U.S., there would have been a riot. In Cuba, it was just how life was. It wasn't like the airport café ran out of coffee.

Diaz said he was also concerned that even if tourists came, they'd have nowhere to go, especially away from Havana, Santiago and the tourist beaches. His town, a speck on the map southeast of Havana and south of the Varadero coast, couldn't handle the occasional missionaries who come to help, much less tourists.

"Where would they go?" he asked. "In Bolondron, they could take a walk and they'd be gone by lunch."

He said the town had little, if anything, to see, and only one private restaurant and no hotel rooms. There was another option the locals liked, but he was reluctant to recommend it.

"You can stay in private houses," he said. "The people here would gladly have you stay in their home. But you couldn't take a shower. They'd give you a bucket of water to clean with. You could drink the water and get sick. I'm afraid if people did that, they would never come back."

Another priest who was in Havana for the ordinations, my friend Halbert Pons from Santiago, said he didn't waste time thinking about the end of the embargo. What happened between his government and mine, he said, was beyond our control. Instead, he talked about what had happened in the eight months since I'd visited him.

He'd paved a courtyard and added some rooms to one of his churches, then scrolled through photos on his phone so I could see. He had stopped work on another church because he had run out of money for the project—temporarily, he emphasized; he was hopeful that would change in time—and he was generally just pushing ahead the same as before Obama said anything.

"Not much has changed," he said.

I didn't see much change myself, walking around Havana in June. The most memorable American moments were the same as moments I'd already had in Cuba, before Obama made his speech.

The dirty little secret of the U.S. trade embargo of Cuba was that it was an obstacle, not a roadblock. Americans had been coming all along. Before the speech, there were eight visa exceptions; after it, a dozen, and that wasn't counting the people who snuck in from Mexico or the Bahamas.

I've flown from Miami to Cuba on an American Airlines jet staffed by an American Airlines crew. A sultry crew, by the way; maybe the rudest collection of airline employees I've ever seen anywhere. But that's beside the point.

The thing is, "American Airlines" didn't appear anywhere on my travel documents, and I didn't get near the American Airlines gates in the airport. I reported to the counter with the name of whatever that day's travel company was, Joke's On You Charters, or something like that, and then went into that terminal in Miami for the charter planes. It was dirtier than the rest, by the way, the carpet more worn, fewer amenities. I bought my morning coffee at a Pizza Hut.

The ticket for the 45-minute flight cost more than the ticket from Richmond to Miami, and Richmond's not a cheap place to fly from. But maybe the cost of flying is taking off and landing; getting from Miami to Havana, there's no cruising altitude. You go up. You come down. You see the Florida Keys. You see the airport in Key West, clear as day. You see a cruise ship, surprisingly large and easy to identify from the air. You see some lush green fields. You see Havana. One minute, you're in the world of easy Internet and ubiquitous everything, the next you're in the land time forgot. You don't even have time for a nap in between.

As long as you could get a visa, you could fly straight over the embargo and go from Miami or Tampa right into Cuba. And not just Havana, either. At the airport in Miami, the departure screen showed flights to five different cities in Cuba: Havana, Santa Clara, Camagüey, Holguin and Santiago. Just like that, and you were there.

You could also sneak in from a third country, which is what I did the first time I went, in 1988. My father and I had flown from Norfolk, Virginia, to Dallas to Mexico City to Havana. But before we flew to Cuba, we had to spend the night in Mexico City, because our route was so stupidly long it couldn't be accomplished in a single day.

Mexico seemed a fitting place. Fidel had gone there, after all, and that's where he bought his boat *Granma*. He kept the silly name and took off with his band of revolutionaries on their unlikely, but highly successful, quest to shape the history of the then-burgeoning Cold War.

And Mexico City is where I learned that people really do drive on the sidewalk. And fast. So fast that if you're not careful, some future generation in your family will have an interesting story to tell about someone they never met.

"My grandfather died before I was born," one of those people will say years from now. "He was run over in Mexico City. Hit by an antique Volkswagen outside a liquor store. No one ever could figure out why he was on the sidewalk."

If you didn't want to be that guy in Mexico City in 1988, you had to stay off the sidewalk. And pretty much off your feet on any surface wide enough to drive a car. The safest place we found, and "safe" was a very relative term that day, was in a car driven by the ex-husband of my stepmother's brother's wife's mother. Or it might have been her father; I'm not sure. He didn't talk much. He just drove. Fast.

No matter the connection, it's good to know people.

So on that trip, I went through Mexico. People still do that as a dodge of U.S. customs. You can sneak in and ask that no one stamp your passport, then you come home and tell everyone, as loud as you can, that you snuck into Cuba. Because once you're home, what are they going to do, right?

People do it from the Bahamas, too, and maybe Canada. I've seen flights land in Cuba from Venezuela and Spain and Germany, too, but that's a long way to go to get around a visa.

Getting in is a lot easier when you can just walk in the front door. The catch was, you needed a copy of your visa to get on the plane in Miami, but some of those visas were sitting in Havana, at the airport, hopefully, and you had to pick them up in person.

Which sounds fine and good and simple, which it would be if things ran in a smooth, orderly fashion, as one always expects. They never do, of course. Airports are maybe the best places in the world to watch the eager, ambitious, overconfident, self-absorbed people of the world crash and burn against those walls of bureaucratic indifference. The guy with the blue latex gloves has the power.

Where those expectations of efficiency come from, no one knows. Go to any U.S. government office thinking someone is going to help you in a polite, orderly fashion just because, and you'll be disappointed, too.

The frustrating part at the airport in Havana is that the system mostly works most of the time.

A friend in a church in Havana told me that once a whole group headed her way landed in Havana and couldn't find the person with the visas, and they all had to fly back home. But that was just the once.

I came close to being the second.

In the fall of 2014, the first time I went to Cuba by myself, I got to the airport in Miami and tried to check in, but the people at the gate couldn't find any evidence of my visa. (Note to self: never again use the travel agent who lives in another town and who doesn't speak English, especially not for a flight scheduled to leave on a Sunday morning when no one is in the office, even if that's the agent the bishop in Cuba has strongly suggested you use.)

The search went on for three hours, stretching all the way from the ungodly early time they tell you to get there all the way to the time when they actually let you leave. I'd been the first in line, and I wound up being last, too.

All the other travelers had come and gone, the Cubans with their shrink-wrapped televisions and bicycles and wheelchairs safely stowed in the hold of the plane and the Americans with their silly straw hats and guilty-as-sin grins. The gate crew had their morning espresso, pumped from a thermos into little plastic cups that looked like the cups on top of bottles of cough syrup, and were quietly chatting when they noticed I was still there. One of them got a puzzled look, then another, and finally someone got the idea to pick up the phone and call someone in Havana and ask about my visa. They reached a woman who had my actual visa in her hand at that very moment. They all smiled at the gate, and a few of them actually looked relieved, and they keyed a few things into their computer and finally gave me a boarding pass and sent me on toward the gate.

Between the charter company's counter and the place where I'd get my full body scan from the guys wearing blue gloves, one of the gate people tracked me down and handed me a replacement boarding pass.

"We're so sorry for the confusion," he said, taking the boarding pass from my hand and replacing it with an even better boarding pass.

They bumped me up to first class.

After all the waiting and the anxiety and thinking I'd be going back to Richmond instead of to Havana, I got to board first. I had the seat across from the door so everyone crowding into the back of the plane had to look at me and wonder, "What's he doing here? That schmuck didn't even have a visa three hours ago."

I settled in and smirked and said "Why, yes, that would be lovely," when a stewardess asked if I'd like a coffee before takeoff.

"It'll be a while, getting everyone settled back there," she said, apologizing for the hassle of having to wait.

I nodded knowingly, politely accepting the fate of the first-class passenger. I sipped my coffee and listened to music on my headphones and watched the others stream by.

It was easy telling the Cubans from the tourists, and not just because the tourists came in neat, matching groups with oversized nametags hanging from lanyards.

Bob from Minneapolis had the look of guilty anticipation, a fanny pack—which do still exist and might be requisite gear on group outings to Cuba—and a reasonable carry-on that he might have been able to stow in the overhead bin, if only the Cubans hadn't boarded first.

Because a Cuban on the way back from the U.S. does not travel light. The entire contents of a Wal-Mart will be crammed into carry-on bags that stretch the limits of physical possibility. It's like a bag of vacuum-packed coffee, small and neat and tidy, until the seal is broken. Then it blows out every direction, expanding to fill whatever space there is.

And the seal is always broken, because there's something in every bag that someone needs before the plane takes off. Only they don't know they need it right away. So the bags go into the overhead bin neat and orderly, with the wheels even pointing the right way. But then they come back out, and the item in question is always on the bottom somewhere, and the whole thing turns into a mess as people start stowing their bags the second time, because by then, they're reaching over the people in the aisle waiting to get to their seats, and they're trying to cram their bags back into places other people have taken.

The well-traveled of the tourists see this coming and stow their bags in the first available space, even if it's 23 aisles forward of their seats. They'll pick it up on their way out.

The rookies wait till they get to their seats, then they hunt backward in the plane for overhead space.

When the plane lands, and momentum pushes toward the sole exit, those people are left stranded waiting for the entire plane to empty before they can retreat three aisles for their bag. Not that they won't try pushing backward into the crowd. But it never works. A row or two back, they're cast aside and wind up waiting in the detritus of someone else's flight: the seat abandoned by someone who knew how to stow a bag, the crushed soda awkwardly crammed into the seatback pouch, the chewing gum wrappers tucked into the seam between seat cushions.

All that positioning takes time, and I finished my coffee before they even closed the cabin door.

But finally, they did, and then the plane taxied out and took off.

Then it landed.

I had spent more time in first class on the ground than I did in the air, but still, I was right up front, and I got to get off the plane first. I only travel with carry-on, and I expected to be on my way within minutes.

All I needed was the woman with my visa.

But she'd disappeared, and I couldn't get past the lobby and through customs without her. So I waited.

Patiently, for a while, as all the cargo hold passengers came off and walked across the tarmac and took my rightful place in line. They fumbled through their fanny packs, taking out passports and putting away the sunglasses they'd had to don for the hundred-foot walk across the tarmac. The tourists stuck with their groups, each member eyeing his or her visa with the wonder of a freshman getting his or her first yearbook. The natives traveled in smaller groups and knew the rhythm of the process better, so they squeezed into the shortest lines and made their way through first.

And still I waited, less patiently, as those people made their way through the opaque doors of the immigration booths and into baggage claim.

And I waited so long, I was not only the first passenger off the plane, but I was also the last passenger in the terminal.

It was like Miami all over again, except no one had coffee on this side.

I waited so long, I could see all the luggage come off my plane, and then I could see the plane get reloaded with the outbound haul, then taxi off and disappear, head back to Miami.

I waited as another plane landed, and a whole flight's worth of passengers made it across the tarmac and into the air-conditioned lobby and through customs.

All the while, the airport guards kept their distance.

The one guy with everyone else's visas would come by on occasion and see me and try to duck away. I'd catch him and ask what was happening, and he'd say, "Wait here. She'll be back."

And she did come back. Finally. She slipped through the door that separated the arrival and departure lounges, but where she'd been, or even who she was, I'll never know. She didn't answer when I asked. She just handed me my visa and walked away like there was nothing to it.

But that's just the way it goes, going to Cuba.

All the lines were empty by then, but still, a guard materialized just in time to point me in the exact direction I was already headed.

"This line," he said, pointing to the single booth that was still open. I smiled weakly and nodded my head. That line, I used.

The agent eyed my visa and my passport, his eyes darting up and down several times to make sure everything matched, like I could have made it past U.S. security only to get caught in Havana. I could hear the ratchet of his stamp hitting paper—my visa but not my passport, it turned out; I didn't get a stamp that trip—and I stepped back and took off my glasses so he could take my picture. Then he pushed a button and I could hear the buzzer that indicated the door was unlocked. I stepped through the wall and into baggage claim and was just three security stops away from fresh air.

A backpack full of camera equipment caused some concern, and I was pulled aside briefly and asked to explain.

"Why two cameras?" the woman asked, her voice firm and accusatory.

"In case I want to take a second picture," I said, using a line Steve Martin used in the movie *My Blue Heaven* when he was caught with a trunkload of stolen books.

The lame attempt at humor was lost on her. Or she just didn't care, the motion of the search being more important than the search itself.

"Okay," she said, still sounding official.

And that was it.

> <

No matter how they got there, some things never changed when Americans were in town.

One day, in a souvenir market on *Calle 23*, five or six blocks up the hill from the *Malecon* and the Hotel Nacional, I watched an alpha guy in his early 20s haggle with a vendor over a painting. He was putting on a show for the lapdog friend he had in tow.

The Cuban had already lowered his price on a painting from $20 to $15 to $12 to $11. The American kept saying "10" and looking at his friend and smirking.

The American, the picture of everything wrong with college fraternity culture, if you're inclined to think poorly of entitled assholes who insist on getting their way just for the sport of it, wouldn't budge from 10. He was the guy with the khakis and the wrinkled oxford cloth shirt and the backwards baseball cap and the sunglasses hanging from the foam thing around the back of his neck. He was the kind of guy smart salesmen would hand off to the trainees.

"It's only one dollar," the vendor said, showing a strain of incredulity not often seen in the usually friendly negotiations with tourists that happen in those markets.

It's a game, and when both sides play by the rules, it's kind of fun. They start a little high, you start a little low, and you meet in the middle, and everyone goes away happy. Because it's all so cheap in the first place—the goods and the prices—and the final negotiation, it's just a dollar to you but so much more to them.

Except with this guy. He had the persistence of one of those people who will bust their ass all day long looking for the shortcut but who won't do any real work, ever, because that's what you have people for.

"Yeah, it's just a dollar," the American said, flashing his asshole smirk to his buddy, who looked increasingly uncomfortable yet somehow resigned to his fate of forever more being the schmuck left to apologize and clean up the mess.

"You won't pay the one dollar more?" the vendor said.

He sounded genuinely puzzled, stymied by a breed of man with whom he'd seldom dealt.

"Ten," the asshole said, his grin getting wider as he shot a look at his friend.

The vendor grabbed the 10 and pushed the painting in the asshole's hands and walked away. The guy wanted to gloat, but the vendor wasn't sticking around for it.

The lapdog friend actually had a larger wad of cash in his hand and wanted to shop and was much less likely to haggle, much less likely to be a jerk about it, and he was left searching for someone to take his money, full price, for the cheap painting he wanted to take back to his mother, or whoever it would be waiting for him, maybe a sister or someone like that. But he didn't have time, because his asshole friend was pulling him away to witness the next great conquest by American superiority.

A few days later, I saw a gaggle of middle-aged versions of the asshole in the airport lounge on their way out of town.

They all had clear, sealed bags of cigars and rum from the duty-free store, and they were wearing out an airport worker about what it meant to have something in a sealed bag from the duty-free store.

"So we have to leave this sealed?" one was asking, holding a bag on which were printed the words *Don't break the seal.*

"They won't take it from us? We can get this back in?"

"What if it breaks?"

"Can I open it here?"

"Can I put it in my bag?"

The Cuban guy patiently answered their questions as a kindergarten teacher would address students who wanted to eat their paste.

It's like they'd never traveled before, had never heard of a duty-free store, couldn't trust a system to work. Dodging the tax wasn't enough

It's amazing, seeing people like that. They can figure out how to get themselves to someplace like Cuba, which wasn't so easy even six months after Obama's great promise, yet they can't figure out how to play it cool with their loot. Those were the guys who'd get busted at customs not because someone found their stash, but because they couldn't help themselves from talking about it among themselves while the agents stood there.

Then it got worse.

They settled into seats near me and started talking about

their Statement, with the capital "S" because it was so important. Because guys who can't figure out the duty-free store have standing somewhere that'll give their Statement, with the capital "S," merit and weight and whatever else statements are supposed to have to make them worthwhile.

It reminded me of the scene in *The Big Lebowski* when The Dude was lying in bed with Maude and trying to justify the importance of his seemingly pointless life. He was, he said, "one of the authors of the Port Huron Statement. The original Port Huron Statement. Not the compromised second draft. And then I, uh . . . Ever hear of the Seattle Seven?"

His struggle for relevance was funny because the whole movie was funny. The Dude, who struggled most days to get out of his bathrobe and pay his rent, had made a Statement.

In the departure lounge of Jose Marti International Airport in Havana, it was much more pathetic than funny. Though, fortunately, the guys were dressed in normal clothes, not pajama pants and ratty robes.

"As soon as we get home, we need to work out what our political statement is going to be," the top dog was telling the other top dogs, none of whom seemed to be listening so much as waiting their turns to make their own pronouncements.

And then the guy paused, just long enough to get the attention of the other guys but not long enough to allow them room on his platform, and he finished it off with the *coup de grace*, the words that cemented his place among the big thinkers in contemporary society.

"Or," he said, stretching out the word and holding it tight for a moment, making sure the others were watching, "or what our *lack* of a Statement is going to be."

Because a half a dozen guys who couldn't figure out how to hold a bag of rum, or how to avoid the cattle call of flying commercial out of an airport that doesn't even offer Wi-Fi, they have a Statement anyone wants to hear?

I grabbed my bag and went to sit somewhere else.

><

In between unpleasant encounters with my fellow countrymen, Havana was Havana as I've come to know it. A little of the same every time, but always a little something new, because I like walking around the next block, too, especially once I know what's down the one.

Mostly walking in Havana is an exercise in being ignored: the averted glances, the heads down, or over, or turned just slightly enough askew to avoid your eyes, because it's still Cuba, after all, and 50 years of watching your step around strangers doesn't go away just like that.

It does make it easy to get around, though, if you don't mind being left alone and ignored and treated like you're invisible.

There's always a little hustle somewhere, someone leading you around the corner to see something no tourist ever takes the time to see. And around those corners, there's usually something pretty cool. And at some point, there's the hustle.

The ones I've seen have been so slow-moving, telegraphed so clearly, they haven't been too hard to dodge. It all comes down to money, and how much it costs for something, usually food, usually for babies, usually being asked by people who don't look or act like they actually have those babies.

I got mine walking down the *Malecon*, minding my own business, looking for sculptures that Diaz, the priest from Bolondron, told me were part of a public art display that had been running for a couple of months.

I made it several miles without seeing a piece of art, from where *Paseo* runs past the Cohiba hotel and ends at the *Malecon*, east past the Hotel Nacional and around the corner to where I was almost in front of the memorial to Antonio Maceo, near where the towering state hospital commands attention.

I'd just spotted the first piece of art when I was approached by Jorge and Tania, both pushing 60, both so friendly and gregarious, I knew they'd work their way up to asking me for something I couldn't or wouldn't want to provide. It would take a while, because that's how it works in Cuba, but the hustle would come full circle.

We quickly worked through the usual "where you from" segment, and Jorge used the words "the U.S." as his entry to an invitation to visit what he said was the home of the original Buena Vista Social Club.

Americans who know of the Buena Vista Social Club usually

know of it as a folklore recording of Cuban music done by the Cuban bandleader Juan de Marcos Gonzalez and the American Ry Cooder, who has made a career of finding mainstream acceptance for music people will buy but not actually listen to, because it's different from American pop music. He did it with an Indian sitar player, too, and some Celtic people playing whatever it is they play, proving anything was possible.

The album featured traditional Cuban songs once popularized, or at least played regularly, by a Bautista-era group of musicians. Joining the outfit was by invitation only, and the guys called themselves the Buena Vista Social Club. The club was more of an idea than a place.

When Cooder went, he focused on recording music played by guys who'd been part of the original club, or who could claim some association to it. It was an excellent album, critically acclaimed and mostly loved, kind of like a foreign film that gets hot for a minute and has everyone reading subtitles while they're eating their popcorn. Some claim it compromised authentic Cuban music by allowing Cooder in, but people will complain about anything.

Since the album came out in 1997, followed by a documentary of the same name two years later, the whole concept has become a piece of kitsch, part of the contemporary Cuban experience of pestering the shit out of tourists with stuff that's supposed to represent the Real Cuba. After a while, it looks like Real Cuba has been filtered through a *Godfather* movie, but that's what most people know, so I guess it's all right for the occasional traveler. The Buena Vista Social Club has been hoisted on me every time I've been to Cuba, except the once when I went fishing, and that was only because the album wasn't out yet.

Every hotel seems to have a Buena Vista Social Club connection, and you can't go two blocks in a tourist area like Old Havana without someone trying to pull you off to some seedy, rundown nightclub they claim is the original home of the music. Because maybe the irony was intentional, the "Good View Social Club" playing in a dump that didn't even have windows?

Even in the big cemetery in Havana, I was treated to the Buena Vista Social Club experience. A guard walked me over to the grave of Ibrahim Ferrer, a singer who had been part of Cooder's album.

But at least that was really a grave; I could see Ferrer's picture on the tombstone, and the slab on top was still snug and secure, unlike many of the others nearby, and presumably, he was still in there.

I wasn't sure of the provenance of the place Jorge was leading me, but I was fairly certain it wouldn't be *the place* as soon as he started dancing and singing the song "Guantanamera," which is supposedly loved by many but that strikes me as the Cuban version of the insidious "Yummy Yummy Yummy (I've Got Love in My Tummy)": pop music played to grave effect on those subjected to it repeatedly, a little more horrible with every spin. If I ever commit a crime in Cuba, it'll be traced back to someone trying to sing me that song.

But before we got there, he and Tania earned their hustle by taking me on a short tour of places I would not have seen if I'd just kept walking on my own along the *Malecon*. It was a hustle with a tour, a nice twist to the usual tourist experience.

The first was the *Callejon de hamel* outdoor art gallery. It stretched the length of a block not far from the University of Havana. It was fronted with a roughly made stone wall that reached to an arch in the middle. There were several openings and what appeared to be a ticket counter just inside the door farthest to the left—you get used to paying entrance fees in Cuba—but it didn't cost anything to walk in and look around.

Nearly every inch of the area was covered in folk art. The buildings on both sides were covered in murals, and there were sculptures and other multidimensional pieces, including a wall in which were set four old steel bathtubs, each displaying a different scene.

There were at least half a dozen other bathtubs, the deep recesses proving perfect as both frame for art and, when cut in half, as makeshift benches.

Atop one building were black and white water tanks, supposedly showing the unity of the races in Cuba. A white tank with a black top was labeled *agua negra* and a black tank with a white top *aqua blanca*. It seemed a touch literal, sitting on a wall covered with an abstract painting, but formal pronouncements of unity usually seem forced in some way.

Stretching more than a floor high, a building over from the

tanks was a painting of a clock face, with the space where the 9 should have been covered with an actual grandfather clock mounted to the wall.

Tucked into another building was a small art gallery with paintings depicting scenes from *santeria*, the Afro-Cuban religion. A round, bearded man stepped in and said it was his workshop, then he reached into a drawer and pulled out a cigar. There was no evidence that work had ever been done in the room—it was oddly clean for an art studio and almost too small to even view, much less create, the paintings—but he didn't stick around long enough to field inquiries. Maybe he knew Jorge and Tania and knew that anyone dumb enough to be tagging along behind them wasn't going to buy his art.

The area also had the requisite bust of Jose Marti, the bleached white head of the 19th century revolutionary set atop a small perch and tucked into a yard behind an iron gate next to the wall of bathtubs.

Jorge and Tania both said something about disabled children and pointed off in the distance, to some building I couldn't see, and the next thing I knew, I was holding two compact discs that looked about as legitimate as those movies you can buy in Chinatown in New York. They were packaged in wrappers that looked like they'd come off a color printer the day it stopped working, all streaked and faded. I was told to pay 20 dollars for the pair, and I could keep them. I did.

After leaving, we stopped briefly at a small corner market, where Tania told a woman to hold up her ration book, which looked like the kind of book paperboys used to use in the U.S. when they still went door to door collecting for their subscriptions.

The woman held up the book without turning to face me, keeping her focus on getting her share of eggs and milk.

Around another corner, we climbed a few steps and walked into an open-air butcher shop. The shops are common in some countries, and at least in Cuba they're inside—in Haiti, I more often saw a carcass hanging from a tree and the butcher hacking off pieces on demand—but it's still an unpleasant sight for an American used to buying packaged meat from a chilled case in a grocery store. I don't eat much meat when I travel.

The butcher looked up and smiled when we came in, and he

didn't object to my camera, so I took a few pictures of him slicing pieces of meat. He was wearing green hospital scrubs.

In a small warehouse next door were fruits and vegetables, discolored and disfigured enough to bring a smile to the faces of those people back home who like paying a premium for organic foods. It looked like that corner of a natural foods market where you always see the fruit flies being shooed away by the women who don't shave. Find yourself there and you know how unpleasant life can be.

The stacks offered the usual: carrots, avocados, bananas, plantains, lemons and limes, grouped together there as in the U.S, as if one of a different color, and a wide assortment of tropical fruits. Plus strands and strands of garlic. So much garlic, you start looking for the Italians. But you never find them, and you rarely see, or smell, any indication that the garlic is used.

Outside that building, on the right was a small stand selling scraggly little chickens. It was like one big cage, with little cages hanging in it.

Jorge said they were destined for use in rituals, though there was no way to know if that was true. It seemed a touch pedestrian, having to buy your sacrificial chickens at market, but who knows? I've never had to search for a such a thing in a busy city.

From there, we passed a small courtyard and rounded a corner and Jorge and Tania both lit up. The hustle was about to kick into high gear.

On one side of the street was a small, closed building they said was the Che Guevara house and museum. We stood across the street and looked at the modest building. I had my doubts.

I've seen Che's house on the other side of the harbor. It's the one with "Che" in large letters on the wall, just across the street from the towering statue of Jesus.

I've seen the Che Guevara memorial mausoleum in Santa Clara. It's so large you have to climb to the top to see the details. And it's so important there's an armed guard keeping watch. On one of my other visits there, I lost sight of my son for a little bit. At times like that, it's good to have an authority figure standing by.

This place they were showing me? It seemed well-hidden for a memorial to one of the country's great heroes. But it was locked up, and they didn't give me time to walk up close and examine it. When I stepped into the street to head over, they pushed me in the other direction, toward a bar that looked dumpy and underwhelming from the street, even less likely a legitimate destination than the museum.

It looked less promising once we went inside.

There was a small foyer with several men lingering. They didn't look guilty, or occupied, or really anything more than awake. Barely. They were just there, sitting in their chairs, waiting for something to happen. Or not. It was a Cuban moment.

The foyer led into a long, rectangular room, which had several tables. On the walls hung a handful of framed snapshots, mostly crappy pictures of generic scenes, a hotel, a beach, that kind of stuff. A little further down the wall, over the tables closest to the bars, were portraits of musicians, or guys who were supposed to be musicians.

Jorge flashed a big, silly grin as he showed me the photos of long-ago men with their horns. Proof, I suppose, that the dive was the home of the Buena Vista Social Club.

"Come, sit, relax," he said, leading to a table in the dark alcove opposite the backlit bar. It was the most private spot in the whole place.

He and Tania conspired for a moment, he sitting opposite me at the table, she hovering over him. Then she turned and walked out.

Jorge said something to the bartender, who had her back to us, and she pulled out three tall, skinny glasses with the Havana Club logo painted on the side and started mixing drinks.

He said something about mojitos, but the woman poured cola into the classes, so I'm not quite sure what she was making. She grabbed for a bottle of rum, but I told Jorge to wave her off. I quit drinking years ago, and that dump, at that time of day, with those two, wasn't when and where I was going to start again. Maybe *because* of them, I'd start again, later, by myself, but not *with* them, then.

Tania came back and handed me a couple of one-peso coins with Che's face and showed me a red Cuban three-peso note, also with his face.

She pulled out a pen and wrote a message across the bill:

Para un amigo de Estados Unidos de unos amigos Cubano

salud y suerto para usted y su familia. "For a friend from the United States: Cuban friends' health and their luck to you and your family."

Then she signed it and handed it to me. "It's for you," she said, smiling. "A gift."

In Cuba, strangers often give you gifts. I've been handed cigars and rum and silhouettes, a favorite trick in Old Havana, where artists quickly draw a black outline on a white piece of paper and shove it in your hand. One guy, once, offered me a woman—"You want a cheeka? Fucky fucky?," he'd said as he peddled me down an alley in his bicycle taxi—though he didn't have her with him.

The gifts are never free.

A few dollars here, a whole lot more there. I'm not sure what the woman would have cost; I was going to spend the rest of that morning with a priest, and I didn't feel good about beginning the day paying for a fuck.

Jorge and Tania started in with the hustle—they focused on the price of milk for babies—and it quickly became convoluted. They wouldn't just come out and ask for whatever it was they wanted, which would have been easy and acceptable. They had a scheme, a seemingly practiced though still awkward routine.

They wanted to take me to a woman who sold cigars. They would earn commission on whatever I bought.

I asked about their babies, but neither offered a clear answer. I went along anyway, just to get back out into the sunshine. The bar had been kind of dreary.

But I wasn't interested in buying a bunch of cigars that I'd have to carry around the rest of the day. Cigars are easy to get in Cuba. Because you're in Cuba, and every person you meet either sells cigars or knows someone who does. Forget while you're there, there's a shop in the airport—duty-free, if you can figure out that mystery—where you can buy all you want.

But I was sitting in a dark bar at 10 o'clock in the morning, not quite sure where I was, and the whole thing was mildly entertaining, and a little amusing and not particularly threatening, so I kept listening. It was like getting hit up for change by your dim-witted uncle and his well-meaning but even more dim-witted girlfriend. You could see them working it through, convinced how clever they were.

Jorge ordered another round of drinks and he and Tania exchanged looks that said "job well done."

Not surprisingly, I got stuck with the check and had to pay $30 for the six drinks, four of which had just been watered down cola over ice. It was less than I had expected.

Counting the compact discs, I was out $50 so far, and we hadn't even met the cigar woman yet.

The whole way over, which turned out to be four blocks, Jorge and Tania kept droning on about the importance of their commission.

It would have been easier if they'd just told me what they were after, but I appreciated the show of effort. When I'd been to Haiti, which I had visited six times, hustling Americans was common, too, but there, everyone always wanted laptops and they didn't play games like pretending they liked you. They just came right out and asked. No friendly "where you from" and no tour of kitschy neighborhoods. Just "Do you have a laptop? I need a laptop. You give me a laptop." Incredibly, I've actually known people who've taken laptops to Haiti for that purpose.

As we stepped in front of the right house, I looked down the street and got my bearings and figured out how to get loose and make my escape, if I needed to, so I stepped in with a sense of ease.

The front room was brightly lit, and the rest of the house was hidden behind curtains. To get in, we had to step over the doorway. It was like moving around on a ship, ducking my head and stepping up at the same time.

We stayed in the front, and I was offered a seat at a small table facing a wall. I was presented with four boxes of cigars and told about quality and how I could apply the tax stamp myself—loose ones came with each box, she said, producing an envelope full of the thin strips—but the one question no one wanted to answer was how much anything cost.

It was like buying a car, where you ask the salesman how much it costs and he flashes his sleazy car salesman smile and asks how much you can spend.

I asked again, and Jorge pulled a whole stack of cigars out of a box by the tissue paper liner and presented the bundle to me for inspection. "Very good cigars," he said.

"I wouldn't know," I said. "I don't smoke."

"Very good," he said, still smiling, still clutching the bundle, still not ready to give in or give up. He made a show of smelling the cigars, bringing the bundle to his face and smiling again, like he was sucking in the aroma of a fine meal. Because that meant something, the knowing nose of a guy who couldn't even buy food for the babies?

I asked again about the price. He balked again.

"Much cheaper here," he said.

"Cheaper than what?" I asked.

"Yes, much cheaper!" he said.

I kept insisting on knowing an exact price, and the woman finally relented and told me the price was $180.

I laughed and pushed myself back from the table and stood up and said thanks. She quickly pushed forward a different box, and then another.

Four boxes later, with the price down to $100, I finally saw enough daylight between Jorge and the door to step through.

I stepped into the street and headed toward a crowd of people on the corner. They gave chase and kept talking about their commission. I finally stopped in the street and turned around to face them.

"Commission for what?" I asked. Calmly, I'll add. I was getting irritated, but I knew the end was near. "We went for a walk."

I knew I was going to pay them something. I love tipping, everywhere I go, especially for good service. And their little tour had been fun, but the growing presumption of them getting a big payday was a little off-putting. I hate to argue semantics when I don't speak the local language, but their word choice irked me, too. Commission? Were they on the clock? Had I assumed their government's responsibility for social welfare?

"The milk for the baby, it's so expensive," Tania said. She tried flashing me sad eyes, but she couldn't quite pull it off. She looked like someone trying to look sad, which is sad in a different way.

Jorge gently but firmly guided me through a door into another small market—behind every door in Cuba, there seems, is another place to spend your money—and Tania followed. She asked the clerk to get a box of milk.

When she stepped into the back, Jorge and Tania both told

that it would cost $26 for the milk.

The clerk came back holding a small cardboard box, in which were several bags of powdered baby formula. She looked at me, then back in the box, then back at me one more time.

Jorge and Tania repeated the words "twenty-six dollars," and I could see them making eye contact with the clerk.

The clerk responded to the cue. She grabbed her calculator—they're in ready supply throughout the country, the primary means of communicating with tourists—and turned it toward me. To prove the cost of the formula, she held out her calculator so I could see the number she had just punched in, right there in front of me. "$26.50," it read. As if the presence of those digits proved anything?

I laughed again and stepped back into the street. Jorge and Tania were on my heels again. They were growing agitated at their inability to close their deal.

I stopped and turned to face them, and they were right there, inches from me. "How much did you think you were going to hustle me for?" I asked.

"Our commission was $40 each," Tania said. She didn't flinch at the word hustle; she just ignored it.

I fumbled through my pocket and tried to pry loose two bills from the outside of the small roll I had. I had a few 20s and some smaller bills.

I pulled out two 20s and I gave them each one. I pressed it into their hands, the way Cubans do when they're giving you something. It makes it harder to give back, once it's crumpled into your hand.

They both opened their hands and looked back at me in disgust.

"No, 40 each, this isn't enough," Tania said, looking at me as if I were trying to cheat her. Jorge's eyes narrowed to a slit, the mean look of a con man about to lose his temper.

"That's it," I said. I turned my back on them again and walked away.

I don't know if they followed. I worked my way into and out of a crowd at a bus stop, then rounded the corner and stepped into the open doors of a church I'd never noticed before, *La Immaculata*.

When I stepped back out, I looked left, then right, all guilty-movie-character-like, hoping Jorge and Tania weren't there.

Then I noticed I was about a block from where we'd started a few hours before, so I could easily resume my little trip down the Malecon in search of the public art that was supposed to be on display. Ninety bucks lighter, but not so bad, all things considered.

> <

Across the street from the church was *Antonio Maceo Parque*, a fittingly grand memorial to "the bronze titan." Second-in-command of Cuba's revolutionary forces, Maceo was a key player in the late 19th century fight for independence from the Spanish and was reputed to be an inspiration to Jose Marti.

The Cubans matched Americans, particularly those from the South, in the monuments they built for war heroes, and Maceo's was among the most ornate.

The general is perched on a horse, the green patina of the bronze visible from high atop a marble base. Just below him are carvings and inscriptions and classical touches like a draped garland. Closer to the ground, and easily reached by climbing on the monument—no pesky guards to give chase there—are figures cast in bronze, including the requisite bare-breasted women in classical poses. If you're going to ride off into eternity, you couldn't have better company.

If you climb the steps and cross over to the pedestals on the edge, you can come eye-to-eye with the women. Standing next to them, you see that several have a detail not noticeable from below: their lips are painted red. Against the weathered green of the bronze, the faint red provides a pleasing contrast, plus a touch of whimsy in a country that's much more whimsical than you might imagine, considering the humorless, left-leaning, political dogma that dominates its government. Cubans like a good joke.

The park is also the site of the only underpass on the entire five-mile length of the *Malecon*. Rather than risking the danger of challenging traffic as you run across—the overpass for the underpass creating one of the few obstructed views along the whole thing—you can duck under and come out the other side.

And that's where I began to find the sculptures I'd gone in

search of in the first place.

Several workers were using a crane to remove a piece of sculpture on the ocean side of the underpass, but it was the only evidence I saw that day that the art was temporary.

As I walked between there and the entrance to the harbor, I saw a dozen or more pieces. Most were on the *Malecon*, but there were also several on the sidewalk on the far side of the street.

There were three wooden stands, each with a seat perched about eight feet high, each beckoning any who dared to climb the rungs.

"Those are so you can kneel and pray, or just look out over the water," Diaz told me the day before. "They're supposed to show the Cubans' connection with the water."

I climbed the first two, sat, watched the ocean and looked back over the traffic and the people walking by below. The view wasn't much different from down there, but the seats did offer a peaceful respite, far enough removed to give a sense of solitude. I tried to close my eyes and really take in the moment, feel it as much as I was seeing it, but the platforms were kind of narrow, and I'm not so good with heights or balance, so that didn't last long. But I did sit and look.

Staring north across the Atlantic from Havana, you can't help but think of America. The geography was all wrong in my mind, but that didn't matter much at that moment. It wasn't like I was going to dive in and swim away. Mostly, I sat there and stared off into the horizon, imagining images of South Beach, in Miami, where I'd been a few days before. There, I'd stared out to sea, too, watching cargo ships pass by in the distance. But mostly I'd stared at the shore and enjoyed the sights on the sand.

In both places, my idea of the map was off. Straight out from South Beach, I'd have headed east and reached South Bimini or the Bahamas, not Cuba. And from Havana, due north, I'd have stretched halfway up the Florida peninsula before landing in Sarasota. Miami was far off to the northeast.

The striking thing about the view was how few boats there were.

The *Malecon* is a five-mile-long seawall separating a city of two million people from the Atlantic Ocean, a welcome mat the likes of which might not exist anywhere else in the world, and there isn't a single boat slip the entire length, not a foot of dock jutting into the water.

It's like opportunity lost, recreation and commerce sacrificed for the sake of solidarity. No one gets in, no one gets out.

You see an occasional oceangoing vessel approach the harbor, tankers heading to the refinery or cargo ships to one of the warehouses that line the banks of the port, but they bring no joy.

I once saw a cruise ship, looming huge and grossly out of place in the narrow inlet, promising a new level of horror to Old Havana, but it was an exception.

There are occasional fishing boats, too, but they bring to mind Hemingway's *The Old Man and the Sea.* They're neither modern nor designed for commercial fishing. I've never seen more than two or three out at a time. There are usually a dozen or more others anchored in the channel, small and dilapidated, the boat version of the little underpowered cars Cubans drive. Most have outboard motors but look sized more for oars. I don't think I've seen one yet that could hold more than two or three men, and they would have to sit on dirty, grimy benches. They're small, open boats that look like they haven't seen a fresh coat of paint in decades. They wouldn't survive an afternoon thunderstorm at sea.

Near where the short *Rio Almandares* flows into the Atlantic, at the western end of the *Malecon*, there are a few larger boats, but even those are modest. They look like charter fishing boats from the U.S., built for sport more than anything.

There are no harbor cruises, no sightseeing trips, no water taxis jetting from one end to the other. There are ferries, but they're for locals, taking workers home to the little towns of Regla and Casablanca on the decidedly tourist-unfriendly side of the harbor. From Old Havana, I've yet to find a way on foot across the channel to the Morro Castle. The coastline in Havana is to be enjoyed from the sidewalk looking out, not from a boat looking in.

Which made the sight of a snorkeler so odd.

I was sitting atop the first of the three stands, staring absently out to sea, when a splash caught my attention.

I focused on the spot where I thought the sound had come

from, and after a minute or two, I saw a pair of flippers surface, then a snorkel and finally a head.

It slipped under again, then reappeared a little ways down.

I'd never seen a snorkeler in Havana, though I'd see half a dozen more before the week was out. Maybe the hope of the end of the embargo had yielded more optimism than I suspected.

The first one seemed to be on a leisurely swim. He was about a hundred feet out and kept a relatively steady distance between himself and the seawall. Every few minutes his head would surface, then he'd disappear again.

I climbed down and kept walking.

I went up the second platform, which had more of a kneeling platform than a seat, and I just peered over the top for a minute before climbing back down. I passed on climbing the third tower. It was a straight ascent, and I wasn't certain the tiny platform could hold my full-size frame, so I stayed on the ground.

I also saw a huge cauldron studded with forks, a piece of art whose message I missed; a blue hand with the thumb up, made out of what looked like aluminum gutter pipes from a house; and a shattered telephone pole spread over the walkway, which reminded me of the East Coast of the U.S. after a hurricane.

Across the street, next to a building, was an ice skating rink. Diaz said it had actual ice, but when I get there, the display was over and the ice was gone. But the subsurface was still in place, as were the walls surrounding it. On the far side, backed up against the building, was a wall of cubby holes full of skates.

Back on the *Malecon*, there was a huge, melting birthday cake. It was probably eight feet high and just as wide and included nearly any color you could imagine. The icing looked so real, glistening in the sun, the grease of the butter ringing the edges on a hot morning, it looked edible.

The most fun of the installations was a beach. At a point where the seawall juts out and forms a rectangle, a little patio was turned into a beach resort. Sand sloped up to the top of the wall, and there were reclining lounge chairs, thatched umbrellas over small tables and palm trees.

Laying on one of the chairs, gazing up town toward the Hotel Nacional, the sight of the palm trees seemed so natural. I took a picture of the scene, and when I look at it, safely back home in the U.S., nothing looks out of place. But a day after I sat on one of the chairs, I passed again and it was all gone.

The midday sun did not deter the fishermen who dotted the wall and the rocks below. No one was catching anything, the middle of the day being the worst time to try to catch fish, but they kept at it.

I stopped to take a picture of one man who was walking along the rocks below the wall, taking advantage of low tide on a calm day. He looked back and waved, then returned his attention to the fish he wasn't catching.

A one-legged man sitting on the wall nearby beckoned me. He was holding a handful of long white paper cones, in which were packed peanuts. He had seen me take the picture of the fisherman and tried to use that as leverage for a sale.

"He's my friend, the fisherman," he said before asking where I was from.

He turned and yelled something at the fisherman, who looked back up at us and waved again. He may have been slightly perplexed, but it was hard to tell for sure from the distance. Either way, he gave up fast and went back to fishing.

The one-legged man had his hook in, though, and he was ready to pull. "Please, one dollar, buy my peanuts," he said, holding out a handful of the paper cones. Only the way he pronounced *peanuts,* the word sounded like *penis.*

I snickered out loud. I may have been 47 that day, but that didn't mean I ever really grew up. A one-legged man offers to sell you his penis, you have to laugh. He gave me a blank stare, not certain what to make of my reaction.

"What do you want me to buy?" I asked.

"Peanuts!" he said, thrusting his hand forward. Only, of course, as he thrust the cone toward me, I thought he was saying, "Penis!" I knew he wasn't, but that's how it sounded, and I just couldn't keep a straight face. I wasn't about to buy a penis, no matter how it was wrapped.

I gave him a dollar anyway and tried to walk away. He insisted I take one of the cones.

"I'm not hungry," I said, offering the universal gesture of rubbing my stomach and shaking my head as I backed up. But he kept at it, and I finally accepted the cone and thanked him and walked away.

I couldn't make myself eat it. I stuck it in my pocket and kept it there until I was way down at the end near the warehouses, far away from the one-legged man. I pulled the cone out of my pocket and snickered again, then I dropped it in a trash can.

The man was the first of five one-legged men I'd see that day. What happened to all those legs, I didn't know. But when one of the men asked me to buy him a new pair of shoes, my first thought was that he should team up with one of the others and he'd get a better deal. But I'm not mean, really, so I kept the thought to myself. But I also kept my money, so maybe I am a *little* mean.

><

I stopped at the mouth of the channel and descended the stairs to the rocks below the seawall to see what it looked like from below.

On previous trips, that area had been crowded with the kind of people who seek recreation on rocky public beaches in areas frequented by tourists—the same in Cuba as in the U.S.; mostly the young, often loud and boisterous, always intimidating in presence if not substance—and I hadn't thought about joining the crowd, but this time, there were few people around. I stepped carefully and stayed close to the wall on the way down to avoid the gaping holes where the steps had crumbled into the water, leaving deep gaps, and I stepped on the rocks.

I hopped from one to another, but the view wasn't much, the rocks were dotted with dog shit and the whole place smelled like piss, so I went back up and walked around the end and along the channel in toward the old part of town.

In the channel, the water had the sheen of petroleum, the shiny rainbow surface, and there was more evidence along the wall where the stains marked the changing tides. It was stained a deep black. In one corner, the trash that had accumulated was also stained black by a coat of oil. It looked like a piece of art, random objects floating together and all painted the same color. There was a flip-flop, the torso from a baby doll, plastic bottles in several sizes and a number of items of indiscriminate origin. The constant was the oil. It could have been a piece left from the art show, a floating sculpture, but it looked too natural, too much like the evidence of environmental neglect, to be contrived. As art, it would have been too exaggerated to be believable.

I passed a line of taxis and almost fell for the ease of riding back home in whatever old American tank I could find, but I decided to keep walking instead and crossed into the square by the San Francisco cathedral, across the street from the old customs house.

I'd been outside the cathedral many times before but I'd never gone in, and I was pleasantly surprised to see the doors open. I paid two dollars to enter, then I spent more than an hour wandering around.

The first floor had what had been the sanctuary, and was currently a music mall with a grand piano on the altar, and a large courtyard, lined on one side by large wooden closets and on the opposite side by alcoves, which had been converted into miniature museums, each showing a different part of the story of the cathedral. The building dated to the 16th century, and there was a lot of story to tell.

On the second floor, looking into the courtyard, was a photo exhibit. It seemed random, mostly landscapes and environmental pictures from around the world. If there was a theme, it wasn't obvious. The photos were nice but not extraordinary. They showed place but didn't really say anything.

Up another set of stairs, there was the balcony looking out over the sanctuary. It had two large glass cases, in which were religious items of some sort, medals and cloaks and things that you know had been bestowed with great ceremony once upon a time. They'd come to rest in a pass-through, forgotten relics from a long-ago time.

And from there, up a couple of more steps, you could step onto the roof. As is the case in so much of the world that's not in the United States, personal safety is a matter of personal interest, not governmental concern, and there were no barriers on top of the cathedral.

From the ledge, easily accessible because you could just walk right up to it, there was a perfect view of the square below. A woman was making money by having her pigeons eat their seeds from the mouths of a tourist boy, a gaggle of whose friends were laughing hysterically at him for being game for the experiment. Other women in garish period attire walked by, their lips painted a bright red. They'd sidle up to tourists and plant wet kisses on their cheek, leaving perfectly shaped marks, then pose for pictures for a dollar apiece. They carried comically large cigars, so big it'd take a torch to light them.

The square also usually had sketch artists who'd do quick, crude silhouettes and push them into your hands and demand money, but I didn't see any that day.

Rising from the roof was the bell tower, appealingly open and accessible. I entered at its base and began the steep ascent up creaky wooden stairs.

At one point, I came across a pair of German tourists posing for pictures. A young woman was standing on a ledge, the upper half of her body inside a large bell, and a man was taking the picture. He turned and offered a sheepish grin, as if to say, "Why not?" Indeed, I thought, why not? I, too, was about to step onto a ledge.

I passed them and went up a level and stepped into one of the large openings, seeing what was to be seen while wedging myself between the bell and the old stone wall. I was pretty sure they didn't still ring the bells.

What was to be seen was a long fall onto a cobblestone road. I stepped back and kept climbing stairs, going as high as I could.

On the final landing that was open, a level below the top, a man sat in a chair and nodded at something.

I stepped through the opening on one side and onto a small ledge and enjoyed, as best I could, another, even higher view of the square. The people looked like the pigeons from that height, and I was ready for a quick retreat when I noticed the man had joined me, outside the opening and on the little slab platform.

He pointed to my camera and then me and made the universal hand gesture for wanting to take my picture. I posed this way and that, at his insistence, and left with three pictures of myself on my camera. I didn't look good, but that was maybe more me than the photographer.

I paid him a dollar.

The view also offered a good perspective on Old Havana. The last time I'd been there, I'd gotten lost wandering through the narrow streets, every way looking like the way before it. But from the top of the tower, it all spread out in an orderly manner and I could see where I wanted to go and map a route there from above. I could also see the route I'd tried months before and how it ended a few blocks short of where I'd been trying to go and how I should have gone right or left and picked it back up. I was with a group then and the others had gotten frustrated, and we floundered our way out. Wandering aimlessly is much easier when you're by yourself.

Back on the street, I made a left when I exited the cathedral, then I took the first right and walked straight until I found the Capitol. Without the burden of a dozen agitated people in tow, I succeeded with ease.

I passed a number of souvenir shops, tucked into the smallest of places, but it was a Tuesday and no one had much enthusiasm for the trade that day. A few people tried calling me over, but no one tried too hard and most didn't budge from their chairs.

"Look, we have what you need," one man said from inside his shop. With a stilted English, he sounded like he was reading from a card in a language he didn't understand.

"We have souvenirs, you like," a woman said. Her words were almost a plea, but they dropped off at the end and disappeared completely as I walked by.

Others just stared but couldn't find the energy for words.

The more interesting sights were the woodworking shops, several of which are in Old Havana, in among the souvenir shops and restaurants and government offices. They make small pieces of furniture.

In one, I saw a display of joints mounted on a board, showing workers the proper way to join corners without having to use fasteners. There was also evidence of work done by hand, the shavings from a plane and crumpled pieces of sandpaper. It could have been the 19th century, the way it looked.

The smell of freshly worked wood is as pleasing there as it is anywhere else, and I stood in a doorway and enjoyed the moment. The workers were all sitting off in one corner, drinking coffee. They ignored me, and each other for the most part, but no one told me to leave, so I took in what I could.

At the next shop, I got to watch grown men making miniature

buildings. I'm not sure of what, or why, but they were laboring over details with nary a concern for the people looking in from the street.

The street emptied onto the *Paseo de Marti* opposite the Capitol, which is covered in scaffolding from a long-running renovation.

The street splits in two, traffic running either direction on the sides. The block past the *Parque Central* becomes the *Paseo del Prado*, with a promenade running down the middle for the final eight blocks, before it ends at the same point where the *Malecon* ends at the mouth of the harbor.

The street is my favorite place in Havana. It's a wide space, with marble benches and trees lining the sides and the middle open for pedestrians.

I've seen a block-long tango there, a public dance spectacle with hundreds of couples dancing to music from a portable radio. I've seen art fairs and artists working *en plein air*, including one man, once, deeply involved in a beautiful landscape that looked nothing like anything in sight. His eyes were in constant motion, one second on his canvas, the next scanning the city in front of him. In his hand, he clutched a brush, and with it his imagination spread across the canvas.

I've seen children on rollerblades and lovers curled up together in the deep corners of the massive benches, too, and all manner of activity in between. The last time, I sat on a bench and watched a man walk by carrying a bird in a cage. He looked so purposeful, a man on his way home after a hard day's work, only instead of a briefcase, he had a birdcage. A little further down, I saw a swarm of bees in a lamppost. The electrical access plate was missing, and thousands of them had moved in. The Cubans steered clear, but I walked right up and looked in. My wife keeps bees, and I'm comfortable around them.

It's a beautiful public space, as open and inviting as the *Malecon*, but with benches and shade. When the day comes that Starbucks opens its branches in Old Havana, this is where people will go to drink their espressos and coffees from large paper cups. (Save your scorn; I like a cup of coffee to go, and I look forward to the day when I can enjoy it on the *Prado*.)

Between the Capitol and the ocean are several hotels,

including the Sevilla, the Parque Central, the Telegrapho and the Inglaterra, among others. It's also the address for the Great Theatre of Havana, a ballet studio and a wedding hall.

There are also crumbling buildings, decrepit storefronts and evidence that people live on the upper floors of many buildings, their telltale laundry strung across the balconies.

The avenue is usually packed full of tourists, but there are enough locals to dilute the mix and make for a pleasing combination.

><

Instead of following the *Malecon* all the way back around to *Paseo*, a walk that promised to be hot and boring, I cut across at *Calle 23*. I'd never gone that way, but I knew the grid of the neighborhood and figured I could figure it out. It was pretty much up and over and back home. I counted three streets before the lettered ones started. From *Calle P* it was just 16 blocks to *Paseo*, then another three over and six down. Walking 28 more blocks didn't seem so bad as long as I didn't count them off.

Between "*M*" and "*N*," tucked into the middle of the block, I found a large street fair full of vendors selling souvenirs. It was the same merchandise that was so prevalent in Old Havana, but here, the clientele was more heavily local, though it certainly drew a strong crowd from the Habana Libre hotel nearby. I couldn't imagine why Cubans would want so much kitsch, particularly the gaudy leather goods stamped with town names and liquor brands and the mass-produced paintings of American cars in front of Cuban buildings, cars that looked better on canvas than they had in person in decades. But the market was busy and most vendors seemed to be doing brisk business. The jewelry sellers were particularly popular.

I made a quick walk through, but I was tired and in no mood for the hassle, so I kept going uphill.

In the next block was the 25-story Habana Libre, one of the larger hotels in Cuba. It opened in 1958 as a Hilton, but less than a year later, Castro took command of the island, and by 1960, his nascent Communist government nationalized all hotels. Since the late 1990s, it has been run by the Spanish company Sol Melia, which manages several other hotels in Cuba.

Another block up, I came upon the *Parque Coppelia*. I'd been there before, but on the previous trip, I'd arrived by bus and had no idea where I was. That time, it was just somewhere else, yet another stop on a long sightseeing tour. Getting there on foot on my own, that was more satisfying.

Coppelia is also a state-run Cuban ice cream chain, and the flagship location in the park takes up an entire city block. Its main building claims to have a capacity of a thousand, but there's never enough room and it's common to see lines snaking down the block, both of *23* and "*L.*"

According to some sources, the shop sells more than 4,200 gallons of ice cream a day to more than 35,000 customers.

When I'd gone before, I'd had the uncomfortable Cuban experience of getting better service because I could pay in tourist currency. There are separate serving areas for tourists and locals, and the peso line for locals is slower. Those were the people waiting in the line down the block.

A little further up the street, I saw the Riveria movie theater, which was proudly advertising *Cake*, a drama starring Jennifer Aniston, whose name was splashed across the marque. She's popular in any language.

The whole street was as busy as any I'd been on anywhere in Cuba, but it was the same in one respect: no one paid much attention to me. Any attempt to make eye contact was unsuccessful, and the people coming at me kept their heads down or their eyes averted and kept moving without hesitation.

><

I finished my coverage of the *Malecon* a few days later by walking west, following its course to where it ends just short of the point where the short, narrow *Rio Almendares* empties into the Atlantic.

Along the way, I bought two cigars from a fisherman who had a story about the high cost of food—always, the food—and stopped to watch yet another snorkeler, this one more daring than any of the others I'd seen. At first I thought he was dead, a bloated body in blue shorts and a billowing striped shirt floating near the surface. But he kicked his feet after a moment and started moving faster. As he passed, I noticed that he was pulling a chicken carcass, held afloat by an empty soda bottle, from a string that was attached to his waist.

There were two fishermen on the sea wall nearby, and I thought perhaps he was trying to drum up business for them, but it was hard to say for sure. Like most fishermen I'd seen along the *Malecon*, they seemed content holding rods or lines; actually catching fish would require a whole different level of ambition and skill.

I crossed the river at *Calle 11*, then stayed as near the riverbank as I could and headed south in search of the next bridge, which I knew would cross back into the Vadedo neighborhood at *Avenida 23*.

For the first few blocks, I could see the river behind the houses that lined the street, but after a while, the road curved and I lost sight of the water. I was about to give up and turn back, thinking I'd somehow missed the bridge, when I stumbled upon the entrance to the *Parque Metropolitan de Habana.*

There were two signs by the main entrance with pictures of dinosaurs and enough tropical plants to give the place a *Jurassic Park* feel, but the hint of majesty was lost in the long riverfront park.

The grounds included a winding dry creek bed, obviously manmade and just as obviously neglected. It showed no hint of recent use.

The park had a small amphitheater, a boardwalk along the river and a cafeteria. One of the arches supporting the bridge, which separated the halves of the park, included murals on two sides. On one was a mix of graffiti-like art of distorted faces and abstract impressions. On the other were various interpretations of the Cuban flag. The two were separated by a parking lot, which was being repainted the morning I walked through. A crew of half a dozen men were applying narrow markings, presumably for motorcycles. A single car sat on the other side.

Havana is a city of parks, and the *Parque Metropolitan* is among the grandest. But early in the morning in the middle of the week, it was also the kind of creepy that large sprawling urban parks are at that time of the day. When I walked up the stairs of the amphitheater, I rustled awake a young man on the lower level. He grabbed a paper sack that held a bottle of something and slipped off without looking up. Elsewhere in the park were random people: one man alone on a bench overlooking the water; a couple of women sitting on stools around the large circular bar in the cafeteria, content to talk as the worker slowly opened shop for the day; another solo man, sitting near an empty playground, talking to himself as he sharpened his machete. Near him were trees, their rotting fruit all over the ground.

One loop was enough. When I circled back around to the dinosaur pictures, I made for the exit.

Leaving there, I climbed stone steps to the bridge, then crossed back into Vedado and followed *Avenida 23* as it wound around a few blocks.

I bought bottled water at a chicken stand just past the bridge and stopped to admire the random piece of bad art: ugly, cartoon-like frogs sculpted atop a rock. It looked like something you'd see in acrylic in a water garden in the suburbs.

I had to wait for the women in front of me to conclude a complicated, lengthy purchase. The clerk apparently couldn't make change, so the woman kept buying until her bill had been used in its entirety. She left with the small package of fried food she'd ordered first, two bottles of liquor in a color like coffee with too much cream and several packs of chewing gum. She seemed happy.

I had exact change for my two bottles, and my transaction was concluded swiftly. The clerk took my money and immediately turned her attention to the next customer.

I drank my water and walked along a few blocks, absent-mindedly heading in the direction of a song I recognized playing from behind a wall across the street. I crossed into the shade, stopped for a moment by the wall and stood under a bougainvillea to listen to Kool and the Gang:

"*There's a party goin' on right here/*
A celebration to last throughout the years/
So bring your good times and your laughter, too/
We gonna celebrate your party with you."

Celebration, and so near the cemetery. The yellow walls of the *Necropolis Cristobal Colon*, supposedly one of the grandest cemeteries in the hemisphere, were visible at the end of the street. I left Kool behind and followed the wall until I found an entrance with an open gate.

I walked past two guards, who were inspecting the trunk of a car on its way out—for reasons I'd come to understand that afternoon—and I kept going. But after a few hundred feet, one of the men caught up with me.

"My friend, you must pay five dollars to come in here," he said.

It was Cuba. I was expecting to pay.

I agreed and offered him the money, but to my surprise, he passed it up to follow protocol. "No, no, not me. You must go out the gate and around to the main entrance."

He tried measuring the distance for me by moving his finger through the air, but he couldn't quite get it. "Long way," he finally said. "All the way around. Follow the wall."

I followed the wall, not certain I'd see it through to the gate. But I kept going, and when I rounded the corner from *Calle 18* to *Zapata* and saw the gate, I kept walking.

The wall had been alternating sections of yellow stucco and iron fence, effective in establishing the boundary but hardly of much aesthetic value. The main gate made up the difference.

It was designed in the grandiose style of the 1870s, when money and materials were apparently of little concern when it came time to honor the dead. Three elaborate arches stretched hundreds of feet wide, and the structure rose several stories high in the center, which was topped with an ornate marble monument.

I paid the five dollars' admission—in exact change, as requested—and another dollar for a map and walked around for a few hours.

The cemetery was an astonishing mix of spectacular statuary, some seemingly new even after desecration and more than a century in the Caribbean sun.

A beautiful yellow chapel with a red tile dome commanded attention in the center, easily visible from the two main roads that intersected the 140-acre grounds in the shape of a cross, and from most other points, too.

The nicest of the monuments lined the road from the main gate to the chapel. Among the most noticeable was a 75-foot pillar and accompanying memorial wall for 28 firefighters who died in an explosion at a Havana hardware store in May 1890.

The white stone glistened as if new, 125 years later, and the decorative metal work had obviously been meticulously cared for through the years.

A heavy chain surrounding the main monument included large gears that represented the hands of the people in mourning, and there were also metal teardrops draped across all four sides. The monument also included a number of cast iron bats, the symbol of the Bacardi rum company, which helped pay for the monument.

A world domino champion was interred nearby, his grave topped with a stone domino showing a double three, the same piece he had clutched as he died of a heart attack during a game.

There were also presidents, priests and any number of soldiers from any number of the wars the country has fought since the cemetery opened in 1876.

But nothing in Cuba is simple or straight or easy, and that's the case, too, here, in a place holding the remains of people whose families fled when Castro took power. The evidence wasn't hard to find. In nearly every direction, there was decay and neglect of varying degrees. Of the more than 500 mausoleums and family buildings on the grounds, not all had been maintained equally.

I saw several that had been boarded up, and on some of those I could peek through the doors in places where the wood had been crudely cut to make room for a chain and lock. Atop graves in those small rooms, I saw work shoes, a wheelbarrow, hoses and other tools, the final resting places having been turned into makeshift storage sheds.

Other buildings were in worse shape, with doors and windows shattered, roofs collapsed and markers missing.

I also saw dozens of open graves, many with their vaults empty. Where the bodies went, I'll never know. Into exile, too, perhaps?

In places, the pathway was paved with pieces of headstones, letters and numbers visible below foot. There was debris everywhere, shards of marble, pieces of cast iron, carved figurines. The head of Jesus sat at the feet of Jesus on one grave. At another, small stone pineapples sat in a heap, near where they had been ripped from the tops of posts surrounding a grave.

The search of the car's trunk hours earlier made sense. You

didn't have to look hard in that place to find souvenirs; you literally tripped over them every few feet. But taking them out, it seemed, was frowned upon.

If I wanted to shoot a movie with a creepy graveyard scene, the *Colon* would offer the perfect backdrop.

> <

The cemetery was a fitting balance to the one I'd seen in Santiago, the *Cementerio Santa Ifigenia*.

There, in a cemetery that predates the *Colon* by eight years, were the bodies and the memorials for some of the country's greatest heroes. There was also the requisite Buena Vista Social Club marker, for the late singer Compay Segundo, but no one bothered to point it out when I'd been there.

In Santiago, there was an air of importance, and a level of maintenance that backed it up. In Havana, there's glamour where people are most likely to look and decay everywhere else, making it a mirror of the city in which it sits.

And in the decay is proof of the difficulty ahead if the U.S. and Cuba are to really establish any sense of normality in relations.

For decades, the Cubans have favored those who have stayed and tried their best to forget those who left. While nearly everyone I've met there has proudly spoken of people they know who now live in the U.S., I've yet to hear a Cuban say he couldn't wait for the others to come home and reclaim their old places in society, or the property they left behind.

"That's going to be an interesting issue," said Diaz, the priest from Bolondron, when I asked him what might happen if old Cubans came back.

In the U.S., there had been much grumbling about the return of property lost during the revolution. But in the 55 years since, that property—houses, office buildings, cars—hasn't sat empty and unused. Whole generations of Cubans have grown up knowing it to be theirs.

But still, whole generations of Cubans have grown up being Cubans. If the Americans come back in great numbers, the Cubans will find a way to cope. And if the exiles don't return, those who stayed will manage that, too.

ACKNOWLEDGEMENTS

THEY'RE RIGHT, THOSE people who put kind words in this space in their own books. None of this is possible alone. I get my name on the cover, but it took efforts large and small from dozens of people to make this happen.

My wife Jennifer, and my children – Caleigh, Jordan, Moses and Madison – get substantial credit for humoring me. I've traveled extensively in recent years but rarely with them, and they've allowed it in a more generous manner than I would have imagined possible. They've listened to my stories, looked at my pictures and generally been supportive of letting me see a world about which they've only heard.

My father, R. Ford Reid, gets credit for instilling in me the love of a good story. I got to grow up listening to him and his friends complain, whine and generally be cynical about so much cool stuff, I never considered any career path but following him into journalism. To him and his friends at the Louisville Courier-Journal, the Virginian-Pilot and a half-dozen other newspapers, thank you for making me the cynical grump I am. Read the book, and you'll know the parts you inspired.

My late stepmother Libby Reid, who died in 2010, made the pursuit of happiness seem such a worthy endeavor. She was always the quiet one in the room – we Reids usually being opinionated to the point of distraction – but she led by example better than anyone I've ever known.

The rest of my immediate family gets bonus points for sitting through I can't remember how many Sunday night dinners and having to listen to me go on about having just gone to some other exotic place to which I'd forgotten to invite them. Thanks for your patience, Phoebe Reid, Silas Reid, Nathanael Reid, Jann Guyre, Amanda Guyre, Amy Guyre, Pete Guyre, Lucy Guyre and Alice Guyre. My two out-of-town sisters, Sarah Phillips in Atlanta and Patience Peacock in Louisville, were spared those stories, but I can't not thank them. They're my sisters.

I enlisted the help of many people in reading all or parts of my manuscript. Some of them actually seemed to read it, and some even offered feedback. I wasn't so good at listening to that feedback, but that's a different issue. Thanks to Robert Antonelli, DeWitt Casler, Aprille Cederquist, Anthony Donovan, Carmen Germino, Bill and Gale Guyre, Kristen Larson, Louis Llovio, Catherine Perrin, Morgan Rowe and Jeremy Slayton.

Two tech savvy friends, Karri Peifer and Christina Wohlers, worked hard to keep me in line and up-to-date and looking and sounding much better than I ever could alone.

Kristen Green was generous in talking about the business of publishing. Before writing the critically acclaimed book "Something Must Be Done About Prince Edward County," which was published in June 2015, she and I sat next to each other for more than a year at the Richmond Times-Dispatch. I happened to know four Kristens at the time, and she was "Loud Kristen." Because she was. But that's good; it was hard to not feel good about being a journalist sitting next to her.

I never would have found this story if not for a bit of serendipity. In the spring of 2010, I had a newspaper assignment to write an Easter story about a children's program at St. James's Episcopal Church, in Richmond, Virginia. I struck up a quick, easy friendship with Kent Duffey, who was in charge of the program. The same year, she invited me to join the church on a work trip to Haiti. That didn't work out, but we stayed in touch, and I wound up going with her to Haiti the next year to build a school. In the years since, I have been on more than a dozen trips with the church.

From Kent, I met Sarah Hubard, with whom I've been to Haiti, DeWitt Casler, with whom I've traveled to Haiti and Cuba, and the Rev. Carmen Germino, with whom I've traveled to Haiti, Cuba and New Orleans. Four better friends, I can't imagine. I've gone on those trips with dozens of others, too. I hate to start listing people for fear of forgetting someone, but two of them deserve special attention. I spent some long, odd days in Haiti with Page Londrey and Andy Smith looking at work projects in places it was hard to imagine people living. That work helped inform the reporting I later did in Cuba. Page's enthusiasm and Andy's steady professionalism are great assets on any trip, and I'd go anywhere with those two.

I also found a Cuban connection to Richmond through the daughter and grandson of the Right Rev. Hugo Blankingship, the only American to have been an Episcopal bishop in Cuba. He died decades ago, but his story has stayed alive thanks in large part to his daughter, Toni Donovan, whom I met in Richmond through St. James's, which she has attended for years, and his grandson, Anthony Donovan, a fellow Richmonder whom I met on the way to Cuba. If I put together a dream team of fellow travelers, Anthony would be a first round pick.

In Cuba, I've made many friends in the past few years. The Right Rev. Griselda Delgado, the Episcopal Bishop of Cuba, made this all possible by being warm and welcoming. Approving my constant requests for visas helped, too. Thanks, also, to her family, her husband the Rev. Gerardo Logildes Coroa; daughter Griselda Edith Tordoya; son Lautaro Martin Delgado; and especially daughter Marcela Beatrice Martin Delgado and her husband, the Rev. Andrei Diaz Dorta. Marcela and Andrei shared their dinner table in Bolondron, and they always share their time when I see them in Havana.

The Rev. Halbert Pons, in Santiago; the Rev. Evilio Perez in Camagüey; the Most Rev. Ulises Agüero Prendes, the retired bishop in Santiago; and Danella Irizar, who never said no to spending a day leading clueless Americans around Havana; were tremendously helpful.

A posthumous thank you to Rosaida "Say" Luya Irizar. She ran the office of the Cuban Episcopal Diocese and knew everyone and everything and had the most gentle way of making you feel special even when you were asking the dumbest questions. She died in February 2015.

In Florida, I've made two good friends who have helped ease me into Cuba. In Gainesville, Marilyn Peterson helped open doors and smooth travel plans before I knew anything about going to Cuba. She and the bishop have been friends for years, and she was kind in sharing that friendship with a stranger. In Miami, Magaly Fernandez is a constant reminder that travel agents are still important and essential in the digital age. I remember once trying to get through the jungle of check-in for a Havana-bound charter flight out of Miami and feeling lost and hopeless. I finally made it to the counter and mentioned her name, and the next thing I knew everyone was friendly and helpful and somehow I wound up sitting in first class.

The staff of the Richmond Times-Dispatch earned thanks, too, mostly for covering me while I was away working on one story or another that wasn't quite on my beat.

My new friends at Koehler Books have also been wonderful in helping me understand the peculiar word of book publishing. Thanks to owner John Koehler, acquisitions editor Nora Firestone, editor editor Joe Coccaro, and designer Kellie Emery.

CPSIA information can be obtained
at www.ICGtesting.com
Printed in the USA
LVOW12s1955160516
488473LV00001B/71/P